Architecture for People

Architecture for People

explorations in a new humane environment

Edited by Byron Mikellides

Holt, Rinehart and Winston   New York

Acknowledgements

NA
2542.36
A7
1980

The Editor would like to express his gratitude to all the contributors to this anthology and to all who have prepared statements and sent material for inclusion in this book.

Grateful thanks are due to: Steve Adamson, London; Gosta Blomberg, Volvo Car Corporation, Kalmar Plant, Sweden; Mrs R. Erskine, Sweden; Suzi Gablik, London; Gallerie Wilde, Köln; Peter Goodliffe, Oxford; Louis Hellman, London; Roger Lindsay, Oxford; Sarah Mikellides; Brian Selby, Oxford; Victor Vasarely, France; John Willcocks, Senior Research Fellow, Leicester.

I would also like to thank Alida Baxter, I. Bentley, I. Davis, J. Hanna, J. Halford, C. Humphrey, E. Jacka, M. Jenks, Y. Rabinowitz, Bob Saxton, and my colleagues and students at Oxford Polytechnic.

The articles by Carl-Axel Acking, Bruce Allsopp, are © 1980 (all rights reserved) to the respective authors. An earlier version of 'Natural Aesthetics' was published as The 'Illusion of Beauty' in *Perception* 1973, vol. 2, 429–439, based on a lecture at the Institute of Contemporary Arts, Nov. 1973. Extract pp. 45–48 from *Community of Interest*. Copyright © 1977, 1978, 1979, 1980 by Oscar Newman.

The Publishers thank the following for the use of illustrations: Aerofilm Ltd: 127; *Architect's Journal* 125 (top, left, bottom), 129 (top); Architectural Press: 42, 129 (top); Australia House: 112; Cavendish Photos Co. Ltd: 70; City Engineer, Newcastle: 136–137; Civil Trust: 134, I. Davis: 56; Richard Davies: 129 (bottom); *Design Magazine*, Design Council: 123; John Donat: 137; Fiddy: 22; Suzie Gablik: 70; P. Goodliffe: 61 (top right and bottom right), 68, 71, 72, 102, 103; Girsbirger: 229; Iderzo and Goscinney Editions: 104; Laus Mango: 134 (both), 135, 141, 142; Bygg Mänskligt: 111, 220; Royal Netherlands Embassy: 50; Eero Saarinen: 108; *She*: 22; Tim Street Porter: 123; Tavistock Publications: 61; *Ur Arkitektur* (*Dansk*) 1; 1970: 111; J. G. Van Agtmaal: 50; Johan an der Keuken: 39 (top centre); Gabrie Wildekoln: 68.

Whilst every effort has been made to correctly credit sources apologies are made for any omissions.

Copyright © 1980 Byron Mikellides

All rights reserved, including the right to reproduce this book or portions thereof in any form.

Library of Congress Catalog Card Number: 79-48067

ISBN Hardbound 0-03-057491-9
ISBN Paperback 0-03-057489-7

First published in the United States in 1980 by Holt, Rinehart and Winston, 383 Madison Avenue, New York, New York 10017.

Published simultaneously in Great Britain by Studio Vista, a division of Cassell Ltd.

First American edition

Designer: David Morley-Clarke

Printed in Great Britain

10 9 8 7 6 5 4 3 2 1

Contents

Preface

I want to design things that people get pleasure in making and want to make things that people get pleasure in using.

William Morris

Architecture for people, people for architecture, humane architecture, building for people, designing for 'human individuals'—these are subtle nuances of meaning which all connote a strong implied message that *we could do better* than we have been doing so far in making our homes, our cities, our biosphere worthy of Man in all his biological, social and cultural peculiarities. This book aspires to capture the mood of this implied message; and to offer both theoretical concepts for understanding the problems involved, and practical suggestions as to how we might make the necessary improvements.

The aim of the book is not so much to provide reasons for the theoretical failure of modern architecture, which has already been extensively discussed elsewhere, but to explore new areas broadly and in depth which could have profound effects on our living environments in the immediate and long-term future. The contributors are world specialists whose ideas and practical work have marked them out as leaders in this area of architectural thought. An international scope has been deliberately sought to avoid parochialism and the rigid attachment to a single solution which has bedevilled much architectural thinking.

The reader will encounter here a wide range of approaches: from biological-evolutionary perspectives on human needs, humanization of factory architecture, research in architectural psychology, to practical architectural solutions that people respond to and take pleasure in inhabiting. The architects who have designed such buildings were invited to write about their work, their motives, their philosophies, their detailed approach to design. It is hoped that readers of this book—and in particular architects—will gain much from these original accounts by leading practitioners.

There has been no attempt to reconcile or summarize the various contributions—either theoretical or practical—in order to present one universally

applicable approach. Each essay could be read independently, though there are certain natural groupings among the contributors on both the theoretical and the practical sides. For example, the pieces on Natural Aesthetics, Urban Aesthetics and Architecture and Emotions constitute one grouping, while another is provided by Housing and Human Needs, Images of Man and The Disappearing Factory. But it is hoped that the reader will be stimulated to make these connections himself.

Before inviting people to write for this book I carried out a survey among architectural students at the Oxford School asking them to give a list of the architects and writers who they thought had done most, in their various ways, to encourage a more humane architecture. At the same time I consulted practising architects, researchers from abroad, and many other, allied groups of people, as well as scrutinizing specialist publications. On these explorations the choice of contributors for the book was based.

Architectural Psychology is celebrating a decade of European history and the Editor's critical appraisal discusses some of the most intriguing findings of this new discipline. Developing a detailed brief through understanding people is illustrated by the work of Aldington and Craig. John Craig has been invited to write a short account of how they translate this understanding in built form for the individual client as well as for groups of people and committees. John Darbourne of Darbourne and Darke takes off from here to illustrate through their design of high density housing that their approach goes beyond answering a brief and towards a formulation of attitudes *to social needs*, within the context of which landscape architecture plays a vital role. Satisfying human needs, encouraging people to become more closely acquainted with their surroundings with each other and with themselves is the theme of the Dutch Architect Herman Hertzberger's statement with examples drawn from his architectural work.

Lastly in this section Bruce Allsopp the well-known historian and theoritician provides us with a historical perspective about the social relevance of art and the crucial task of educating the client.

Oscar Newman is both a practising architect and writer. He is author of the influential book *Defensible Space* and the President of the Institute of Community Design Analysis, New York.

Dr Nicholas Humphrey is one of the most prominent young scientists in England today. He is Assistant Director of the Department of Animal Behaviour, University of Cambridge, and a regular contributor to *Nature* and *Perception*.

Dr Peter F. Smith is a practising architect, Director of Research in the Department of Architecture, University of Sheffield, and author of *The Dynamics of Urbanism* (1974), *The Syntax of Cities* (1977) and *Architecture and the Human Dimension* (1979). In most of his writings the aim has been to establish the relationship between the various brain sciences and architectural design, particularly in respect of aesthetic perception and symbolism. Although Smith's theories have not been verified directly they offer a new perspective in urban design and one we are most likely to hear more of in the future as research in neurophysiology is increasingly dominating work in perception.

The leading researcher in Architectural Psychology in Sweden, Dr Rikard Küller has turned towards neurophysiology in his own work. Dr Küller has been working during the past 10 years trying to establish the factors or dimensions we employ in perceiving and responding to our built environment, using various methods of investigation.

Prof. Carl-Axel Acking was invited to contribute a piece based on the wealth of his lifelong experience as a practising architect, former Professor of Interior and Furniture Design, author, researcher, and founder of the Department of Theoretical and Applied Aesthetics at Lund (in 1964) until his retirement in 1976.

Charles W. Moore is a prominent practising architect and Professor of Architecture and Urban Design at the School of Architecture and Urban Planning at the University of California in Los Angeles.

Robert Maguire of Maguire and Murray, is both a practising architect and Head of the Oxford School of Architecture. Their buildings have been acclaimed by many independent observers as fine examples of buildings for people on very low budgets and has been the basis of 'Humanes Bauen', a circulating exhibition in Europe.

Mats Egelius is a promising young architect and author of the book *Ralph Erskine: A Human Architect* (1979). His genuine concern for people started when he was a student at Oxford and then followed by working in Ralph Erskine's office; Egelius considers how Erskine's projects satisfy basic human needs as defined by the Danish psychologist Ingrid Gehl. Ralph Erskine himself has kindly redrawn for this publication his original comments for an open plan office for Pågens, Malmo, in an uninhibited Anglo-Swedish form which illustrates very vividly his concern for individuals as they are.

Humanizing work-places is by no means an easy task; the development of the industrial estate as opposed to the old Victorian industrial city has produced problems deeply entangled among political and socio-economic factors. Have management and labour consultants and engineers taken over the role of the architect beyond the design of glorified offices? Kenneth Frampton, Fellow of the Institute of Architecture and Urban Design, currently holding teaching jobs at Columbia University, New York and at the Royal College of Art, London considers in depth these general issues with specific reference to the Volvo experiment at Kalmar, Sweden as well as the relationship between the nature of industrial work, the effect of management style, ergonomics and the design of the buildings.

Lucien Kroll is a well-known Belgian architect who has made much use of the principle of user participation. Kroll considers his philosophy behind the well-publicized participation exercise at Mémé (Student Building for the Medical Faculty of the University of Louvain). His motto *'L'architecture est faite pour l'homme: c'est une affair entendue'* (Architecture is made for man: no one would deny it) is consistent in all his work. At Cergy, Les Vignes Blanches, Atelier D'Urbanisme et D'Architecture, L. Kroll as one of the prize-winners of the competition 'Town Houses' declared: 'No inhabitant participation, no plans'.

Walter Segal is a veteran architect builder. 'To my way of thinking the creator is primarily a craftsman who breaks with the techniques of his craft after years of apprenticeship and practice as in the painters' workshops in the past.' Building cheaply and quickly; teaching clients all the tricks of the game in a simple and refreshing manner are some of his special trademarks. Segal also discusses Bureaucracy and Politics as they relate to ongoing experiments in housing in Lewisham.

Peter Stringer is one of the foremost theoreticians and researchers in the field of Architectural Psychology, regular contributor in International conferences and author of several books and articles on the subject. He believes that our view of what *Architecture for People* really involves will differ from individual to individual depending on our assumptions about the nature of man and whether we see him as an active, passive or rational human being.

Finally, Gösta Ehrensvärd formerly a distinguished Professor of Biochemistry in Sweden and now in the U.S.A., looks in an exciting way at the present and future relations between Man and Biosphere. In his letter accepting the invitation to contribute in this collection he writes:

'This is obviously easier said than done and I am fully aware that Mankind has made very few inroads in the whole complex of thoughts on this matter. Yet the whole idea behind the planned book is encouraging as a step in the right direction: Man searching for a Truly biological *niche* in the Biosphere; not by conquest but by symbiosis. This concept will be emphasized in future ages, when *materials for buildings and utilities*—including Transports—will be scarce, even with an abundance of energy. Here we have a connection between the views of the biotechnologists and architecture, and this is my field of interest. How much could we take out in renewable material from the biosphere without disturbing its delicate balance? In view of the fact that man cannot live in the rigid patterns outlined by insect-societies, what could we envisage a suitable organization fit for encompassing the *diversity of human beings. . . .*'

It is also hoped by the Editor that this wide diversity of human beings will be reflected in this anthology of ideas and practical solutions. Variation is not only the raw material of evolution but the lifeblood of humane living environments.

Oxford, March 1979

Architectural Psychology and the Unavoidable Art

Byron Mikellides

In the field of architectural psychology, when research findings confirm our preconceptions they are superfluous; when they contradict them they are obnoxious.

In March 1969 at Dalandhui in Scotland, the first Conference of Architectural Psychology was held. Since then interest in this study has been growing rapidly and another four International Conferences have been held in Europe, the proceedings of which were subsequently published. There have also been nine E.D.R.A. (Environmental Design Research Association) Conferences in the U.S.A., each of which has taken published form in two large volumes of papers and workshop discussions. There have also been several symposia, weekend meetings and seminars, organized by various bodies such as the S.S.R.C. (Social Science Research Council) and the British Psychological Society, as well as commercial interests. Over 1,000 papers have been published at the conference level and over 400 relevant publications, books and articles are quoted quarterly in the *Architectural Psychology Newsletter*, which was established after the Dalandhui Conference in 1969.

This voluminous outpouring of empirical research has been heavily criticized on various grounds in different quarters. In America in particular, the pressure to publish, irrespective of content and applicability, is quite strong, and it comes as no surprise that the published work is of no significance to us. Ask an architect, a planner, or an urban designer what use he can make of this gigantic outpouring of research in environmental psychology, architectural psychology, environmental perception, the ontoperivantic aspects of psychostructural environics, or whatever you may decide to name it, and the unhappy fact would most probably be that many, if not most of the potential consumers of such work feel that this kind of research is constantly asking the wrong questions in the wrong ways and that it is at best irrelevant and at worst inaccurate and misleading.

Many architects also feel quite sarcastic about the investment of time and energy spent in work which usually comes up with such *obvious* conclusions that we could have guessed most of the results through commonsense anyway. The main criticism of research in these areas has been that it only puts into complicated form observations with which sensitive architects and planners are already familiar. The reader of this book may be helped in gauging the truth of this attitude by inspecting some typical research findings and carefully observing his own reactions to them. A brief list of such findings is given below, with short interpretive comments that are intended to bring into sharper focus the probable reactions of many readers:

1 Introverts have higher privacy standards than extroverts. (We all know that a typical introvert is a quiet, retiring sort of person, introspective and fond of books rather than people, whereas the typical extrovert is sociable, likes parties, has many friends and needs people to talk to. It comes to us as no surprise therefore that an introvert does require more privacy than an extrovert.)

2 Red and yellow are the more exciting colours, and blue and green the more calming colours. (We are all well aware that red and yellow are mostly associated with fire and blood, green with nature, and blue with the colour of the sky.)

3 As the pupil size is considered an accurate indicator of arousal, we would expect that the pupil would grow larger in a complex room than it would be in a simple room. (It is well known that increasing complexity results in increased visual interest, hence this increase in arousal as measured by the pupil size.)

4 After natural disasters such as earthquakes, floods or hurricanes, morale is likely to be low, with looting and other forms of deviant behaviour. The public will show signs of panic, inactivity and the situation will rapidly deteriorate into chaos. (We see this on TV all the time.)

5 When staff and factory employees in a British tobacco factory were asked whether they wanted to have separate dining facilities, they overwhelmingly preferred to share their facilities on

a communal basis so that they could meet with each other. (If only we would ask people what they want before we design for them!)

6 A socially-planned community is likely to show a reduction in the incidence of neuroses (minor mental illness) and show no change in the incidence of psychoses (major mental illness.) (One often hears of 'suburban neurosis' and 'new town blues' due to unsatisfactory and poorly planned environments, but one does not expect to change the deep-seated, largely inherited mental illness of psychoses.)

7 Crowding results when there is lack of space. (Overcrowding rats or mice in conditions of 'standing room only' is bound to cause considerable stress and complete disruption in social function.)

8 The moon appears larger when on the horizon than when it is high up the sky simply because it looks closer to us than when overhead. (Most of us have seen the 'moon illusion'.)

9 There are differences between full-size and scale-model study bedrooms in the assessment of lighting quality. (There is no substitute to real environments for finding out how people perceive and respond to them.)

10 Visually handicapped people, on being introduced to 3 different rooms, gave different impressions of the different characteristics of these rooms from people with normal sight. (Unfortunately, one would expect this.)

We have here, in these few examples the most intriguing findings of this developing empirical science of architectural psychology. Most readers would probably agree that they found most of the conclusions obvious to them, some irrelevant, as well as finding a few of the questions misguided. Why, then, since they are so obvious, is so much effort and energy consumed in schools and departments of architecture to establish such findings? Why is so much money from public funds spent by the s.s.r.c. and other research awarding bodies when the money and effort could be more fruitfully deployed elsewhere?

Before we answer this complex question, the reader should be informed now that *every one of the ten statements listed above is the direct opposite of, or significantly different from, what was actually found.*[1] Extroverts have higher privacy standards than introverts, which suggest that extroverts feel more conscious of the need for visual privacy than introverts. Green is no more calming and tranquilizing than red, provided that we compare colours with equal saturation and brightness; in other words the most critical factor for excitement is not hue but the chromatic strength of the colour. There were no differences in pupil size in the response to a complex room compared with that to a simple room. Immediately after natural disasters, people's attitudes are far from helpless, for the instinct for self-preservation instigates a phenomenal degree of resourcefulness, and for facing up to the new realities in a cool and philosophical way. Tobacco factory and staff workers opted for separate dining facilities; what may be considered a socially desirable objective or a cherished ideology may not be what people want. There was no evidence of the 'suburban neurosis' or 'new town blues'; social planning appeared to have no effect on neurosis, but did reduce the incidence of psychosis. Crowding can be defined as the perception of excessive social stimulation and not merely the lack of space; the enormous cross-cultural differences in the perception of being crowded illustrate this point, for some cities in India and Japan make Western crowded cities look like paradise. The moon illusion depends on terrain, and specifically on the distance effect of terrain; according to principles of size-constancy, if two objects form images of equal size, the more distant must be the larger—which is opposite to the explanation mentioned above. There are *no* differences in the assessment of lighting quality between full-size and scale-model rooms. And the visually handicapped, in an environment where there is no perceptual conflict, can compensate for their lack of sight in a non-visual manner, and make judgements which are not appreciably different from those made by people with normal sight.

If the actual results of the investigations had been given first, rather than the opposite results I provided, the reader would have labelled these as 'obvious' also. Obviously something is wrong with the entire argument about 'obviousness'. It should really be turned on its head. Since every kind of human reaction is conceivable, it is of great importance to know which reactions actually occur most frequently, and under what conditions. Only then will a more advanced understanding of the man/environment relationship emerge, which will undoubtedly have beneficial effects upon our lives.

Having satisfied our obvious curiosity about obviousness, we must now turn to the more complex question of relevance. How relevant should research be to solving the type of problems the architect is facing? This is a particularly difficult question to answer because of the imprecise definitions of the word 'relevance'. Architecture involves the pulling of many strings and can be seen on many multi-dimensional levels. Is understanding people's individual differences—their personalities and emotions in the psychological sense—of more relevance than understanding 'why we see what we see', which is the fundamental question that perception psychologists have posed? Or is it of greater importance to ask how we make sense of the world in terms of strategies, cognitive maps and spatial schemata? Is the value of psychology more relevant at the design conceptualization stage or at the point where we want to obtain objective feedback from the way people use our buildings?

This diversity of information which could be considered important, depending on our particular idiosyncratic needs, is the first difficulty therefore in our definition of relevance. Some people will consider the effects of colour on our emotions to be of the greatest significance, while others may contemptuously treat this as a matter of mere cosmetics while considering the real challenge to be the political and social factors involved in participation exercises.

The second difficulty we encounter in our attempts to define relevance is that there is a considerable number of variables involved in each research situation. The answer to a problem in England could be of no direct bearing on an apparently similar problem in Peru because of the differences in the political and socio-economic climate of the two countries. Before a designer could use the findings in a design, further comparative research would have to be undertaken to ensure that the results in one country could be cross-validated with the results in the other. In addition, many environmental conditions are difficult to quantify and the use of subjective judgements is questionable. Furthermore, the large number of variables which interact with these conditions are, to a large extent, interdependent. Humans respond not simply to one stimulus at a time but to the total event; and that response depends on one's age, sex, experience and general emotional state. Variables such as these make psychological analysis even harder.

Thirdly, the degree of confidence we place in the results of an experiment will influence their relevance. Even if the results are statistically significant and we are fairly convinced by them, we may feel somehow unable to accept them because we may suspect an independent or intervening variable which has not been controlled or cannot be quantified. In the world of medicine it is not child-birth which causes tooth decay as it used to be thought, but calcium deficiency. In the same way, drabness does not cause vandalism, nor does colour cure it; colour, however, may mediate towards a solution by triggering off certain biological and social mechanisms.

Sometimes we may even find the 'relevant' answer to a problem without understanding why—that is, without understanding the intricate relationships of the underlying principles involved. In general, psychologists are interested in what are called 'second order' problems: they try to unravel these underlying principles and to answer the question 'why?'. Second order problems are usually of a general nature and at first sight may be considered to be completely irrelevant and to have nothing to do with design. On the other hand, architects are interested in 'first order' problems, which deal with very specific questions and are extremely difficult and dangerous to generalize about, just because of the number of very specific variables involved. According to Ivor Stillitz, one of the early researchers in environmental psychology, work on first order problems is relevant not only on practical grounds but also for its heuristic value. When we have a number of solutions to such first order problems we can also proceed to formulate valid and soluble second order problems.

Psychologists have stated some of the problems related to research and applicability in terms of the 'data paradox': the better defined and more specific the problem is stated, the more remote to everyday life it is, though at the same time it will be scientifically respectable; on the other hand, the greater the number of variables involved the more relevant it will be to everyday life, though of a dubious scientific respectability.

Architectural psychology is not unique, of course, in this matter of relevance. The issue is of topical importance to most branches of academic inquiry. It is a favourite topic in the behavioural sciences.[2] A recent bibliography listed over 4,000 publications on 'small groups research'—an attempt to bridge the gap between psychology, which studies the individual, and sociology, which concentrates on the properties of institutions and social classes. Lott and Lott described 400 different studies on the concept of 'group cohesiveness' alone.[3] Leading social psychologists such as Michael Argyle believe that little remains to be done and nothing very exciting has been discovered. R. D. Mann, a psychotherapist, considers such research misleading and irrelevant to his needs and to those of other group therapists and teachers.

One of the strongest protagonists for more directly applicable research is Liam Hudson, author of *Contrary Imaginations* and *The Cult of the Fact*, who considers that far too much effort is spent in British and American universities in tackling second order problems. On the other side of the fence Donald Broadbent of Cambridge defends the empirical science of psychology: 'Against the perspective of 2,000 years the speed of our advance in studying human nature seems more cheerful. At a rough guess, two hundred more years may bring the study of behaviour up to the level which physics reached in Newton's time'.[4]

The architect will perhaps find this confusing state of affairs depressing. What with the difficulties about obviousness, the relevance of such diversity of information to design, the large number of variables involved, the degree of confidence when looking at the results, the 'data paradox', the first and second order problems and the general level of controversy within the behavioural sciences, he may be convinced that the best and easiest way out is to forget the whole thing and design completely by feel. Compare, however, the role of the architect to that of the psychiatrist: a useful analogy could be made on at least two levels. The psychiatrist has still insufficient knowledge from psychology as to the best way of treating a patient; he cannot wait until the year 2000 to obtain more valid scientific knowledge of the Broadbent type before he treats his patient; he also knows that 'prevention is better than cure' and works accordingly. He has studied as part of his training what we do know about the psychology of people and he separates fact from fiction. At the same time he follows his own personal philosophy and predisposition as to which psychological school to belong to (behaviour therapy, psychoanalysis, group therapy). The architect also starts from a position of insufficient knowledge in all the related fields. He too considers that prevention is better than cure and within the time constraints has to produce a 'treatment'—a building which has to meet many diverse criteria. The most fundamental difference, however, between the two roles is that the architect is not trained and *educated* to distinguish which is fact and which is fiction, and the easiest way out is to build his own preconceived ideas, theories and design philosophy. In fact, in certain quarters, the architect is built up to this expectation through a stereotyped, grandiose image of his profession.*

The architect is trained to appeal to three well-known philosophical methods: the methods of

*See the piece by O. Newman p. 45–48.

Authority, Tenacity and Intuition. The method of Authority states that something is true because somebody says it is true, usually a well-known figure such as Le Corbusier—but if the source is wrong, so are those who cite it. The method of Tenacity is to believe something is true simply because one has *always* believed it—but continued belief could be continued error, and moreover produces a biased observer. And by the method of Intuition a statement is felt to be true because it is self-evident—whereas we have already seen that something was clearly wrong with the entire argument of obviousness, for some of the findings which were undeniably and obviously true were the direct opposite of what was actually found.

In addition, the architect-philosopher bases his thinking on the famous Laws of Thought without reference to place and time: the law of Identity (if something is z, it is z), the law of Contradiction (a thing cannot be both z and not z), and the law of Excluded Middle (anything must be either z or not z). These laws have been notoriously misused in the past because no reference to place and time has been made in stating them both through the lack of knowledge and through careless logic. (For instance, if we take as an example of the second law, a man cannot be both tall and short at the same time; yet a five-foot man would be considered short in the West and tall among pigmies!)

Our short digression in philosophy and logic has

not been intended to condemn the architect who practises on the basis of his own personal design philosophy or by applying his own creative talent. What is wrong is that unlike the psychiatrist he does not test his ideas against what we *do* know about people both from psychology and from those architects who have succeeded in designing pleasing and humane environments.

The most vital contribution (or 'unquantified relevance') of all the psychological work is towards a change in attitudes—a redefinition of the role of the architect, in relation to his understanding of people. A 5th-year architecture student writing, introspectively in 1968, about why he embarked on the Architectural Psychology option in the course at the Oxford School of Architecture considered its main value: 'To convince people that they are content with what you are providing for them'!

The psychologist, Brian Wells, writing in 1965 commented on these attitudes and the state of Architectural Education: 'Architects and Engineers are concerned crudely with the physical creation and control of the environment, while psychologists and managers are with its effects on human beings.' He then went on to say: 'I am not sure that many, if not most architects, would repudiate the simple role of the creative engineer and claim that their pro-

1 *Dalandhui*, 1969: 'Courtship in the House of Blackdell.'

fession bridges the gap between these two groups, but there is little evidence that their present education and training prepares them at all seriously for this wider role.'[5]

Compare these views with that taken 10 years later from a typical answer by a 3rd-year student taking his B.A. Honours Finals in June 1978, who had studied psychology as part of his architectural education. The comment illustrates very clearly the growing change in attitudes towards the role of the architect:

Psychology? What the hell has that got to do with architecture? Architecture is designing beautiful buildings full of fantastic qualities; that's design. Architecture is something which will enable me to express myself—blow my mind without any constraints. It will revolutionize design. This was the naïve yet understandable attitude towards psychology that I personally had in the first year. This attitude has undoubtedly changed dramatically to one where I now have a healthy interest in some aspects of the subject. However, it is only in three years of gradual change that this has happened. . . .

Architectural psychology seeks to find out why people react to buildings differently. Why are some buildings and environments liked more or hated less. . . .?'

These questions inevitably lead us to architectural education. In its contribution to such a complex discipline as architecture we need to be clear about our definition of psychology. Teaching methods, projects and educational technology are of fundamental importance since they influence the content of the psychology syllabus and the way that architects experience the world. We have seen in recent years serious attempts in primary education to influence the quality of teaching: activity methods, simulation, vertical grouping, team teaching and learning through experience are just a few examples of new directions. In an attempt to train better family doctors the McMaster University, Ontario, has abandoned the traditional process of lectures and exams in favour of methods designed to provide awareness and experience of the human problems of sickness and clinical symptoms.

There is a great difference between reading about human behaviour and *understanding* it in a fashion which will be useful for design. The Oxford School Psychology Syllabus[6] is an attempt to encourage this understanding-through-experience to which we should devote more time and energy. The study of psychology will be an important factor in the development of new attitudes among architects towards their role and image in society. It may

2 *Kingston*, 1970: 'Apprehension in the Convent.'

contribute to overcoming one of the obstacles which Bruce Allsopp, in his book *Towards a Humane Architecture* (1974), identifies as preventing architects from adopting human values and from creating a comfortable, familiar environment which people can enjoy: namely, their professionalism and narrow outlook.

Psychology also seems to me to be making a contribution to architectural education in a number of other ways. The science has a general educational value in that it increases the student's knowledge in a relatively new discipline. The subject matter of psychology, such as perception, personality and proxemics, is of value to designers whose interests are in predicting behaviour in the environments they design. And it is in this understanding of individual differences and how the individual relates to society that the present day architectural students seem to be interested, rather than in single-variable experiments: it is the general awareness that we are dealing with people, not merely applying new techniques or advocating new theories, that they consider important in their work. Psychology is a discipline comparable to architecture in that it integrates information from other sciences (physiology, physics, engineering, zoology, anthropology, sociology and others) in an attempt to understand people. The strong emphasis on the scientific method enables the student to recognize the limits of our knowledge and look critically at new research.

It is important that the architect should be able to work within groups of specialists such as psychologists, engineers, quantity surveyors. The lack of communication between architects and psychologists at the moment forms a strong barrier to appreciating what constitutes useful information for the designer, or what information the designer should ask for. The inclusion of psychology in architectural curricula will increase such communication.

Psychology will also provide the architect with training in social skills. There has been a lot of work recently in interpersonal behaviour, by Michael Argyle at Oxford and others, which can be taken as constituting a 'new approach' in social psychology. The traditional interest amongst social psychologists in 'small group research' has expanded into areas such as kinetics and paralinguistics. A specialized knowledge of this kind of work by architects (to be taught in the first year of training) could increase the quality of social interaction both in the architect-client situation and in architectural group projects, where an understanding 'group dynamics' may avoid conflict and the final dissolution of the group. The ability of the architect to draw upon a repertoire of social techniques, both lexical and non-lexical, will enable him to deal especially effectively in interpreting or obtaining a brief from his client. The work done by Aldington and Craig, who emphasize the need to understand the client and through this understanding to develop a brief, exemplifies a process we could teach to all newly recruited students of architecture.*

'Social interaction is a fascinating and baffling object of study: on the one hand it is immediate and familiar, on the other it is mysterious and inexpressible—there do not seem to be words to describe it, or the concepts to handle it.'[7] Michael Argyle in his book *The Psychology of Interpersonal Behaviour* (1967) has provided us with some of these words and concepts in the analogy he makes between motor skills and social skills. Just as we learn to drive a car or play tennis, we could learn to interact with different people and develop diverse social skills—both verbal and non-verbal. Analyzing social motives which energize and direct social behaviour, bodily contact, paralinguistic aspects of speech, self-image and self-esteem; and analyzing different types of feedback in interaction through use of video types—all this should be an essential part in such training.

Yet another contribution that general psychology may make to architectural education is that it can lead towards an acquaintance with recent work in *architectural* psychology. The formal programme in psychology should enable the student to be critically aware of what is going on, to value the

*See the piece by Aldington and Craig, pp. 27–33.

15

diversity of approach in the field, and to evaluate attempts to build up theoretical models of the Man/environment relationship. Such a new understanding will foster the dialogue between the architect and psychologist, and will help towards an overall increase in communication between the two disciplines.

It seems timely at this stage to look at this research as reflected in the content of all the European International Architectural Psychology Conferences which I have attended in the past ten years. The aim is not to consider all the relevant research findings, nor to summarize them: this would be an impossible and superficial task. In this volume the reader may obtain a flavour of the conferences from the papers of Rikard Küller, Peter Stringer and Peter Smith; while N. Humphrey's paper is by an outsider whose ideas and experiments architectural psychologists find fascinating and relevant. Instead of close paraphrase, my intention here is to provide laconic representational images of these conferences which will perhaps capture the content of the papers given, the predominant themes in discussion, and the atmosphere of these gatherings. To achieve this, I have invited the best-known architectural cartoonist, Louis Hellman, to translate the images in black ink!

3 *Lund*, May 1974: Revitalized hope in Diversity (and Herring).

1 *Dalandhui, 1969: 'Courtship in the House of Blackdell'* This was the first conference of its kind in Britain: a friendly and enquiring conference which provided us with new hope in the dialogue between psychology and architecture. We saw the development of the *Architectural Psychology Newsletter* as a vehicle for communicating information and research. The most significant themes were: architecture, psychology, the game's the same: do we need a theory?; visibility and privacy; pupillary response to architectural stimuli; the assessment of room friendliness.

2 *Kingston, 1970: 'Apprehension in the Convent'* The number of participants trebled. The formal dialogue between architecture and psychology expanded to include design criteria for underwater habitats. George Kelly's 'personal construct' theory (how Man translates his life and environment into a form that he can understand) was taken up from the first conference. There was also a strong emphasis on lighting research and the use of semantic differential scales (measuring the connotative meaning of concepts). The more informal discussions took place in a convent. Papers given were on topics including: social ritual and architectural space; perception of the human environment; a linguistic model; the semantics of security and the dream of community; housewives' attitudes to shopping centres; and attention structure of pre-school infants.

16

3 *Lund, May 1974: 'Revitalized Hope in Diversity' (and Herring)*

Following a lapse of three years the Lund Conference proved invigorating and worthwhile. Although this was the largest conference so far, informal communication—including the tasting of various herring varieties—amongst participants was well fostered by the organizers: this was the main feature of the conference. The diversity of papers was phenomenal, and the flavour was truly international, ranging from the therapeutic effects of architectural activity in a children's home in Northern Africa, to children's images of Harwich. Topics covered were: colour psychology in space; participation and gaming; privacy; building evaluation; space networks; aesthetics; unobtrusive methods of investigation; and attempts to move beyond semantic measurement.

4 *Surrey, October 1974: 'Psychology First, Architecture Second'*

Just three months after Lund we were faced with yet another conference: 'Psychology and the Built Environment?' This was more of a psychologists' conference than an architects' one. The emphasis was on theory and experiment and improved methodology, including better and more accurate methods for measuring thermal comfort, wind, rain, temperature, and the effects of a new motorway on residential areas. We also considered: multi-dimensional scaling techniques; cross-cultural evaluation of houses, and in particular, Japanese apartments; and individual differences in repertory grid measures for a cross-section of the female population.

5 *Sheffield, 1975: 'Education, Participation and Karl Marx'*

'Education for the Urban Environment' was the title of this Conference. Papers were presented on public participation and its rewards, environmental education and education for designers, urban language, and professional and research roles. The emphasis was on application and on several current projects. It was inevitable within this context of professional ideology and public participation that politics was discussed.

6 *Strasbourg, 1976: 'Space Appropriation—Misappropriation'*

In line with the best French tradition, the *'Appropriation de la Space'* conference was located in the finest restaurants of Strasbourg. Setting aside variations of meaning especially between northern and southern Europeans, the term 'appropriation' implies an active image of man, by which space is considered basically as a means to various ends. The conference discussed the modes of appropriation and its applications in the home, in

4 *Surrey*, October 1974: Psychology First, Architecture Second.'

workplaces, and in institutional places. Appropriately the discussion centred in appropriation, differentiation, alienation, participation, appellation, degustation, symbolization, identification, expropriation, and finally mis-appropriation!

Although my tone may seem critical in places, the concern of this review is not an all-round attack on the evolving new science of architectural psychology. The crucial task for architectural psychologists is to tell architects and planners the truth: how much we do know and what we are likely to find out in the near future in the pursuance of our empirical science. We need to establish which experiments have direct or indirect design implications, what type of work is helpful in identifying problems, and which studies are interesting or stimulating.

Nor should we pursue further the question of relevance. We must accept that some findings will and some will not be relevant to us. It would be presumptuous at this early stage of development in a new discipline to define the limits of *diversity*, or to state categorically what specific relevance the work should have. It would be rather like criticizing a child for not being an adult. 'Modern psychology has no history, just a past,' C. A. Mace wrote in the early sixties, referring to the empirical nature of psychology. This is even more so in the case of architectural psychology, which has a mere ten years of development. To assess its impact on architecture and planning would be premature, as some of its effects will be felt in the long term, especially in the changing attitudes of architects and planners towards people. In the short term, we have seen develop a healthy interest in the subject, a new climate of acceptance of the new discipline, and improved methods of study both observational and statistical. For example, factor analysis and multidimensional scaling techniques enable us to discover more subtle interrelationships between variables. In the study of colour we have moved far ahead of asking people to put six 'colours' in order of preference and (if there was some agreement among them) proclaim a universal order of preference. For by controlling the dimensions of saturation and brightness and treating the findings statistically we are able to reject the earlier studies and provide evidence that there is greater variability of preference *within* each hue, depending on its chromatic strength and lightness, than *between* different hues. In addition, there have been several first order solutions to problems of a specific nature which are of interest in their own right, though we cannot generalize from these results until we build more case studies and relate them to a theory. Feedback from people who live in buildings and neighbourhoods is more forthcoming now and is taken more seriously than before by architects and planners.

Participation was made a more respectable area of study after a whole section was devoted to it at

5 *Sheffield*, 1975: 'Education—Participation and Carl Marx.'

the Lund and Sheffield Conferences. Getting people involved at all levels of decision-making, from social planning to the later stages of architectural and urban design, so that they feel they are an active and contributing part of the environment they live in, has led since then to become the subject of a serious and ongoing debate. The word 'democracy' means that the decisions about people are made by the demos, i.e. by the people themselves. In our attempts to translate these ideals we have developed many political systems which claim in their own way to be a closer interpretation of them. Within each democracy—however loosely defined—the way in which participation and involvement is effected by people in their day-to-day affairs depends primarily on political, economic and social conditions, and so it is inappropriate and misplaced to suggest 'participatory models' which will be universally applicable. What could be said, however, is that within each political and socio-economic framework there should be some attempt to *improve* the real (as opposed to phenomenal) working of participatory mechanisms. The constant revisions of the law, the restructuring of industry, and some political manifestos, are attempts towards this improvement, and although outside the scope of this account they very much affect the decisions taken by the design professions. Some argue that architects and planners have very little to do with the way in which people's lives are influenced by their designs, and that the quality of life is overwhelmingly the product of political and economic considerations. However, such arguments debase what people can do as individuals and what they can do in their professional role as the active manipulators of the environment. It is a defeatist attitude based on a passive rather than an active image of Man, and I strongly believe that both architects and planners have a major say in participatory democracy.*

Planning for People is the title of the book by M. Broady in which he advocates that people, through voluntary associations and other bodies, should be much more involved in social planning. Planning has to be thought of not only as a matter of physical design and economic policy, but also as an educational social process which seeks to encourage the contributions which people themselves can make to the improvement of their own social environment.

In the field of architecture, Paul Rudolfsky wrote a book exclusively on *Architecture without Architects*, and John Turner, in his books *Freedom to Build* and *Housing for People*, stressed the vital importance of giving people a say in their environment, a view which was based on extensive studies in Europe and North and South America. He concluded:

'When dwellers control the major decisions and are free to make their own contribution to the design, construction or management of their housing, both the process and the environment produced simulate individual and social well-being. When people have no control over, nor responsibility for key decisions in the housing process, dwelling environments may instead become a barrier to personal fulfilment and a burden on the economy.'[8]

'Participation', 'citizen participation', 'consultation', are fashionable phrases at the moment and many people feel that much too much is being said about the process and that very little has been done about it. The importance of real participation in practice can hardly be over-estimated, provided that the right participatory approach is used in the right circumstances and is acted upon *after the problem has been identified*. Participation must not become a mere cosmetic attempt to appease people or to hide other considerations.

Mats Egelius's project (advisor Kiell Palmeby) in Uddevalla for his Goteborg firm v.b.b. is an example of a successful participatory exercise. His deep concern for people led him to convince his firm that there was architectural and social value to be gained from user consultation on a venture involving one hundred dwelling units developed for rented accommodation. The participation was with a representative group of 47 users who met fortnightly for three hours. Each gathering started with

* Consider in this respect the work of Lucien Kroll, p. 162, Walter Segal, p. 171, and H. Hertzberger, p. 38.

a short summary of the progress made during the preceding weeks, and was followed by group discussions on prepared topics. The first five meetings concerned how the users wanted to arrange their living environment. Subsequent discussions centred on site lay-out, dwelling lay-out, equipment standard, cost, communal buildings and landscaping. During coffee breaks slides were shown and discussion encouraged of other housing schemes, so that the people were made aware of their relative merits. Finally, the results from different subgroups were summarized and agreement was sought for future action.

This experiment proved very stimulating and worthwhile for all the three parties concerned; the prospective tenants, the housing association and the architects themselves. The close relationship that was formed between the people and the architects over a period of more than a year proved particularly invigorating. The cost of the whole exercise was approximately 100,000 Kr., which divided by one hundred dwellings comes to 1,000 Kr. or £100 per dwelling—a mere fraction of the total cost of each unit. Yet it was the first time in Sweden that participation had taken place for rented accommodation.

This was a successful form of participation because the problem was first identified and then analyzed carefully: the architect moved and worked from within the firm, changing existing attitudes

6 *Strasbourg*, 1976: 'Space Appropriation—Misappropriation.'

where necessary and convincingly arguing in architectural, economic and social terms that made sense to his employers. If the pressure had come from outside (for example, by way of a community action group, as may have been appropriate in a different set-up) this well-organized participatory exercise may not have been possible.

What is an appropriate form of participation for rented accommodation in Goteborg may be more similar to a comparable scheme in Alaska than to participation involving owner-occupier development in another part of Sweden. Identifying the particular problem in its context may be of more critical importance than political, economic and social considerations at a national or international level, or the intricate relationships between the central and local governments concerned.

Troubleshooters to natural disasters, such as Ian David of Oxford who has travelled in the past few years to such places as Nicaragua, India, Guatemala and Yugoslavia to bring architectural expertise to post-disaster housing, have realized that the issues involved are not primarily architectural. The efforts of certain relief agencies to house people made homeless by natural disasters are often misplaced. In the Guatemala earthquake some Western aid was so useless that it now has to be burned or buried. Analyzing people's needs, exploring their local coping mechanisms, and then filling the gaps from outside by providing expertise in safe construction techniques, tools and components, is the procedure which Davis sees as the only realistic role for external helpers.[9]

One of the most important lessons of this work, and of participation in general, is the directive towards the redefinition of the role of the architect. Without ignoring aesthetics (which has been unduly out of fashion lately, but underlies so many of our everyday decisions), the architect should fill a basically support role, helping people to be more resourceful and to identify and participate with their environments in every possible way, and liberating their latent creativity, so often suppressed in our industrialized society. The idea of 'home' should be extended to encompass the semi-private space outside or the trees that the occupant has helped to plant beyond his own garden.

One should see this redefined role of the architect within the context of other professionals in our society. Should we learn to do our own conveyancing, or should lawyers help us in a similar supportive fashion? Should accountants, economists, doctors impart to us some of their skills so that we could derive some pleasure of self-accomplishment? Surely there is an area within every profession open to the layman to develop according to his or her interests. Television, educational broadcasting (the Open University) and the increasing level of communication are all directions which could further this end. However, such redefinitions of roles would upset some fundamental and deep-seated values within society; and questions of competence, restrictive practices, all inevitably entangled among economic and political considerations, would also come into play.[10]

It seems timely, after considering the role of the architect, participation and the general relationship of psychology to architecture, to look more closely at the general area of 'human motivation', or 'human needs' as it is increasingly referred to in current architectural work.

By referring to human needs the architect might aspire to understand people better. But the danger is that he will become more confused than ever, or even that he will take up the false position of eloquently justifying his design decisions by reference to some obscure conscious or unconscious human need. The complexity and richness of personality patterns, the multiplicity of biological and socio-cultural determinants make his task of formulating an adequate understanding of personality extremely difficult until he tempers his knowledge with real-life experience. The most likely outcome is that he will tend towards one particular standpoint, one particular theory which will suit him best, instead of attempting to understand the diversity and richness of human needs. We will consider very briefly some of these possible approaches in the Appendix.

What are human needs? Are individual needs different from social needs? Do modern environments satisfy basic human needs? How far are architects and planners responsible for these environments? Do buildings or the lay-out of our cities *influence* our living needs and habits? Can we say that they affect or even *determine* our daily life? Or is it merely a question of the environment inhibiting or facilitating some of our routine behaviour until, after some time, the human capacity to adapt enables us to re-establish control of the situation. Perhaps environments only provide the context in which the more important influences of social and economic conditioning determine our behaviour: for some people argue that to consider that the environment *determines* our behaviour is anathema, an insult to our intelligence. But now look at the magazine article illustrated overleaf (fig. 7) and see whether Alida Baxter, a housewife, agrees with our discussion in the 'wall-game' she plays with her neighbours every day and night. Accounts of the same problem may be found in numerous (usually comic) plays and novels, and may be verified by our own and our friends experiences. The American sociologist Ervin Goffman, in his books *The Presentation of Self in Everyday Life* (Edinburgh University Press, 1956)

The wall game

ALIDA BAXTER's neighbours are such very close friends

SKETCHES BY FIDDY

Having thin walls is when a neighbour tells you she's got cystitis and you say, "Yes, I know".

For the past 15 months, my husband and I have lived in one cell of one of the largest blocks of flats in Europe. We only know our neighbours' names because we receive their wrongly-delivered mail, but I could tell you more about their personal habits than those of my best friends, and I hate to think what they could tell you about us.

The couple on the right talk to each other only after midnight, are addicted to TV sport and Wagner, play hide-and-seek, judging by their rubbish, live on Schweppes Tonic and potatoes. They have muttered rows (we all learn to mutter, eventually) about whether their bedroom window should be open or shut and practise Yoga over the weekends (probably the effect of two solid days next to us).

The girl on the left believes in quantity rather than quality, has giggly conversations with girls in her kitchen and sexual intercourse with men in her living-room. Her bathroom is always full of people relieving themselves, talking to each other and, thank God, frequently drowning whatever it is we're doing in our own bathroom at the time.

My most embarrassing moment occurred a week after we'd moved into our lovely (sic) new flat, when I was sitting on the loo spending a penny and someone 6″ behind me, hidden by green tiles and the bathroom cabinet, started doing exactly the same thing. After a few agonised staccato bursts, the anonymous one and I both gathered up our drawers and fled. By now my bladder control is exquisitely discreet.

My husband's worst moment was lying in bed telling me a filthy joke and hearing the people next door laugh at the punch line before I did. He's learned to speak so softly everyone at his office thinks he's got laryngitis.

It's as if every room were bugged, and we're reduced to secret agent tactics. If we want to have a private conversation we get under the shower, draw the curtains and splutter our confidences at each other through the drizzle. Apart from anything else, it's costing me a fortune in hairdos!

Entertaining is a nightmare. We spend the whole evening stopping our friends' mouths with alcohol, food and kisses, in the desperate hope they won't end up blackmail victims as the result of some unguarded comment. The girl next door stomped past us in the corridor, eyes averted, for weeks after a friend of ours had been to dinner and given us a detailed account of what he did in Gay Lib when he wasn't being a curate.

We're painfully aware of our sexual inadequacies, since we've heard what goes on six or seven times an evening on one side of us and three or four times a night on the other. I don't mind listening to other people doing it, but I don't want them to hear me. Since I had to put a creaking board under my bed because of my slipped disc, we've whiled away countless hours waiting till they all go out so that we can leap at each other without fearing they've pulled up their chairs for a bedside seat. But even this frustrating ruse isn't foolproof. Languidly wiping

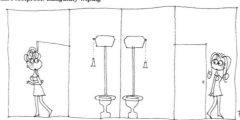

away the perspiration one afternoon, I suddenly heard a smothered noise behind the wall.

"The bastards!" I hissed. "They sneaked back in!" A stifled chortle confirmed the accusation.

My husband thinks I'm getting neurotic about our lack of privacy, possibly because I don't have as many orgasms as the girl next door. But *nobody* has as many orgasms as the girl next door.

One evening when we hadn't needed to turn the TV sound on at all because it was being supplied so adequately through the walls, we made the mistake of registering a complaint. Since then it's been total war. From the moment we grope for *Today* and one or other flank slams into Radio 1, it's ear-to-ear combat with no walls barred.

Both hating getting up, we have our most historic rows in the morning, drowning Robert Robinson's sarcasms with bitter insults, slammed doors and dropped milk bottles. Our neighbours sit palpitating, a couple of feet away from us, and we can always tell when they're listening because they go so quiet. If we pause for breath, they rush off to turn up the volume on everything from Tony Blackburn to a cassette of the last Nigel Gresley A4 locomotive coming through the Welwyn tunnels.

There's a ceasefire while we're at work, followed by transfusions of gin between 6.30 and 7.30, and then the hand which turns the switch rules the block. Whatever you want to listen to, get in first, if you don't feel you can bear crouching with your ear up against the loudspeaker in order to catch a word or two of your chosen programme.

From midnight on, the floor is clear for the insomniacs and the couple above us come into their own. They do their exercises in the early hours (at least we think it's their exercises), grind and percolate coffee by the gallon, and then play Linguaphone records on the learn-while-you-sleep principle. Unfortunately *we're* still wide awake, but even so my French has never been better.

Sitting hunched in our living-room, with *Match of the Day* thundering through from the flat on the right and almost drowning the keening of the girl who lives to our left having yet another climax, I try to understand why people want to live in communes, and I fail. Surely you only have to move into a flat in central London and all society's silly, artificial little barriers are immediately stripped away. There's no such thing as insularity when you belch in an empty room and a disembodied voice says "Pardon", but oh, how I wish there were. I know I'm just a neurotic hermit vainly searching for a cheap method of sound-proofing, but am I really alone? Is there anybody else who wants to go back to the days when you had to drill a hole in the wainscoting if you wanted to spy, or have modern builders brainwashed you all into accepting wall-to-wall eavesdropping? It may be a boon for earplug manufacturers, but it's driving me nuts.●

and *Behaviour in Public Places* (Glencoe Free Press, 1963), argues that despite our ability to communicate across boundaries such as a door or a window or even a thin wall, we learn through social conditioning to honour certain conventions which he calls 'conventional situational closure':

A glimpse of these conventions can be obtained by noting a fact about socialization: children in our middle-class society are firmly taught that, while it is possible to address a friend by shouting through the walls, or to get his attention by tapping on the window, it is none the less not permissible, and that a desire to engage anyone in the region must be ratified by first knocking at the door as the formal means of making entry.

Consider now Alida Baxter's behaviour in the light of Goffman's observations. Not only do we find that the social conventions are not maintained, but open recognition is given to the communication possibilities and her behaviour becomes completely dependent on what the neighbours do. If on the other hand, our Mrs Baxter were Mrs Yoshi Moto, thin walls would cause no problems. She would be perfectly accustomed to paper walls as acoustic screens, as the Japanese learn to rely on their own powers of concentration to screen out sound. Yet it is plain that the sensitive European finds it very difficult to cope with and adapt to thin walls; and as E. T. Hall convincingly argues in his book *The Human Dimension* he differs from the Japanese in responses to olfactory, tactile and thermal space as well as visual and auditory space. To the inquiring mind and the architect who wants to go beyond satisfying basic user requirements, it is obvious that we must distinguish between needs to which we have a biological predisposition and needs which, together with the way in which they are manifested, are the product of learning through socialization. It might then be possible to introduce new creative designs in the knowledge that people could adapt to them or come to appreciate them — perhaps through programmes of re-education; and by the same token the architect will recognize and understand certain limitations in design when dealing with needs deeply rooted in our biological make-up.

Human needs have been explained both by single-drive theories of motivation (for instance, by Sigmund Freud) and by multi-drive theories. A fuller account of Freud's theories, as well as of more sophisticated theories such as those of A. Maslow and G. Allport, is provided in the Appendix. There the hereditary and biological influences upon behaviour are mentioned, together with others. The relative importance and intensity of each specific need or instinct may be considered as hereditary, or drastically affected or suppressed by the environment, depending on which theory we uphold. For Maslow the satisfaction of the 'lower needs' is a precondition of the emergence of the 'higher needs'. Lewis Munford wrote in 1956 that 'to live in the highest sense is to be freed from the pressure to survive'. Yet according to R. Ardrey the need of identity is more important than the need of security and stimulation. Indeed, we could find many individuals from our own experience who do not follow Maslow's sequence or order.

Given the present state of knowledge, it would probably be futile to attempt a synthesis of these diverse approaches to produce a final list of needs or motivational goals, or to try to reduce these goals into categories. Anthropologists, social psychologists and sociologists have made it clear that goals vary considerably from culture to culture, and also differ between sub-cultures within each culture. Indeed, according to some of the psychological theories we have looked at, the organization of goals and needs is so distinctive and unique for each one of us that classification is clearly impossible.

Turning to more practical matters, we may ask if architects and planners can provide the environment for satisfying all these needs and goals? Can they work with others to create the right framework for every person's ultimate self-actualization'? Or are they too much motivated to actualize themselves when they produce a 'building'?

Unfortunately, we cannot answer these questions decisively as we have no objective criteria on which to base our judgements. Maslow has defined some of the characteristics of the 'self-actualized' person: he is independent, self-contained, spontaneous in behaviour and inner experience, creative and non-conformist—he does what he pleases. An architect with these qualities, of course, ignoring inhibitory social customs, could be truly creative if he 'rhymes with reason'. But by the same token he might be spoiled by too much creative freedom, 'self-actualizing' at the expense of everybody else. In fact, the chances are that an architect who looked at our lists of psychological needs could pick several which would exactly suit his pre-conceived schemes or justify any of his design decisions.

How we go about deciding the *degree* to which these needs are satisfied is yet another matter. And it is more difficult still to establish the complex dynamic inter-relationships between these needs. A psychologist would regard it as basic to anticipate that there will be significant individual differences towards participatory exercises, allowing a few people to pursue more egocentric 'self-actualizing' than the rest.

When Le Corbusier built his chapel at Ronchamp, was he satisfying the need of self-actualization or, in McClelland's theory, the need of achievement? Perhaps it was Adler's 'striving for superiority', or, most likely, Allport's 'functional autonomy' as it became a motivational influence in its own right and inspired the creator to create new masterpieces. And what about the old parishioners who commissioned the architect: which of their needs did the Chapel satisfy? Were their needs similar to those of the children who live near the Chapel or the shop-keepers who sell souvenirs nearby? Is it possible that the building has acquired a particular meaning over time?—that is, has it become a signifier, a symbol, a sign, a referent, an icon (to borrow but a few terms from the semiotician's language), and is it now part of an ideology, a morality, with an acquired motivational force of its own?

If the reader is not confused by now, he may not have been reading these theories carefully. In writing about human needs we referred to 'drives' which energize and direct behaviour, motivational forces and goals, energies, instincts, hereditary pre-dispositions, biological and innate tendencies, acquired drives and environmental influences. All these phrases and the more specific terms that theorists have attached to each of them, are labels, used to describe psychological drives or hypotheses about human needs, none of which has yet been firmly established on scientific grounds. In a sense the labels are 'makeshift', and to discuss and distinguish their meaning would take up a theoretical volume in itself.

The reason we spent some time in accounting for these diverse theories is mainly that one sees over and over again in architectural briefs and other writings some reference to 'human needs'. Some accounts define these needs simply in terms of safety, ventilation, sun, sleep, rest, etc., with no reference at all to any of the psychological needs we have considered here. It is to be hoped that architects who are unaware of work in this area will find this summary (including the emphasis on individual differences) revealing, and that they will follow it up with further exploration and incorporate some of the findings in design.

Others who are already more informed, and who may adhere to their own preferred hierarchy of human needs, perhaps run risks of a different nature. It may be appropriate to stress here that human needs have to be understood and studied *within the framework of each design problem*, and that familiarity with a theoretical framework is by itself totally insufficient. It is one thing to know about needs (and even to be able to recite from memory Murray's list of twenty) and another thing to isolate the relevant ones for a defined problem within a particular cultural context. *Knowing* about human needs is an important first step, *understanding* these needs a vital second, but evoking and expressing them through their *translation* in built form is a culminant third. It is at this stage that the creativity and sensitivity that is demanded of the architect becomes the critical factor. At this point the architect needs to be inspired by nature and art together, perhaps reading Nick Humphrey again to recall how Man's aesthetic sensitivity evolved,* and

* See pp. 59–73.

going out into nature to learn from experience what natural structures men find beautiful. Then he may return to his drawing-board and try to emulate these structures in design not by the naive way of mimicking natural objects, but by being inspired by the 'relations between the artificial elements exhibiting the felicitous rhymes of natural beauty'. It is at this stage too that we might all breathe a sigh of relief, as there is obviously no single solution; there is no prescribed answer to a design problem, and a building cannot be based on an unvarying systematic approach. Architecture is still an art, the 'unavoidable art' referred to in the title of this paper.[11] Some architects sometimes feel that when scientists or even laymen tell them what to do it interferes with their creative role, and they may resist this intrusion in a domain they consider as their exclusive reserve—after all *they* are the professionals and they know more about architecture than anyone else. The answer to this conflict lies in the definition and image of the architect's function. His creative role has to be tempered by his understanding of human needs. Just as he takes into account building and planning regulations, economic and other such considerations, he cannot these days produce a work of art *per se* at the expense of the people. It is in this marriage of interests, and in his understanding, that the architect's truly creative role resides.

We will be looking in the pages that follow at the practical work of architects who after going through the first two stages of knowing and understanding human needs, expounded them and then tried to translate them in their designs. There is no clear-cut case that architects who build *for* people are more humane than architects who build *with* people or 'barefoot' architects who *help* people build their homes. Whether the architect decides to locate his office on the site for continuous consultation, or chooses to live and work with the users or meet them informally over 'cake and beer' sessions depends entirely on his idiosyncratic feelings about the best way he *and* his team-mates can understand their client. The feeling of involvement and identity can be achieved right away in the initial stages of

design, or in rented accommodation at the stage when the tenant moves in for the first time to his new home. The final test, of course, rests on the verdict of the people themselves who live and use the buildings and obtain joy from their environments. This was in fact the test used in the choice of the people asked to write in this book: all of them have either built architecture for people or have, through their writings, the sacred ability to inspire the creation of a more human environment.

Notes to the text
[1] A. Hill, 'Visibility and Privacy' in D. Canter (ed.), *Architectural Psychology*, Proceedings of the Dalandhui Conference, (RIBA, London, 1970), pp. 39–43. (2) L. Sivik, 'The Language of Colour' in T. Porter and B. Mikellides (ed.), *Colour for Architecture* (Studio Vista, London, 1976), pp. 123–42. (3) I. Payne, 'Pupillary Response to Architectural Stimuli' in D. Canter (ed.), *Architectural Psychology* (1970), pp. 35–9. (4) I. Davis, *Shelter After Disaster* (Oxford Polytechnic Press, 1978). (5) B. Wells, 'Architectural Psychology: the evolution of a technology', *Architectural Association Quarterly*, July 1969, pp. 44–9. (6) S. Taylor and Lord Chave, *Mental Health and Environment* (Longman, 1964). (7) J. Desor, 'Toward a Psychological Theory of Crowding', *Journal of Personality and Social Psychology*, no. 21, 1972, pp. 79–83. (8) L. Kaufman and I. Rock, 'The Moon Illusion', *Scientific American*, July 1962, vol. 207, no. 1, pp. 120–30. (9) J. Lau, 'Differences Between Full-size and Scale-model Rooms in the Assessment of Lighting Quality' in D. Canter (ed.), *Architectural Psychology* (1970), pp. 43–8. (10) Carl-Axel Acking, 'Reduced Visual Ability and Environmental Experience', *Swedish Building Research*, no. S67, 1976.
[2] A recent Oxford examination question invited discussion of the proposition that 'Psychologists know more about rats than human beings', and Cambridge candidates have been asked to comment on the view that 'Taking a Ph.D. is a modern counterpart of the gentleman's tour of Europe in the nineteenth century, but is probably more harmful'. At the 1972 Postgraduate Conference in the Behavioural Sciences in Britain, there were papers on such diverse themes as 'Food and Fidelity in Frigate Birds', 'Prey Capture in the Golden Hamster', and 'Treatment of Couples for Sexual Difficulties by a Combination of Behavioural Techniques and the Methods of Masters and Johnson'.
[3] A. J. Lott and B. E. Lott, 'Group Cohesiveness as Interpersonal Attraction', *Psychology Bulletin*, vol. 64, pp. 259–309.
[4] D. E. Broadbent, *Behaviour* (Methuen, London, 1964), p. 204.
[5] B. Wells, 'Towards a Definition of Environmental Studies—A Psychologist's Contribution', *Architects Journal*, 22 Sept. 1965, p. 678.
[6] Reproduced in *Architectural Psychology, Newsletter*, no. 4, December 1975.
[7] M. Argyle, *The Psychology of Interpersonal Behaviour* (Penguin, Harmondsworth 1967).

[8] J. Turner, *Housing for People* (Marion Boyars, London, 1976).
[9] I. Davis, *Shelter After Disaster* (Oxford Polytechnic Press, 1978).
[10] 'In England the whole population of about forty seven million could be housed at an overall density of twelve houses to the acre, four persons per house, on 1,521 square miles, that is a square of thirty-nine miles. The area of the whole country is 50,869 square miles, so the area of such housing would be three per cent of the land surface. These figures are given merely to indicate the nature of the problem and put it into perspective: it would be silly to advocate housing everybody on twelfth-of-an-acre plots, and there are much better ways of planning homes, but even in densely populated England one may doubt the necessity for high-rise housing to be imposed upon people who do not want it. The root of our trouble lies in the scale of priorities and the unmitigated extravagance of industry in the use of land. This is abetted by planners who seem to delight in spacing-out industrial establishments on trading estates with a prodigality which would be condemned where it lavished upon housing.' (B. Allsopp, *Towards a Humane Architecture*, 1974.)
[11] This phrase is attributed to Dr Peter F. Smith.

Understanding People and Developing a Brief
Aldington and Craig

We find that a highly detailed brief is essential from which, and on which, to 'grow' a design. It is vital to determine the limitations. When they are truly defined—and understood—then one is free to work.

The brief contains all the normal data—physical requirements, like sizes of actual existing things, lists of accommodation for objects and people. It also contains psychological information. This mostly qualifies the physical data. It informs about feelings, states of mind, worries, likes and dislikes. It includes background information—almost anything interesting about the client, his job, her job, spare time, the site, the local traditions, and so on.

For us the psychological information is the most important of all, and it is this category of data that has the most profound and far-reaching effect on the 'physical' aspects—orientation, form, materials—of the building.

This experience reinforces the view that a brief is not a brief unless it not only *states* the problem but also *understands* it. This is the first stage of the creative process—UNDERSTANDING.

You are of no help to a client if you merely state his problem 'in your own words'. Many buildings are simply statements of problems, problems perpetuated in built form. In a good building the designer, by understanding, has used the problem and helped it to give birth to its own solution. The problem is there, inherent, but absorbed and enjoyed, in the final goal.

We find that conflicts are often very fruitful. Husband and wife are sometimes in conflict, simply because their natures are different; perhaps this forms part of their attraction.

A small and simple example of a resolved conflict can be shown by two people for whom we built a house on a beautiful hillside in the country. He is a professional man, fond of his wife, longing to live in, and on, this hillside. He brings accounting work home, goes through gardening catalogues, is enthusiastic and untidy. His wife—who used to be a managing director's secretary—very keen to have the new house, shares her husband's love of the country and gardening, is very conscientious, almost obsessively tidy, very, very clean and careful.

He said: 'I need a study to work in but I hate being in a room away from my wife, and anyway I want to enjoy this hillside. I have to have a study but I'll hate using it, and I'll probably bring the papers out into the living room and work there.'

She said: 'I'm not having a brand new house littered up with bits of your papers and books—it'll look awful. You've got to have some sort of study and *use* it because *I* want to look at the hillside without continually being put off by a lot of mess.'

They were, of course, describing the difficulties in terms of 'rooms', as this was their previous experience of existing buildings and they couldn't see how the problems could be resolved in other ways.

The solution was brought about by designing a living area (they wanted to be together most of the time) which included the 'living' activities of cooking, eating, sitting, reading, watching and so on. Certain feelings and physical requirements also made themselves felt—the clients wanted their eating/dining place to have a small, enclosed, 'cosy' feeling; the cooking part close to the eating but 'separated', the tables easy to lay, and so on; it must be possible to see the view from both areas; the sitting area must be the larger, more spacious in size and feeling, and nearest to the view and the hillside; again it must be separated to some extent from the other areas. And what about this 'study'? This was placed in a central position, not as a room but as an open box with steps either side connecting all areas (separating them too). The height of the box was carefully chosen. *He* can work and see *over* to his wife cooking and sitting, or to the hillside. *She* can work or look at the view and talk to her husband, and his 'clutter' is confined *in* a tidy enclosure. If he leaves something lying about it can be picked up and put in the 'box' without opening a door to a 'room'.

Our clients were very sceptical about this idea, and even more when they saw it being built. At this point it would have been all too easy to have lost an important part of the building. We had to persuade our clients that an act of faith was needed until the work was finished, and we undertook to remove it if it still worried them.

The house was completed and after three weeks of living with it they said it was the best thing in the building and christened it 'the doghouse', which it remains to this day. This eight-foot by five-foot work-station solved the problem and became the pivot for the whole living area of the house. The problem gave birth to the solution and the physical form of this part of the house was dictated *entirely* by an understanding of: feelings about a hillside, desires to live in a certain way, and a seemingly irritating psychological conflict about tidiness.

Comment is often made that detailed and personal briefing is relatively easy when dealing with a private client, but that as soon as one is faced with a group of people or a committee then de-personalization sets in and this is exacerbated further still if a building is being designed for, say, a large professional or local authority group where the personnel are unknown or may change frequently. It is a widely accepted fallacy that a building designed for a speculative or universal use will inevitably be of a soulless character.

1a-b House near Barnstaple, England. Photographs by Richard Einzig.

However, in our experience, what is required in such situations is that the architect should take even greater care to make sure that his brief is 'human'. It is too easy to fall into the trap of thinking that as one does not necessarily know the building user one must therefore make a nondescript building in order that it may suit everybody, and in its characterless way offend no-one by being easily adapted to the 'average' person. But who is the average person? The average person doesn't exist, and so by designing buildings for the average person one is designing for non-existent people. There is no need to say more—just look around you.

As an example of group briefing, the following may be of interest with regard to a small medical group practice we built in Oxfordshire. We were asked by the clients (who had some unusual ideas about the effects of buildings on patients) to provide accommodation for two doctors plus a treatment room, reception, etc.; and to look very carefully at the relationship between doctor and patient. The doctors felt strongly that the waiting 'room' which they used before had a bad effect on their waiting patients. This room—so characteristic, with its two rows of chairs facing each other, with the out-of-date magazines on a table in the middle, where people, embarrassed and worried, are forced to look at other equally embarrassed and worried people opposite, seemed to put the patients waiting to go into the consulting room in the worst frame of mind possible. Would it not, therefore, be a good idea to design something that did precisely the opposite?

The other major factor in the briefing was the importance of the confidentiality of the consultation. For these doctors this was the very kernel of general practice. The patient should not only be able to sit in an acoustically and visually private room, but actually be able to feel it. There is a big psychological difference here. Further to this, there was a requirement that the patient waiting in an area which gave a sense of freedom instead of a sense of imprisonment should be overlooked and reassured by a receptionist. At the same time the patient should not have contact, until called, with the doctor, whose own particular area should be

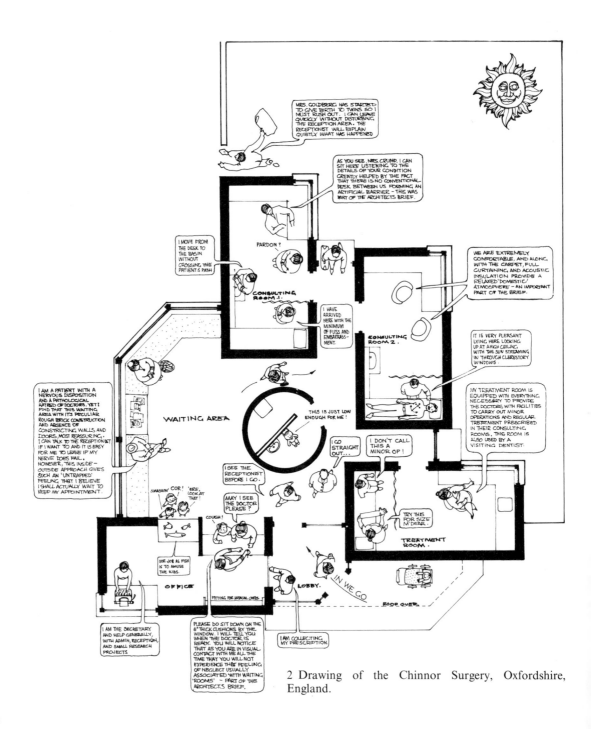

2 Drawing of the Chinnor Surgery, Oxfordshire, England.

3 The Chinnor Surgery, Oxfordshire, England.

kept away from the waiting area. Further to this, the patient should be routed out of the building via reception (without passing back through the waiting patients), so that the receptionist would know that he had left or be able to remind him of the necessity for another appointment. (See figs 2 and 3.)

The solution started off as an open space combining waiting and circulation to see if these could actually be amalgamated. At the same time the consulting room activity was closely examined to see what it should ideally consist of. It proved to be divided into basically two activities. The first was consultation, that is, a conversation between two people, rather than an interrogation, with a desk in between. The other activity was a physical examination requiring a couch.

Qualifying these basic needs were the further requirements that patients should enter through a door that was in the doctor's view and be able to sit down very quickly, against a wall to give a feeling of security. Natural light should fall on the patient's face but *not* from behind the doctor. Doctor and patient should sit across a corner of a writing surface. The patient should be able to get to the couch and undress easily without crossing the path

of the doctor, who should be able to get to a basin, wash his hands and then to the couch without crossing the path of the patient. This produced the double-square consulting room lay-out shown in the diagram.

Once the double-square was accepted, the acoustical privacy requirement was answered by producing this form as a separate building rather than a room inside a building and so the consulting room appeared as a little brick box with its own roof. The requirement for natural lighting over the couch without overlooking produced a 'monopitch' tilted roof with a clerestory window. Privacy with 'imprisonment' was implied in the lay-out and scale of the window over the desk. This was kept low and domestic in size with normal curtains reinforcing the general feel. The rooms were orientated so that they all looked out onto a small garden without overlooking each other; there was thus no need for obscured glass or blinds.

The requirement for acoustical privacy meant that the room had to be designed with a roof which was integral with roofs of other private or public areas, so the waiting area and circulation areas had their own roof levels, lower than those of the consulting rooms. The other problem was that of creating privacy between waiting area and consulting rooms without turning the waiting area into a prison. This was achieved by placing the services and toilet in a circular tower which effectively cut off the view of the patient from the doctors' areas, *but did not give the patients the feeling that they were being kept out*. This is important.

The finishes of the building, which are the basic materials of construction rather than applied finishes, also reinforce these points. The consulting rooms are little buildings and the waiting area is essentially an external space although it is under a roof—therefore all the materials in the waiting, circulation, outside area of the consulting room, are external materials. Once inside the consulting room the materials change. There is carpet, plaster, timber, curtains, all the things associated with being *inside*. The doors are effectively sealed. The feeling of quietness and privacy is reinforced.

Outside, the waiting area, with its freer forms and external materials, gives the patient the feeling that

4 Health Centre, Wellingborough.

he is welcome but not imprisoned, that he can go or stay as he wishes. People will stay if they know they can leave!

The treatment room and the office/reception areas were, in this instance, able to follow the same pattern as the consulting rooms, as they shared the same requirements. The form of the consulting room generated the form of the other two areas, so that a consistent aesthetic and plan form were set up. Their requirements fell quite happily into these forms: they were not forced.

This was the first time that such an approach had been used with a small group practice and the building created a good deal of comment. Feedback from patients and doctors was extremely favourable. Many patients told the doctor that they looked forward to visiting the surgery, whereas before they had to screw themselves up to do so; and the doctors were satisfied that the building was now working as a positive medical tool rather than something which merely exacerbated a patient's anxieties.

What we want to emphasize is that the building form, although answering certain physical needs and the demands of certain activities, was mainly generated by the emotions and feelings of the users. As designers we feel the important thing is to allow these emotions and feelings to work upon our imagination so that they can be intensified into a solution which celebrates rather than merely paraphrases the requirements.

The doctors who originally commissioned the scheme have now been replaced by other doctors who work equally happily in the building, and of course many of the patients have changed too. The new doctors and patients do not find the building design constricting because it was designed for others, and in answer to the question of particular buildings for particular people which will not therefore fit their successors, we would only say that this view seems odd when people will pay twice as much for a mill or a barn to convert into a house as they will for an ordinary house. It seems somehow contradictory that people should wish to live in a building designed for industry. Why do they? Surely because people react very favourably and strongly to a sense of character and are willing to go half-way to meet a building that has one. If a building has no character, if it is built for the non-existent average person, then the sense of dissatisfaction and frustration will be expressed in carping complaints.

The approach used for the Oxfordshire surgery was also applied in the design of a medical centre for 17 doctors, and all their attendant administrative staff, with a large treatment area in Northamptonshire. The problems here were different. The scale was very much bigger and the resultant built form was different. But the approach was the same as were the requirements on the part of the doctors to regard human beings as human beings, to do away with the institutional corridor and the anxieties it produces in the patient. Some of the experience gained at the smaller surgery was used in the larger one, but it was not simply converted like a carbon copy. The result has been a building which works happily for the doctors and the patients, although again many of the original people have since left.

These experiences have convinced us that you cannot design for averages and that it is pointless to try. The important things are statements of problems followed by understanding, and bringing to both understanding and design the exercise of imagination.

1 Housing at Pershore, Darbourne and Darke. The footpath through the central green is deflected around the existing trees.

Social Needs and Landscape Architecture
Darbourne and Darke

As architects we believe that if we balance against each other an exhaustive analysis of a design project the recognition of our inheritance and the necessity of economic restrictions, we arrive at an attitude towards architectural character—namely, that it cannot be either a recreation of the past nor an over-accelerated view of the future. Our fundamental philosophy is to try and discover the behavioural and psychological requirements of the individual or group in order to extend the demands of the brief. This approach applies to all types of building. On the other hand, the personality of the site, in its physical and cultural aspects, gives invention to the physical form and directions to architecture in general.

Our concern goes beyond the confines of answering a brief towards a formulation of attitudes to *social needs*. We recognize that the creation of new housing has failed to live up to the brave post-war aspirations. With the growth of heavy-handed, standardized development we increasingly felt that the integrated and sensitive balance between social responsibility, economy and, no less important, the *quality* of our surroundings, could be fully realized only through detailed diagnosis and finely tuned solutions. At the same time political and professional debate was giving indications of a movement to modify forms of tenure, subsidy, public and private ownership and so on, which led us to the conviction that the form and fabric of building should attempt to accommodate these future possibilities. The density of people living on a particular area of ground, or the number of inhabitants in a neighbourhood, has been one of the primary theoretical guides for planning control or development. Existing densities in many cities well exceed 200 persons per acre, and even some attractive and popular provincial towns have surprisingly high population densities within their most sought-after historical districts. The exodus to new towns is no complete solution for the majority of housing stress within cities. The continuation of high densities has therefore been understandably accepted, with the additional justification, apparently, that it has preserved family roots and maintained community facilities. The high blocks of the post-war era seemed to be the only way of creating the high-density housing that such an argument called for. Although the high blocks have largely been discredited, alternative methods of achieving high densities within low buildings have been found possible and it is arguable that these methods have

2 An exhaustive search for influences and constraints is considered essential to the design process and the physical characteristics of the site and its surroundings will almost certainly direct form of the solution.

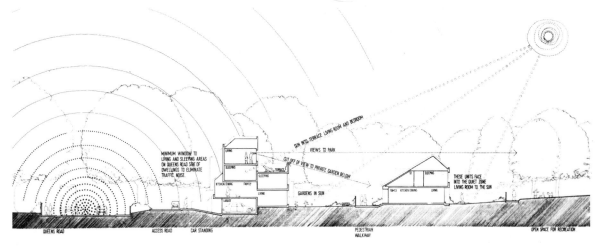

realized a more acceptable standard of social amenity. More families can now have gardens.

Given all this, it is worrying to witness the panicked over-reaction which has resulted in the issue of blanket, standardized directives aimed at almost halving original densities for outer and inner city redevelopment. Conversely, rehabilitation, rightly growing in importance, continues an automatic acceptance of high densities. This is surely an anomaly in attitudes or at least an understandable questioning of that over-reaction. Unfortunately, the present popularity of rehabilitation is not, in our view, always based on objective comparisons: it is often the result of a disillusion with bad modern design and a scepticism about the benefits of change.

In a state of crisis—the condition in which housing and other social services regularly exist—or in the competitive world of the 'market', economic considerations quite predictably hold a major dictate. Our work has been, and quite rightly so, subject to extensive restrictions in this respect.

Risking a generalization, we can say that this factor has often been responsible for our consistency in the choice of materials: the common view that this relates to totally subjective preferences is over-simplistic. A concern for economy of resource stabilizes a particular architectural interpretation, which is often of necessity fairly 'neutral'. To compensate, we therefore look towards the *landscape* concept which is developed as an integral part of any scheme.

Few will dispute that landscape architecture demands both scientific and artistic skills. This may sound pretentious in the context of so much of our work, yet these skills are required. The travesty of this principle is that not uncommonly the design of external spaces is seen as a cosmetic afterthought involving the capricious planting of trees, placing of plant boxes, and other accessories. Instead it should be integral to the architecture.

3a-b The Marquess Road Estate in Islington, London which succeeds in giving most of the tenants the feeling that they are living in houses rather than flats.

Shaping the Environment
Herman Hertzberger

It would be something if everything we made encouraged people to become more closely acquainted with their surroundings, with each other and with themselves.

This implies arranging things differently, so that the world, in so far as it is amenable to our influence, becomes less alien, less hard and abstract, a warmer, friendlier, more welcoming and appropriate place; in short, a world that is relevant to its inhabitants.

It is hardly possible for a more human architecture to concern itself with other than ordinary everyday things. Things apparently too unimportant to have far-reaching consequences, but which are in any case practicable and above all comprehensive.

We must combat the barrenness of the ever-expanding no-man's-land around us, by providing people with an appropriate environment with scope for everyone.

The more influence a person is able to exert on his surroundings, the more committed he becomes.

One becomes attached to things only when one is able to relate to them, when so much of one's own effort and feeling has gone into them that they become one's own, incorporated into one's own world of experience.

Architects can provide the basis for such a relationship by stimulating each person to make his own efforts to do something with his surroundings, according to his own point of view.

1a–b *Below:* Old people's home '*Die Drie Hoven*', Amsterdam. (a) Public space occupied by individual inhabitants.
(b) Interior street department for permanent care (tentative to avoid the usual hospital atmosphere).

2 Dwellings at Delft type diagoon 1967–1969. The concavities in the periphery could be built in with additions, and as such are an invitation to those inhabitants wishing to enlarge the inside of their houses.

The idea determining the carcase houses, 8 prototypes of which have been built in Delft, is that they are on principle uncomplete. The plan is to a certain extent indefinite, so that the occupants themselves will be able to decide how to divide the space and live in it: where they will sleep and where eat. If the composition of the family changes, the house can be adjusted and to a certain extent enlarged. What has been designed should be seen as an incomplete framework. The carcase is a half-product which everyone can complete according to his own needs.

Many people are of the opinion that, because of their relatively high building costs, these houses do make much sense as an experiment, and indeed we have not been able to prevent them being occupied by a group that is much too select in terms of income and motivation. And apart from that it is a very limited number of houses, so that whatever conclusions we make cannot be taken as generally valid.

It is an attempt to get away from a number of persistent stereotypes which still dominate housing. They are meant as prototypes to show what should be possible to-day as an answer to the sort of housing demands we suspect many people have.

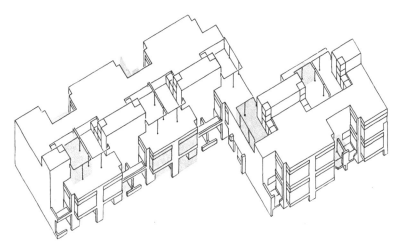

3 Office building Centraal Beheer, Apeldorn.

'Form must improve conditions, or rather, must lend a helping hand to people, inciting them to make their own improvements.'

'Architecture is able to help to improve living conditions, by clarifying the responsibilities and relationships of those involved with it, and bringing to light the amount of scope each person has for freedom of action, as well as showing where, by whom, and in what ways he is oppressed.'

'What we can do is to open up the scope of form, so that revaluation becomes easier, thus enabling established ideas and values to be phased out and replaced, in order to make way for better relationships.'

Let us try and contribute to an environment which gives people more chance to impress it with their own individual characteristics. It must also be responsive to loving attention, thus enabling it to be taken over by each person as an essentially familiar place. The more involved a person is in the shaping and maintenance of his surroundings, the more appropriate they become and the more easily appropriated by him; but just as he takes possession of his surroundings so will they also take possession of him.

This care and solicitude creates a situation in which a person appears to be needed by his surroundings. Not only does he have some control over them, but they in turn are a reflection of him, and have some control over him too.

In this way, form and user interpret and adapt to each other, each enhancing the other in a process of mutual submission.

Put like this, the relationship between the built-up environment and its users is analogous to that between an instrument and its player.

In principle the instrument contains as many possibilities as can be drawn from it while being played. It is up to the player to draw as much out of the instrument as he can, within its range. So both instrument and player continually reveal their ability to complement and fulfil each other. Form as instrument offers each person the scope to do what he most desires, and above all, to do it in his own way.

That is why form must allow for both individual and communal activities, and their significance and associations. It should, moreover, be able to call forth in each person fresh ways of using it.

Therefore, form itself has to contain the incentive that provokes each person into making the choice most appropriate in his current circumstances. This unusual kind of hospitality is the feeling for people, their values and their dignity which should be inherent in everything we make.

Educating the Client

Bruce Allsopp

If I am to make a valid comment it can only be in the context of my thinking about the social relevance of art which has been developed in a series of books since 1955 and most recently in *Ecological Morality* (1972), *Towards a Humane Architecture* (1974) and *A Modern Theory of Architecture* (1977), in all of which I have maintained that art is a necessary human activity; a means of understanding ourselves and nature, a means of creating and a means of communication.[1] Architecture has rightly been regarded as one of the arts and, as such, it employs a medium to which it gives order and significance. The medium of the architect is building; but whereas the painter's materials need cost him very little and the poet uses the free currency of words, which only acquire value by the use to which he puts them, the architect almost always depends upon the expenditure of large amounts of other people's money. Naturally the patron has had a say in the design and, in some cases, he regarded the architect as a useful servant for implementing the patron's own ideas. In religious, as well as civil architecture, constraints upon the architect were strong and design was achieved by a close relationship between architect and patron which assured that the human needs of the patron, as he himself saw them, were not disregarded.

It happened that the modern movement in architecture coincided with the rapid decline of the personal patron and his replacement by a *client*—a word which implies a different relationship: moreover this client is now seldom an individual person. More and more building is promoted by boards, committees, councils and institutions, and these multiple clients depend increasingly upon institutional finance—the investments of insurance companies, banks and pension funds. Cost-effectiveness and profitability have become major constraints and relatively rarely is the client going to be the actual occupier of the completed building. In these conditions much of the design-thinking, previously done by the patron, has had to be done by the architect.

The gain in autonomy by the architect was, in some ways, gratifying but the tensions which had

automatically related architecture to people were relaxed or removed. Early in the present century, under the influence of the Arts and Crafts Movement, sympathy with materials, the disciplines of hand craftsmanship and the basic assumption that pleasing decoration was an integral part of architecture, had established formats which were socially acceptable and lasted until the 1930s. The alternative ideology of the Modern Movement attempted to give aesthetic value to functionalism; but with anything so multi-functional as a building this was abortive.[2] Form followed fashion, derived to a large extent from admiration of machines such as aeroplanes and motor cars, and the developing science of aerodynamics.[3] Architecture was cut off from tradition and from any viable aesthetic theory.

One answer was to abandon the notion of architecture being an art and model building on the motor industry which was producing sleek, socially acceptable models, anonymously designed and differentiated, from year to year, by an evolutionary process activated by fashion, which was influenced by a few 'top designers' of very expensive models. This manifestly elitist system was closely analogous to the clothing industry and reduced the great art of architecture to the ephemeral level of costume. In comparison, Gilbert Scott's belief that architecture is the art of decorating structure might seem to be respectable!

In the ruinous wake of the Second World War social-utilitarian architecture flourished, most of all in Britain where concern for people set aside artistic considerations and required decent accommodation. 'Houses before offices' and 'Farms before motorways' are still valid slogans in a country which is in the forefront of experiencing the after-effects of a world-wide industrial revolution which it pioneered. For other industrial countries Britain is a demonstration on a laboratory scale of the problems which lie ahead, and not least in architecture.

Social-utilitarianism largely displaced formal functionalism in the 1950s. An enormous amount of building was contrived (I cannot say designed) by people whose artistic ability was negligible—

worthy, well-meaning people though they were. The resultant quality of environment is, in many cases, appalling and though one might have thought that at least such buildings would have had commodity and firmness, this is not always so. It seems that socialism without art, when applied to building, does not satisfy basic human needs.

Some architects have recognized that what the public requires and expects from them is that, as architects, they should produce beautiful buildings, and despite the enormous philosophical difficulties which we cannot discuss here,[4] 'beautiful buildings' means architecture which people admire and enjoy, buildings which give beloved identity to places. At one end of the scale there are buildings like St Paul's Cathedral in London, Sydney Opera House and the Royal Liver Building in Liverpool: at the other end there are pantiled cottages, a market cross, a Victorian public house, a classical *mairie* in France, a needle-like copper spire in an alpine valley, or just a row of terrace houses which have, in some way or other, a 'little bit of character' which differentiates them and those who live in them from the abyss of anonymity.

Unhappily this awareness of the need for architecture which is art, at whatever level—from the sublime to the vernacular—became enmeshed in an extraordinary phenomenon of our time, the widespread belief, propagated in most schools and in many colleges of art, that art *is* self-expression.

The naïve idea that, in making a work of art, the artist is merely expressing himself cannot be discussed here, but this is not what art is about. Certainly in architecture the idea that an architect's art is an expression of himself can only be sustainable, in a social context, if he actually believes that by expressing *himself* he is benefitting society. Art is not self-expression but in the present social climate many people attempt to relieve the pent-up feelings generated in modern society (and partly as a result of the inhumanity of modern architectural environments), by performing para-artistic activities which may well be a valuable form of psychotherapy. It would be foolish to suppose that the results of this treatment are comparable in nature with the works of art produced by Michelangelo, Mozart or Wren. They are different in kind. They are valuable as an activity, not for what they produce. Unhappily architects of considerable talent have been caught up in the wave of self-expressionism which has affected the other arts.[5] But great artists are rare: even competent artists are uncommon, and yet people expect of architects, among whom possibly 0·1% have high artistic talent, that they should produce artistic architecture. If 99·9% of architects are to have no firmer aesthetic base than self-expressionism the outlook is bleak; 'doing one's own thing' is, indeed, antithetical to doing what other people want.

Though architects will fiercely deny this, there is not enough talent to go round. The answer to this problem is provided by history. All the great civilizations, with their virtues and their faults, have accumulated architectural formats in which two things are possible. *Firstly*, the architect of genius can amplify the format and, *secondly*, the format, carefully studied as a system of design within socially acceptable limits, enables minor architects to do good work.

But how are we to create a format comparable with the great systems of Classical, Gothic or Islamic architecture? Certainly not by imposing upon people what we believe to be good for them, no matter how good our sociological, religious, psychological, ideological or aesthetic reasons may seem to us to be. If we are to have humane architecture which 'speaks to the condition' of people as they are, and not as we might think they ought to be, we must learn to serve through architecture, not impose ourselves for our own satisfaction. The simple answer is that to achieve architecture architects must be humble to their art and love their fellow men. But this also applies to all who build, to bankers, insurance companies, speculators and governments, local and national.

I do not see how we can hope to restore the productive safeguards of the old patron-to-architect relationship, so we need to create a group of people with a body of knowledge, based upon genuine understanding of and feeling for the real and changing needs of people. Perhaps in our institutionalized society we should have professional clients. Architects cannot produce good architecture all on their own. I believe they want to satisfy humane requirements: they will not, and I would think cannot, become proficient in doing so on their own without impairing their ability as architects. The failure of modern architecture in recent years is only partly the fault of architects. The main burden of blame for inhumane architecture must rest upon clients who have failed to educate themselves for the great responsibilities they undertake.

Notes to the text

[1] B. Allsopp, *Ecological Morality* (Frederick Muller, London, and Bunri, Tokyo, 1972) (also published as *The Garden Earth*, Morrow, New York, 1972); B. Allsopp, *Towards a Humane Architecture* (Frederick Muller, London, and Bunri, Tokyo, 1974); B. Allsopp, *A Modern Theory of Architecture* (Routledge & Kegan Paul, London, 1977).
[2] B. Allsopp, *Art and the Nature of Architecture* (Pitman, London, 1952).
[3] See Le Corbusier, *Vers une Architecture* (Paris, 1927).
[4] B. Allsopp, *Art and the Nature of Architecture*; and *The Future of the Arts* (Pitman, London, 1959).
[5] In *The Future of the Arts* I thought that functional and social restraints would preserve architecture from self-expressionism which I then saw as a danger to the other arts, but I was wrong.

Whose Failure is Modern Architecture?

Oscar Newman

In response to growing public disaffection the modern movement in architecture has become the subject of increasing attack by architectural critics and the practising profession. Peter Blake, for twelve years editor of the prestigious *Architectural Forum* and author of *The Master Builders*, a 1960s' series which deified Frank Lloyd Wright, Le Corbusier and Mies van der Rohe, has now joined the ranks of defilers in his new book *Form Follows Fiasco: Why Modern Architecture Hasn't Worked*.

Brent Brolin, representing both the new generation of young architects and the promising breed of environmental designers, has expressed equal disillusionment in his *The Failure of Modern Architecture* (London and New York, 1976). Philip Johnson, recent recipient of the highest award bestowed by the profession, the Gold Medal of the American Institute of Architects, and a man whose seminal work on Mies van der Rohe (1947) brought modern architecture into prominence among the *cognoscenti*, has, in his New American Telephone and Telegraph Building, subjected his otherwise modern building to the symbolic appendages of the Roman Empire (fig. 1).

In my view the current self-flagellation of the architectural profession and its critics is not the consequence of a considered reassessment of the modern design philosophy but simply the voguish abandonment of a style which has dominated architectural design for half a century. Unfortunately the social values and planning methods of the modern movement, which were its *raison d'être* and are its saving grace, are also being forsaken. There are some European critics who claim that the only facet of modern architecture that received transfer to America was its style. In that light it isn't modern architecture that has failed but the straw man that was made of it. It is possible too that the failure runs much deeper: that the architectural profession has been unable to perceive and adopt a relevant role for itself in twentieth-century society. The modern movement in the thirties provided both the insight and the vehicle to allow such an evolution, but it was shunned. The general practitioner, because he persisted in viewing himself in the traditional role of Renaissance man, failed to appreciate the new functions required of architectural form in the twentieth century: modernism was thus reduced to the status of a new style. To understand the current malaise one must look to the origins of the modern movement in Europe, examine the buildings of the twenties and thirties that were its best achievements, and then follow its descent and usurpation by practitioners who could not relinquish their cherished historical roles even at the expense of facing obsolescence.

Modern architecture became the predominant style of building in America after World War II. In all of our schools of architecture it replaced the Beaux Arts tradition of the eclectic use of historical styles. It was heralded by the practitioner as a major breakthrough: a design philosophy which would allow industrial technology to receive direct expression in building. With a modern architecture, it was reasoned, architects could remain true to the inherent capacities of the new materials, and buildings would cost less because they would not have to be distorted into contemporary configurations of past monuments nor covered with fake ornament. The naked function of a modern building and the bones of its structure would be its final form. Finally, modern architecture, in allowing us to answer our spatial needs through uncluttered forms, would also become the symbol of a society which was able to shear away the old rituals and restrictions of the past and to attack the problems of the present boldly and directly.

But this is not what happened. Despite their designers' commitment to 'functionalism', many modern buildings have proven impossible to use and have had to be either drastically modified or completely torn down. Pruitt-Igoe, the 2,700-unit public housing project in St. Louis that was demolished a few years ago, is the most often cited

1 *Opposite* The proposed new AT & T building by Philip Johnson. In the chaos that has resulted from the current disenchantment with modern architecture, Philip Johnson has been able to return to his first love and give free vent to monumental Classicism.

example—although Louis Kahn's medical laboratories at the University of Pennsylvania, Philip Johnson's dormitories at Sarah Lawrence, and Ralph Rapson's Cedar Riverside housing development in Minneapolis are more important failures, in that little cost was spared in their construction.

Buildings constructed in the service of the modern style have not cost less than conventional buildings because, in the architects' concern for expressing the structural elements, they have had to abandon the traditional two-stage process of building. Contractors normally assemble buildings by first putting up the rough structural, mechanical and electrical components, with no concern for neatness. They then bring in a new crew of skilled craftsmen to cover up the rough work with costly finishing materials. With an architectural style which demands that the steel and concrete of a building's structure be exposed, the work previously classified as rough now became the finished product, and so had to be installed with great care by highly skilled and expensive craftsmen.

The final irony is that for low- and middle-income groups—the user-group thought to be the most important beneficiaries of modern architecture—these spare buildings have not symbolized the new progress and directness but rather the provision of basic needs in the most uninspired and unadorned fashion possible.

The search for a modern style was not born simply of the pursuit of new fashion. It was initiated as a result of architects having become consciously aware of four things: that in the new industrial society the mass of people attracted to the large industrial centres replaced the rich and the established institutions as the architects' new client; that the buildings their new clients needed were not palaces, temples or mausoleums but housing, schools, factories and office buildings; that if architects were to provide the quantity of these buildings needed to satisfy the new, urban mass society, they would have to do it expeditiously, the new industrial technology would have to be the source of the materials and the means for putting materials together into buildings. The fourth new area of

consciousness that one detects in the first modern architecture is their growing discomfort with the use of traditional styles. They perceived that the draping of schools, office buildings, and factories in steel and concrete replicas of Greek temples would be a disservice both to the activities to be housed and to the materials and technology employed.

One of the more important attributes of the modern architecture style was the freedom it gave architects to plan the interior areas of buildings without regard to the previous conventions which required them to house activities within contemporary duplicates of building forms out of the past, whether Classical, Gothic or Romanesque. The modern style also gave architects licence to expose the materials used rather than to cover them in plaster appliqué columns. With the new style, architects could open whole wall surfaces to light and air. They were freed to assemble their new materials within the framework of a new form language that owed more to modern art and the form of ships, airplanes and warehouses than to the rule systems for applying the old architectural orders.

The pity is that few architects were able to rise to the occasion—they were unable to cope with the formal liberty that modern architecture gave them. The old architectural styles may have been a hindrance, but they were also a crutch. In the absence of these aids many of the lost generation sought out a new order. The restrictions of the old were soon to be replaced by the restrictions of a new, codified style. The activities of the new society were to be regimented into a new formal order; the satisfaction of the spatial needs of the buildings' users were again to be relegated to secondary importance. Much of the form language of Mies van der Rohe, for instance, is as restrictive as would be attempting to house such activities within a Greek temple. The minutia of a Mies steel detail is also as taxing as the ordering system of the Baroque and, I must add, as unrelated to the inherent capacities of the materials used (fig. 2).

Philip Johnson's recent dismissal of the modern idiom and his adoption of a new Classical style

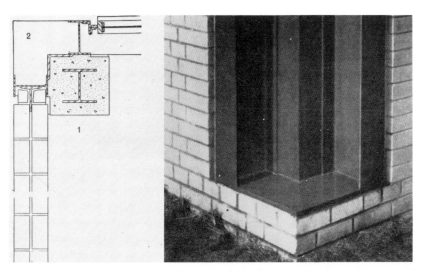

2 Photo and detail drawing of a corner of Mies van der Rohe's, Alumni Memorial Hall at I.I.T. The external column and its complex connections to the brick wall are unnecessary artifacts. The detail reveals the internal structural steel column buried in the concrete to meet the local fire codes. The external steel column and brick walls are non-load bearing.

3 Crown Hall in the I.I.T. Campus, by Mies van der Rohe.

appears to have surprised and shocked the practising profession and its critics. But from his writing and work it is clear that Johnson was always disdainful of both the social concerns and planning methods of modern architecture. His selection of Mies van der Rohe as his master, and as the architect with whom he would introduce modern architecture to America, is consistent with his stylistic predilections. For of all the identified pioneers of the modern movement, Mies van der Rohe in his language of forms and planning method is the most Classical and geometrically constrictive. His architecture is less concerned with the activities that are to be housed than with maintaining the purity of his forms. Some of Mies van der Rohe's buildings at the Illinois Institute of Technology are little more than monumental sculptures which

incidentally and almost *post facto* also house things like administrative offices and classrooms (fig. 3).

Most of Philip Johnson's buildings also fall into this category. It is clear that his primary interest is with the visual imagery of his buildings and not with satisfying the spatial needs of the buildings' eventual users. Johnson's major architectural successes have as a consequence been buildings in which the programmatic needs were simple and could be satisfied in virtually any kind of large open space—his churches and exhibition galleries (fig. 4). How, then, do Johnson's obsessions and predilections differ from those of the architects of classical times? Very little. How are his buildings

4 Philip Johnson's, Amon Carter Museum of Western Art, Forth Worth, Texas, 1961.

modern? Only in that they appear to be done in what, in America, has been loosely termed the modern style. The buildings of Mies van der Rohe and Philip Johnson, evaluated in terms of their planning freedom, their ability to serve their clients' needs, and their use of contemporary technology, are not really modern. Johnson's current decision to place an open Greek pediment atop his new American Telephone and Telegraph building does not make this building fundamentally different from any of his previous, so-called 'modern' buildings: he has just come out from being a closet classicist.

In the four or so generations of architects that have been produced by American schools since World War II, following the adoption of modern architecture as the current vogue, it is hard to find very many American practitioners who are aware of the sociopolitical roots of the modern movement or of the planning and technical disciplines that were its foundation. Modern architecture in America has simply been: the modern style. The prevailing ignorance of these roots in America is not surprising. The European practitioners who fled the holocaust to introduce modern architecture to America were not willing to live through another witch-hunt. McCarthyism was running rampant in this country just at the time when modern architecture was beginning to come into its own. It would not have bode well, at that time, to have referred to its social concerns. Hitler had already labelled modern ar-architecture as *Kulturbolschewismus*; who knows what McCarthy would have called it had he been made aware of its origins.

But in fairness it must be admitted that the very birth of modern architecture in Europe was itself steeped in philosophical conflict. From its earliest discernible signs, at the turn of the century, there was already evidence of two distinct schools of modernism. Where one school was determined to use the new technology and materials to address the needs of the new urban populace, the other became enamoured with the forms of the new machines and engineering structures. The form language of transportation, machines and factories became an inspiration for the creation of a new style. Both

schools talked of the liberating qualities of the new architecture—but their work suggests that each meant very different things by it.

I have labelled one group the 'social-methodologists'—both for making their central concern the definition of the building needs of the mass of society and for their evolution of a design methodology which strove for an unrestrictive development of a building lay-out and straightforward use of the new industrial techniques. The other group I have labelled the 'style-metaphysicists'—first for making their prime interest the creation of a new architectural style, and second for their belief in the deterministic qualities inherent in the intangible symbolism of spatial and formal configurations. Assigning particular architects, or groups of architects, to one or the other of these two schools is a more difficult task than the identification of the values of each school. Many practitioners and theorists managed to keep a foot in each camp—often to their own continuing imbalance and dismay. Walter Gropius was certainly one of these, while Le Corbusier—the crowning achievement of the style-metaphysicist camp—at times produced exemplary buildings in the other tradition.

The social-methodologists recognized the potential benefits of mass production and the availability of products at a mass scale as a means of providing for the needs of a mass society. They were committed to the use of the new technology to provide the new working and middle classes with decent housing, schools, hospitals, factories and recreation areas. This group can be recognized as early as the turn of the century in the Arts and Crafts Movement in England, the Chicago School in America, the German Rationalists, and the Dutch School of Berlage, Berhrens and Loos. The practitioners of the 1920s and 1930s who followed in their footsteps were the Germans Hugo Haring, Mart Stamm, Ernst May and Hannes Meyer; the Dutchmen B. Bijvoet, J. Duiker and L. C. van der Flugt; and the Finn Alvar Aalto. Their buildings are noted for the freedom with which the various facilities to be housed are positioned on the site and placed adjacent to each other so as to be of greatest utility to the building's users. The internal uses dictate the shaping and assembly of spaces and the final building mass. Yet in spite of the fact that a formal mishmash might easily have resulted from such a method of shaping and grouping areas, these architects succeeded in creating a form language which gave their buildings a satisfactory unity. In addition these buildings are noted for their direct use and expression of contemporary materials. The new building technologies (the ability to span large distances and to free walls of their load-bearing function) are also employed to produce internal spaces which have more natural light and greater flexibility of organization. The Zonnestraal Sanitorium by Bijvoet and Duiker (1928, fig 5), the workers' housing of Ernst May (1926), and the Van Nelle Factory of Brinkmann and Van der Flugt (1928, fig. 6), are all excellent examples of the social-methodologists' school of modern architecture.

The style-metaphysicists, on the other hand, chose to see in the new technology, the new materials and the rapid growth of cities a liberation from the traditional stylistic and technical restrictions of the past. They saw in the forms of factories, trains, ships and planes a new esthetic, a new style that could be applied to the three-dimensional art of architecture. Instead of seeing the forms of ships and air-planes as direct expression of their own particular utilitarian func-

5 The Zonnestraal Sanatorium in Hilversum, by Bijvoet and Duiker, 1928. The reinforced concrete construction allowed large sections of the building's peripheral skin to be clad in glass, where sunlight, view and association with outside areas were deemed desirable. The form of the building grows from the assembly of the building's internal areas. This occasionally results in very complex facades which the architects have nevertheless been able to reconcile into an acceptable formal composition.

tions (the equivalent of which would have to be found for schools, housing, etc.), they saw in the stylistic language of these machines forms which could be cut out and applied to buildings independently of any consideration of their function (fig. 7). The fact that many of the 'new' buildings, such as houses, also fulfilled rather traditional functions was obviously somewhat bothersome. Those who were troubled by these contradictions reconciled them by turning a group of houses into a massive tower and conceived of homes as machines for living. For the style-metaphysicists, the stylistic purity of their new form language became their dominating concern; the activity to be housed within their buildings was relegated to secondary importance—it was either straight-jacketed into the new form or only minimally provided for (figs 8 and 9). Having justified the revolution in architecture with claims that the old revivalist schools

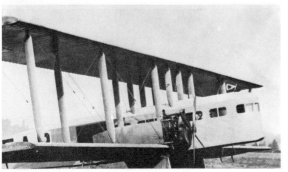

8 Rietveld's house at Utrecht. For all the planning freedom this formal geometry allowed the architect (a rationale he employed to justify its style), it is disappointing to find the house poorly laid out; its various functional requirements were seriously compromised to serve the formal idioms.

6 The Van Nelle tobacco factory, Rotterdam, 1928, by L. C. van der Vlugt. The factory provides natural light and ventilated work areas for both office and factory workers. It also includes recreation rooms, lounges and dining facilities. It compares well with the best of contemporary, humane working environments.

7 Illustration from Le Corbusier's, *Towards a New Architecture*, first published in London in 1927. The forms of the new airplanes were used as direct source material in devising a new form language for modern architecture. The style-metaphysicists did not study the forms of the new machines in light of the jobs they had to perform and then try to find an equivalent for buildings, they simply stole the machine forms and applied them to buildings directly and, often, inappropriately.

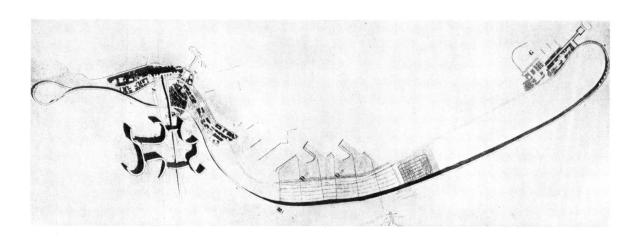

put impossible restraints on the planning of contemporary buildings, they in turn fell into exactly the same trap; the stylistic demands of their band of modern architecture soon made it difficult to address their design problems straightforwardly.

In their search for a way to use modern technology to address the building needs of the new concentration of urban populations, architects had sought a form language that would not require costly hand labour and ornamentation. The richness and pleasure in form was to come instead from the geometric play of proportions, colour and materials. The spareness of means evoked the search for and heralding of the spare style. But the new style soon became mistaken for its purpose; the medium had become the message.

In the planning of housing developments the style-metaphysicists saw only the opportunity to design on the grand scale, to wipe out the relics of the past—the traditional buildings and endless rows of single-family workers' houses—and to replace them with an architecture that reached up to assume in height its relative proportion to the horizontal spread of the city. They designed buildings that could be seen for miles, that moved along highways the length of a city, that housed the new masses in a mass architecture. The architects advocating this philosophy labelled themselves NeoPlasticists, Purists, De Stijl, and included the practitioners

9 Le Corbusier's City Plan for Algiers. The project was entitled 'shrapnel', 'with the intention of breaking through, for once, all the administrative red-tape and to establish in city-planning the new scales of dimensions required by contemporary realities.' (*Le Corbusier, 1910–1960*, p. 299 Girsberger, Zurich, 1960).

Rietveld, van Doesburg, Mies van der Rohe, and Le Corbusier.

In the early 1930s there appeared to be little conflict between the two philosophies. To each of their proponents they seemed united by a common goal. Their dispute was with a common enemy: the traditional practitioner still caught up in the endless application of NeoGothic, NeoClassical, and NeoRenaissance styles. But as one traces the association between the members of the two groups, their differences become more clear and their conflict and parting become inevitable.

The International Congress of Modern Architecture (CIAM) was, from the late 1920s to the mid-1950s, the organization which was both the arena for and spokesman of the modern movement. Gropius, Giedion, Mies, Le Corbusier and many others were among its founding and active members. From its inception it managed to serve the interests of both the stylists and the methodologists. But after their initial meeting in 1928 one can trace the increasing rivalry, misunderstanding, and dominance of first one group, then the other, to the final dissolution of CIAM at the Dubrovnik conference in 1956.

The purpose of the first CIAM conference, which took place in La Sarraz, was to frame the Association's aims and statutes, and to enunciate some general working principles:

'It is the destiny of architecture to exhibit the preoccupations of its time; works of architecture cannot help but be reflective of their current circumstance. Modern architecture therefore can only move into a direction determined in concern with economic factors.

The ratio between housing areas and areas set aside for parks (including play areas) and areas required for circulation are determined as a consequence of the current social and economic milieu. The very act of establishing a housing density effectively predetermines the social class of the user.' (Excerpt from the CIAM La Sarraz Declaration, 1928)

The theme at the 1929 Frankfurt meeting was 'Dwellings for the Lower Income Groups', and the work presented on that occasion can be considered as nothing less than a revolutionary approach to the problems of contemporary housing. The Frankfurt meeting laid a foundation for modern architecture much beyond the limits of the immediate problem tackled. The same theme was taken up again in 1930 at Brussels and extended to the town-planning scale. Walter Gropius' speech, summarizing the most recent experiences of German rationalism, raised for the first time the question of the relationship between flats, buildings, neighbourhood units and the town, and offered a precise set of formulations for discussion.

In 1933 CIAM met in Athens on the theme 'The Functional City', and issued the 'Charter of Athens'. This document represents the conclusive outcome of a period of concrete and fruitful work— the results of what must now be viewed as a golden age in modern architecture. For the first time in the history of architecture a group of architects from every industrialized country in the world devoted themselves to a survey of the problems of human settlements and recognized the shortcomings of architectural action which did not proceed from an understanding of the urban phenomenon in which it found itself. The 95 articles of the Charter examine these many questions in concrete terms; no question of a modern style is raised, only questions of method. The question of style and the metaphysics of space appear several years later at the Paris meeting in 1937, when CIAM began to rest in the shade of Le Corbusier's prestige.

In 1947 at Bridgewater, the meeting was devoted to re-establishing contacts severed by World War II and to reviewing the past ten years. From now on the style-metaphysicists would dominate the Congress. The theme of the Bergama meeting· in 1949 was 'The Architecture of Settlement', but the main interest was in Le Corbusier's *'Grille'*, a graphic system devised by Le Corbusier and his disciples in which to render all presentations of projects so as to make them conform to a uniform style. While a war-devastated world grappled with the enormous task of reconstruction, CIAM discussed the usefulness of the Le Corbusier grid, how to employ the grid, the best way to pack the grid. The credibility of the architectural profession in lending knowledge and method to problems of reconstruction was at stake.

The theme of the 1951 meeting in Hoddesdon was 'The Core of the City'. The report which was drafted at the meeting contains such a collection of inaccurate statements and idle speculation on the relationship between urban problems and built form that one wonders how so many of those who also participated in drafting the Charter of Athens ever put up with it.

Looking back at the workers' housing of Mark Stamm and Ernst May presented at the CIAM conference in Frankfurt in 1929, it is so clear, by contrast, what a solidly grounded theory of architecture could accomplish. The workers' housing in Frankfurt is a model relevant to the needs of low-income groups even today. Stamm and May labelled their projects 'Existence Minimum', by which they meant to define the minimum home and its accompanying environment that should be provided each

family—regardless of income. Theirs was an architecture which employed contemporary materials and technology to produce, at very low cost, a decent house in a well-planned community for even the poorest family (fig. 10). When in 1959, at the dissolution of CIAM, the philosopher-architect Aldo van Eyck stated, 'Existence Minimum be damned; we are not interested in minimums, we are interested in maximums,' he was speaking as a middle-class Dutchman in a post-war Holland—a country that had managed to rebuild its cities, eradicate its slums, and provide a very desirable minimum of housing for all its population. Holland, like Van Eyck, was ready to consider the next step, but most of the rest of the world, including America, was not anywhere near ready.

The major weakness of the social-methodologist school was that the form of their architecture was not poetic enough; it was prosaic by definition and

10 Low-income housing scheme in Frankfurt—Bruchfeldstrasse 1926–28, by Ernst May, the City architect. The housing is grouped around a court which leads to the community center.

subservient to the building program, the materials used and the cost. Their form language was not allowed to run off and pursue an inner lyricism. As a consequence it could not easily inspire nor win over the new generations of young architects. In its bid for their loyalties the social-methodologist school lost. That problem is still with us today, even as we have become aware of the bankruptcy of the methods, ideas and form language of the style-metaphysicists. For example, in the design of housing, young architects are trained to acquire a visual perception which makes them appalled by the endless sprawl of suburban development. They are not taught to be inquisitive enough to learn whether most families living in single-family houses in a suburban tract find their homes the closest image of their affordable ideal—whether their homes satisfy their aspirations and represent, in tangible form, what they have worked for all their lives to achieve. Architects and urban designers may be outraged by the endless visual monotony of suburban tract development; but the families that occupy them do not see the overall tract; they see only the glory of their own individual homes. For them, their single-family house is symbolic of arrival. For the architect or urban designer driving by, or flying over, these tracts, they form a boring, endless, uninspiring landscape. Architects and architectural historians have been damning the suburban tract development since the 1930s, but social scientists and realtors will tell you that these tracts continue to be the most sought-after and the most successful form of moderate and middle-income housing ever built. The hardest lesson for architects to learn is that: for the consumer the least important of requirements to be satisfied in housing is the visual composition created by the total assembly of a hundred or more units. And yet, the satisfaction of this very requirement—the production of an overall inspiring urban view—is the primary, self-imposed criterion for the architect involved in the design of mass housing. For he knows that it will be the first criterion that will be used by his peers and critics in evaluating his design (fig. 11).

By the late 1940s the modern movement in architecture had become dominated by the style-metaphysicists and their desire to institutionalize a new architectural form language. The incomparable creator and master of the new architectural style, Le Corbusier, so captivated and mesmerized the architects attracted to the modern movement that he succeeded in becoming at once creator, impresario and finite master of the entire movement. Toward the end of his career the social-methodologists could only see him as the man most responsible for leading the modern movement off its main track and down the siding of stylistic showmanship. On the other hand, his followers saw him then, as they do now, as the supreme being who codified the modern movement and gave it its final form and international recognition and acceptance.

A further weakness in the stylists' overriding concern with image is that it prevented them from giving much thought to the institutional and financial framework necessary to seeing their plans implemented. Le Corbusier's obsession with design on the grand scale required him also to advocate a centralized bureaucracy of businessmen necessary for achieving it. His grand designs, which relegated the home of the individual man to insignificance, would take a bureaucracy of a similar size, and lack of concern for the needs and aspirations of individuals, to implement them. This is a fundamental weakness in Le Corbusier's thinking and in the thinking of contemporary architects intrigued by the practice of urban design. Socially conscious disciples of Le Corbusier have difficulty reconciling the fact that he looked to what he called the 'captains of industry' to ultimately build his vision of the future city.

The French communists termed Le Corbusier's futurist city—*Ville Contemporaire*—fascistic because it implied a strong, central government and an elite corps of businessmen to run it. This was a rare group of communists indeed who could perceive the dangers of large, centralized government and appeared committed to the rights of individual men and their separate actions. Or perhaps it was only the ogre of a centralized government by 'capitalist' businessmen that they were objecting to so strongly.

It is interesting that today's newly emerging schools of self-identified 'Marxist' planners and environmental psychologists are strongly advocating that the ownership of *all* urban land be assumed by the state, as this will greatly facilitate large-scale planning and development. They argue that the problems currently attending the assemblage of endless tracts of small, individually owned parcels of land could thus be avoided. Whether from the right or from the left, the average citizen must take heed of those who would deprive him of his quarter-acre of land—for the plans that are being made for the physical counterparts of the brave new societies will make his place in the sun as insignificant as the social role that is being planned for him. He is being

11 Habitat '67. Once it is understood that this model for supposedly dense urban housing only achieves a density equivalent to single family row-houses, it becomes clear that the architect's concern was with producing exciting visual forms. Habitat '67 costs more than ten times what conventional single family row-housing would cost and deprives everyone of their own yards and children of immediate access to the ground. Only an architect could have conceived of such a costly waste and only other architects are able to applaud it so uncritically.

rendered a pigeon in a pigeon-hole. There will be little to the new form of the physical representation of his place on earth that will satisfy his need for individual recognition. His identity will be obliterated in the grand scheme. The form and character of the large redevelopment schemes we have been witnessing these past thirty years suggest that we could do much worse as planners than enable the average citizen to prevent such developments by the very gist of his individual ownership of a small parcel of land in the middle of it.

Conceptualization of the grand physical plan always necessitates the establishment of the large autocracy needed to implement it—whether the autocracy is a centralized revolutionary government, a state housing agency with powers of eminent domain, or a consortium of large industrial companies. Le Corbusier was politically astute enough to realize that only a large, autocratic, centralized authority—whether of the left or the right—could martial the resources and maintain the singularity of purpose over time to implement one of his urban megastructures. Only such a centralized institution would be able to suppress the personal preferences and actions of thousands of individuals necessary to force compliance with the grand plan. Perhaps the most difficult pill the socially concerned urban designer, architect and planner must swallow is that, at the urban scale, what he perceives as visual disorder may be the ultimate expression of a pluralistic society in which each individual is free to implement his own plan because he controls enough of society's resources and land to be able to satisfy his own needs.

It was the belief of the style-metaphysicists that the modern style itself could be liberating and that a modern, collective society could be achieved by housing people in new, communal environments. It was almost as if the poor could be at once both liberated and politicized by being introduced into mass housing designed within a Mondrian or Corbusierian format. But these were also physically complex environments which required sophisticated communal social structures to survive in and operate. In contemporary American society, when the poor are housed in such environments, the projects are run paternalistically by large housing bureaucracies. There is little liberation, no autonomy and no separate identity for the individual family.

The unanswered challenge being posed to the architectural profession today was formulated in the first CIAM conference: can we harness the new technology and our social awareness to provide the majority of people with a living environment which answers both their needs and their image of themselves? Modern architects seem to have dropped that challenge. Is it because the task is too difficult or simply that the solutions are too obvious and, therefore, uninteresting?

In their search for a new form language the pioneers of the modern movement sought to symbolize the values and aspirations of the new industrial society in building forms. But little thought was given to the question of variation in the values and aspirations among different segments of the population. Given these variations, whose values were to be embodied in the forms of the new architecture? As the only values and aspirations that the architects were familiar with were their own, these are the only ones they addressed. It should come as no surprise then that the form language of modern architecture symbolizes little of the values of most of society—and least of all those of low and moderate income groups.

The architectural education process produces severely disoriented practitioners. Not only are young architects kept ignorant of the tastes, values and perception of the client groups they will be serving, they are intentionally trained to be antagonistic to them. I recently attended a community meeting in which a young black architect was presenting a preliminary design for a housing project to be built in the neighborhood he grew up in. He was representing a large firm, and to make his link with the community evident he brought to everyone's attention the fact that his mother was in the audience. He then went on to present a very contemporary, concrete, high-rise scheme. The community rejected his plan. His mother's astonishment at her son's design was only aggravated by her public embarrassment.

Most of our architectural schools are geared toward turning out the occasional genius—the future master of the new style—the next generation of tastemaker. His competence in addressing his clients' needs is given secondary importance. Architectural students are not familiarized with the principles governing the lay-out of various building types, whether houses, schools or office buildings. Their studio masters delude them into thinking that in the design of any building they must themselves rediscover the 'essence' of that building type from scratch. Little effort is made to have students first familiarize themselves with the work of other architects and developers who have built such buildings previously. There is no discipline or method that says that the development of a few new changes to further perfect existing models is a worthwhile pursuit. For most architects commencing the design of a new building, the work of all other architects is studiously avoided so as not to taint themselves with the sin of plagiarism. As a consequence, we turn out professionals who design housing projects, dormitories, schools and office buildings which may be handsome, and which will win design awards, but which will also likely prove impossible to live or work in. The full extent of this tragedy is best appreciated when we realize that the most recognized of architects are often those who turn out the most dramatic failures. Such architectural genius works best in designing buildings which are predominantly non-utilitarian. Society should not reduce the esteem in which it holds its most prominent architects by requiring them to concern themselves with the building chores of domesticity.

In summary, I have identified three functions required of the new form language of modern architecture: that it be open enough to allow freedom in the planning and laying out of areas but still sufficiently uniform to result in a recognizable totality; that it allow the *expressive* use of contemporary materials—not only in enabling the new building materials to be revealed (exposed) but in allowing an expression of the work the new materials were capable of (spanning large distances, opening up walls to light and air); and finally, that the form language symbolizes the aspirations of the building's user, both in linking the building to those of the past he desires to identify with and in the employment of materials and colors that are evocative of well being.

It is clear that in asking the new form language to answer the third function (the symbolization of the aspirations of the user) the designer often comes into conflict with some of the requirements of the second function (the expressive use of contemporary materials and technology). How does the designer reconcile this apparent conflict? With skill and good humor. It must be possible to have a recognizably modern architectural form which, in addition to answering the first two requirements, can occasionally make use of traditional formal elements and materials to enrich it and address the needs of the client. Examples of art which is unmistakably modern even though it makes important use of traditional formal elements do not come to mind easily in architecture, but they do in other art forms: music, dance, painting. It cannot be that difficult to create the equivalent in architectural form of what the Beatles and Bernstein have produced in music.

The revolution in architecture of the 1920s and 1930s was a revolution in planning methods and in the adoption of social concerns. The challenge posed then is yet to be understood or assumed. Modern architecture is not dead, as our critics claim; it is yet to come alive.

Natural Aesthetics
Nicholas K. Humphrey

'There's no disputing tastes.' Maybe. But that men have tastes there's no disputing either. Aesthetic principles, often unformulated, continually affect the way we lead our lives. My room has objects in it, coloured objects, shaped objects, objects arranged in space—why those colours, those shapes, that arrangement? A gramophone in the corner is making a noise—why that noise? When I stop writing and go for a walk I shall take a particular path— why that path? In few cases has the answer to do with utility alone. Many of the books on my shelves are useful books but none the more useful for having coloured covers; the curtains across the window keep out the cold but are none the warmer for the curious pattern on them—and the flowers on the table, the pictures on the wall—what *use* are they? So far as I've been free to I have selected the sounds, sights, smells and other feels around me because I find them pleasant in themselves. All men do as much, in greater or less degree. There is the puzzle.

It is the prerogative of a biologist to ask simple-minded questions about human behaviour. I make no bones about treating aesthetics as a biological phenomenon, and my question, simple-minded certainly, is fundamental: 'What is the function of Man's appreciation of beauty?' Function has a special meaning for biologists—the function of behaviour is the contribution it makes to biological survival.

'What happens', wrote C. A. Mace, 'when a man, or for that matter an animal, has no need to work for a living? . . . In the state of nature a cat must kill to live. In the state of affluence it lives to kill. . . . When men have no need to work for a living there are broadly only two things left for them to do. They can "play" and they can cultivate the arts.' The logical extension of this statement would be this: if in the state of affluence men live to cultivate the arts, so in the state of nature they must cultivate the arts to live. This is my starting point. In this essay I shall put forward some ideas about why men (and animals) respond to 'natural beauty' and I shall explore the implications of these ideas for artistic design.

I do not mean to trivialize the concept of aesthetic preferences by including within it examples of behaviour which are clearly related to the satisfaction of primary biological needs. The preferences men show for the taste of good food, for bodily comfort or for sexual stimulation may properly be excluded from discussion. I go along with others in regarding one of the defining criteria of aesthetic preferences as their irrelevance to obvious needs. Gautier's dictum that, *'Il n'y a de vraiment beau que ce qui ne peut servir à rien'* might seem unduly negative. But Kant was near the mark: 'When the question is whether a thing is beautiful, we do not want to know whether anything depends or can depend, for us or for anybody else, on the existence of the object.'

Yet in the quest for a functional explanation it would be self-defeating to deny aesthetic preferences *any* useful role. If the response to beauty in one form or another occurs regularly and consistently within the human species it is fair to assume that it confers some biological advantage. Biologists work on the assumption that Nature gives little away for free: if men take pleasure in looking at particular sights or hearing particular sounds we may expect that the consequences of their doing so—whatever they may be—are beneficial, though the benefits may well be indirect and the beneficiaries may be quite unaware of them.

Seventy years before Darwin published the *Origin of Species*, the Scottish philosopher Thomas Reid, in 1785, suggested how a modern biologist might proceed:

'By a careful examination of the objects to which Nature hath given this amiable quality [of Beauty], we may perhaps discover some real excellence in the object, or at least some valuable purpose that is served by the effect which it produces upon us. This instinctive sense of beauty, in different species of animals, may differ as much as the external sense of taste, and in each species be adapted to its manner of life.'

Yet it is easy to dismiss Reid's manifesto. The injunction to 'examine carefully' the objects of beauty would be fine were it true that different individuals of the same species did find the *same* objects beautiful. But one of the central problems of aesthetics has always been that, in man at least, there is no clear consensus. The point was forcefully made by Maureen Duffy in her review of Jane Goodall's book *In the Shadow of Man*. Jane Goodall had written: 'But what if a chimpanzee wept tears when he heard Bach thundering from a cathedral organ?' To which Miss Duffy replied: 'What indeed if an Amazon pigmy or a nineteenth-century factory hand wept tears at such a minority western cultural phenomenon?'

The way out for some critics when confronted with the diversity of individual taste has been to react with the cynicism of Clive Bell, stating that:

'Any system of aesthetics which pretends to be based on some objective truth is so palpably ridiculous as not to be worth discussing.' (Bell 1913)

But William Empson scorned such anti-rationality. He wrote,

'Critics are of two sorts: those who merely relieve themselves against the flower of beauty, and those, less continent, who afterwards scratch it up. I myself, I must confess, aspire to the second of these classes; unexplained beauty arouses an irritation in me . . .' (Empson 1930)

The problem of looking for common principles behind apparent diversity is not peculiar to aesthetics. Very similar problems have arisen in other disciplines, notably in linguistics and in anthropology. The break-through in these fields came through applying the methods of *structuralism*. I believe that a structuralist approach is the key to a science of aesthetics.

In his discussion of the analysis of myth, Lévi-Strauss (1963) wrote as follows:

'. . . the contradiction which we face is very like that which in earlier times brought considerable worry to the first philosophers concerned with linguistic problems. Ancient philosophers did notice that certain sequences of sounds were associated with definite meanings, and they earnestly aimed at discovering the reason for the linkage between *these*

sounds and *that* meaning. Their attempt however was thwarted from the beginning by the fact that the same sounds were equally present in other languages although the meaning they conveyed was entirely different. The contradiction was surmounted only by the discovery that it is the combination of sounds, not the sounds themselves, which provides the significant data.

He went on to say: 'If there is a meaning to be found in mythology, it cannot reside in the isolated elements which enter into the composition of a myth, but only in the way those elements are combined.'

Following this lead, it would seem fruitful to search for the essence of beauty in the *relations* formed between the perceived elements. As it happens, just such an approach was proposed in 1808 by the philosopher Herbart:

'The conclusion is that *each* element of the approved or distasteful whole is, in isolation, indifferent; in a word, the *material* is indifferent, but the *form* comes under the aesthetic judgement. . . . Those judgements which are commonly conceived under the name of taste are the result of the perfect apprehension of relations formed by a complexity of elements.'

But it is one thing to point to the importance of relations, another to say *what* relations are important and another still to say *why*.

Lévi-Strauss himself, in so far as he has had anything to say about aesthetics, has tended to regard works of art merely as a special sort of myth. For him the work of art is a 'system of signs' which conveys a message. To understand the message we must make an equation between the *relations* among the signs and the *relations* among the things signified.

No doubt such myth-like works of art exist. We know for instance of a Chinese scholar, Lyng Lun, who 2,500 years before Christ strung together five tones of oriental music, explained them, formed them into a system, and gave them strange names, every tone being called after a social stratum from

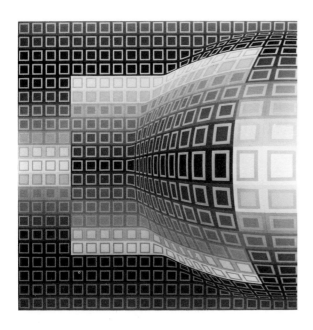

1 *Above:* 'Bika Zeπ' Victor Vasarely, 1976.

2 *Above right:* Paving stones, Rome.

3 *Right:* Canal scene, Venice. Photo P. Goodliffe.

4 *Buryat Ongon*. '*Ongon* of the two girls of the Khori lineage'. A magical drawing presented to a Buryat girl on the occasion of her marriage. The elements of the drawing, perceived in relation to each other, tell a story which serves to protect the girl in her new home.

5 Chestnut fan.

the emperor down to the peasant: *kong*, the emperor; *chang*, the minister; *kyo*, the burgher; *tchi*, the official; *yu*, the peasant (Pahlen 1963). Within such a system almost any piece of music must, if interpreted in a structural way, have carried a potential social message. In the field of graphic art, Caroline Humphrey (1971) has recently shown how the magical drawings of the Mongolian Buryat people embody structuralist devices which make the drawings effectively into 'visual texts'. And almost certainly similar sign-systems are at work within the mainstream of western painting. Christopher McManus and I found evidence that Rembrandt, for instance, may have made use of a simple sign system in his painted portraits whereby the social status of the subject of the portrait was indicated by the left or right turn of his head (Humphrey and McManus 1973).

But be that as it may, these sign systems where they exist serve primarily a semantic function, not an aesthetic one. They do not lend *beauty* to a work of art. If structuralism is to help in pointing to relations which are *aesthetically* satisfying it must take a different turn.

Few people have written with more insight about beauty than the poet Gerard Manley Hopkins. Hopkins is hardly to be called a 'structuralist' since the name had still to be invented in his lifetime, yet not only did he see that the essence of beauty lies in certain relations but he attempted explicitly to define what those relations are. In 1865 he wrote a paper for his tutor at Oxford in the form of a 'platonic dialogue' between a student and a professor in a college garden. The two of them fall to discussing the beauty of the garden and they dwell in particular on the leaves of a chestnut tree. The professor holds forth on the structural relations within the chestnut-fan, pointing out how each leaf is a variation with a difference of the common pattern, how the overall shape of the fan shows mirror symmetry, the left half being a perfect reflection of the right, whilst in other ways the internal reflections are tantalizingly irregular—each of the large oblique leaves, for instance, being reflected by an exact copy of itself in miniature; and he discusses too the relation between the leaves of the chestnut and the leaves of other trees, drawing attention to the way in which the chestnut leaf, being fatter at the distal than the central end, is the opposite shape to the common shape, shown say by the leaf of an elm. The professor continues:

'Then the beauty of the oak and the chestnut-fan and the sky is a mixture of likeness and difference or agreement and disagreement or consistency and variety or symmetry and change.'

'It seems so, yes.'

'And if we did not feel the likeness we should not feel them so beautiful, or if we did not feel the difference we should not feel them so beautiful. The beauty we find is from the comparison we make of the things with themselves, seeing their likeness and difference, is it not?'

Before long they move on to the subject of poetry:

'Rhythm therefore is likeness tempered with difference . . . And the beauty of rhythm is traced to the same causes as that of the chestnut-fan, is it not so?' . . . 'What is rhyme? Is it not an agreement of sound—with a slight disagreement?' . . . 'In fact it seems to me that rhyme is the epitome of our principle. All beauty may by a metaphor be called rhyme, may it not?'

In 1909 Christiansen coined the word *'differenzqualität'* to refer to what Hopkins had called, 'likeness tempered with difference'; and shortly afterwards the writers of the school of Russian Formalism propounded a system of aesthetics based on essentially similar structuralist ideas. In England the philosopher Whitehead wrote of rhythm:

'The essence of rhythm is the fusion of sameness and novelty; so that the whole never loses the essential unity of the pattern, while the parts exhibit the contrast arising from the novelty of their detail. A mere recurrence kills rhythm as does a mere confusion of differences. A crystal lacks rhythm from excessive pattern, while a fog is unrhythmic in that it exhibits a patternless confusion of detail.' (Whitehead 1919)

Here then we have the beginning of an answer to what relations lie at the heart of beauty. 'All beauty may by a metaphor be called rhyme.' What is rhyme like? Well, let us have an example:

Jill rhymes with hill
'Jack and Jill went up the hill'
Jill does not rhyme with street
'Jack and Jill went up the street'
Jill does not rhyme with Jill
'Jack and Jill went up the Jill'

Taking rhyme as the paradigm of beauty, let me turn at once to the fundamental question: Why do we *like* the relation which rhyme epitomizes? What is the biological advantage of seeking out rhyming elements in the environment?

The answer I propose is this: considered as a biological phenomenon, aesthetic preferences stem from a predisposition among animals and men to seek out experiences through which they may *learn to classify* the objects in the world about them. Beautiful 'structures' in nature or in art are those which facilitate the task of classification by presenting evidence of the 'taxonomic' relations between things in a way which is informative and easy to grasp.

Three steps are needed to justify this argument. First, an explanation of why classification should be important to biological survival. Second, an explanation of why particular structures such as those exemplified by rhyme should be the best way of presenting material for classification. Third, evidence that men and animals have a propensity to classify things and that they are attracted in particular to the presence of rhyme.

In order to be effective agents in the natural world, animals require the guidance of a 'world model', an internal representation of what the world is like and how it works. This model enables them to predict in advance the characteristics of 'recognizable' objects, to anticipate the likely course of events in the environment, and to plan their behaviour accordingly. The role of classification in this context is to help organize sensory experience and to introduce an essential economy into the description of the world. An effective classification system is one which divides the objects in the world up into discrete categories according to criteria which make an object's membership of any particular class a relevant datum for guiding behaviour: the objects in any one class may differ in detail but they should share certain essential features which give them a common significance for the animal. Such a classification system will reduce the 'thought load' on the animal, expedite new learning and allow rapid and efficient extrapolation from one set of circumstances to another.

We may be sure that any animal which could not or did not classify things effectively—which could not recognize the likenesses between things—would not have a chance of surviving for long. And so, in the course of evolution, there must have been very strong pressures on animals to perfect techniques of classification, on a par perhaps with those that have made eating and sex evolve into such efficient and dominant activities. I shall argue that, just as with eating or with sex, an activity as vital as classification was bound to evolve to be a *source of pleasure* to that animal. Both animals and men can, after all, be relied on to do best what they enjoy doing.

But I am anticipating. The next step of the argument is to demonstrate the relevance of rhyme. The young animal's task of imposing a system of categories upon the world is comparable to that which faces a zoological taxonomist when he sets out to classify the animal kingdom. We may assume that the goal before the animal is in some sense 'given', that he has an innate predisposition to develop *a* system of categories, but that the actual system he arrives at must be largely based upon his own experience. How does the animal—and the zoologist—proceed? I would suggest he works through the following stages:

(1) he makes a preliminary reconnaissance and from this forms certain hunches about how his world is constituted, what kinds of classes of objects it contains and what are the distinguishing criteria.
(2) he seeks further evidence to test the 'validity' of these criteria and at the same time to acquaint himself with the diversity which may exist *within* each class.
(3) to the extent that his criteria prove successful he adopts them as permanent guidelines for future classification, while to the extent that they fail he abandons or revises them.

Imagine that the taxonomist is concerned to classify warm-blooded vertebrates. In making a preliminary survey he meets a cat, a dog, and a hen and he notices that the cat and the dog are covered with hair whilst the hen is covered with feathers. On this basis he sets up two putative classes, called mammals and birds, defined respectively as animals which have hair and as animals which have feathers. His next step is to look for further examples to test his ideas. Suppose that the next animal he meets is a horse and then a rabbit. Applying his criteria he discovers that these animals fit neatly into the category of mammals. Then perhaps he meets a sparrow, then a mouse, and then a parrot and he is pleased to find that whilst the mouse is clearly a mammal the sparrow and the parrot fit the definition of a bird. Looking further he meets another cat, but on this occasion he pays it little attention since it tells him nothing new. Later on he meets a spider, but since this is not a warm-blooded vertebrate it can provide no evidence either way and again he shows no interest in it. Slowly, by accumulating evidence, he establishes that his criteria do indeed serve to make unambiguous distinctions, and at the same time he becomes familiar with the range of different animals that fall within each class. It remains of course for him to show that his classification is a useful one, i.e. that it serves some purpose to group mice and horses or hens and parrots together.

Certain principles of how to gather evidence emerge. The zoologist needs to prove that his criteria serve both to *group* different animals together and to *separate* one group from another. Accordingly he looks for two kinds of examples: (i) sets of animals which share a particular distinctive feature, and (ii) other sets of animals which share a contrasting feature. Thus he looks in effect for 'likeness tempered with difference', ('rhyme'), and for *contrast* between sets of rhyming elements. But he is not interested in seeing repetitive examples of the same animal, nor in seeing an animal which is altogether different from the others and thus lies beyond the scope of his classification—'a mere recurrence kills rhyme, as does a mere confusion of differences.'

Pursuing this metaphor of the taxonomic 'poem':
horse 'rhymes' with dog,
hen 'rhymes' with parrot,
horse and dog contrast with hen and parrot,
horse does not rhyme with horse, nor hen with hen,
neither horse nor dog nor hen nor parrot rhyme or contrast in a relevant way with spider.

Now to the nub of my argument. I believe that the same principles which apply to the zoological taxonomist apply to every animal who needs to classify the world about him. If it is helpful for the taxonomist to look for 'rhymes' in his materials, so it is helpful for the animal to do so. It is for this reason that we have evolved to respond to the relation of beauty which rhyme epitomizes. At one level we take pleasure in the abstract structure of rhyme as a model of well-presented evidence, and at another we delight in particular examples of rhyme as sources of new insight into how things are related and divided.

Let me move onto the next stage of the argument and give evidence that men and animals do indeed take pleasure in classifying things and, on that account, are especially attracted to rhyme.

'Learning', said Aristotle, 'is very agreeable, not only to philosophers but also to other men.' (*Poetics* IV). What evidence is there that classification—the core of learning—is agreeable to men and to animals also?

For experimental evidence of a general kind we may look to the many studies of exploratory behaviour. Comparative psychologists have found that, in almost every species studied, animals will work to be exposed to novel sensory stimuli. Indeed, 'stimulus novelty' is the most universal reinforcer of behaviour which is known. In my own work with monkeys I have found that monkeys will even work to look at abstract paintings and prefer such pictures to pictures of appetizing, but familiar, food. Recent experiments strongly suggest that when monkeys work to look at pictures they do so because the picture presents them with a challenge to incorporate new material into their model of the world: pictures of familiar objects hold their attention far less long than pictures of objects for which they have no readily available category. But while they do not spend long on thoroughly familiar things, neither, I should say, are they interested in looking at a total jumble. And that leads me on to the question of rhyme.

The significance of rhyme was in fact recognized by experimental psychologists some time ago, though they called it—and still call it—by the cumbersome name of 'stimulus discrepancy'. In the early 1950s a theory was propounded called the 'discrepancy theory', the gist of which is that men who have been exposed for some time to a particular sensory stimulus respond with pleasure to minor variations from that stimulus (McClelland *et al* 1953). And confirmatory evidence has come from a number of studies. For instance, human babies who have been made familiar with a particular 'abstract' visual pattern take pleasure in seeing new patterns which are minor transformations of the original (Kagan 1970). Among animals, it has been shown, for instance, that chicks who have been 'imprinted' early in life on an artificial stimulus soon come to prefer new stimuli which are slightly different from the one they are familiar with (Bateson 1973). Neither babies nor chicks are attracted to stimuli which are wholly unrelated to what they have already seen.

I have been pursuing my own research with monkeys along these lines. But this is not the place to report the details of experiments. And it is not in fact to experimental evidence that I want to give most weight in this discussion. For there is much in the evidence of anecdote and common experience to substantiate the view that men, at least, take pleasure in one form or another of classificatory activity.

As we might expect, the tendency is most pronounced in children. Children have a thirst to know 'what things are'. They love especially to learn *names*, and to prove the power of their vocabulary with new examples. Picture books for children often serve no other purpose than as practical exercises in classification. The same animals—rabbits, hens pigs—appear in the pictures again and again. 'Where's the bunny?' asks the child's mother, and with a smile of pleasure the child points a finger to yet another rabbit which rhymes with those he has already seen. The ability to name becomes tangible evidence of the ability to classify, and when the name for an object is not available children will often invent their own. The poet Richard Wilbur tells this story:

'. . . I took my three-year-old son for a walk in the Lincoln woods. As we went along I identified what trees and plants I could. . . . After a while we came to a stretch of woods-floor thick with those three-inch evergreen plants one sees everywhere in New England woods, and I was obliged to confess I didn't know what to call them. My three-year-old stepped promptly into the breach. 'They're millows', he told me, 'Look at all the millows.' No hesitation; no bravado; with a serene Adamite confidence he had found a name for something nameless and brought it under our verbal control. Millows they were.' (Wilbur 1956)

Yet while children may manifest the tendency most clearly, adult men often show an equally innocent delight in classifying, not least in naming. A poem by Robert Bridges called *The Idle Flowers* mentions 83 different flowers by name in a poem only 84 lines long!

I have sown upon the fields
Eyebright and Pimpernel,
And Pansy and Poppy-seed
Ripen'd and scatter'd well.

And silver Lady-smock
The meads with light to fill,
Cowslip and Buttercup,
Daisy and Daffodil;

King-cup and Fleur-de-lys
Upon the marsh to meet
With Comfrey, Watermint,
Loose-strife and Meadowsweet;

And all along the stream
My care hath not forgot
Crowfoot's white galaxy
And love's Forget-me-not. . . .

And the reverse of the coin is the ridicule that is heaped on people who make mistakes with names. A. P. Herbert tells a story against himself, again to do with flowers:

' "The anemias are wonderful," I said. My companion gave me a doubtful glance but said nothing. We walked on beside the herbaceous border. "And those arthritis," I said, pointing to a cluster of scarlet blooms. "Always so divine at this time of the year." Again the dubious glance, and again no utterance except an appreciative "Um." I came to the conclusion that the young lady knew no more about flowers than I do.' (Quoted in Hadfield, 1936).

The concern with naming, carried to such an extreme in Bridge's poem, finds echoes in another remarkable aspect of human behaviour—the passion for *collecting*. Collecting, whether the material of the collection be postage stamps, antiquarian books or engine numbers, is to my mind yet another manifestation of the pleasure men take in classification.

Curiously, there is only one psychologist I know of who has deemed collecting worthy of comment. That man, surprisingly enough, is Pavlov. In an essay called 'The reflex of purpose', he characterized collecting as, 'the aspiration to gather together the parts or units of a great whole or of an enormous classification, usually unattainable." and went on:

'If we consider collecting in all its variations, it is impossible not to be struck with the fact that on account of this passion there are accumulated often completely trivial and worthless things, which represent absolutely no value from any point of view other than the gratification of the propensity to collect. Notwithstanding the worthlessness of the goal, every one is aware of the energy, the occasional unlimited self-sacrifice, with which the collector achieves his purpose. He may become a laughing-stock, a butt of ridicule, a criminal, he may suppress his fundamental needs, all for the sake of his collection.' (Pavlov 1928).

Collecting, though its practitioners are not usually credited with aesthetic sensitivity, is not, I believe, far removed from the appreciation of beauty. Consider for a moment the nature of a typical collection, say a stamp collection. Postage stamps are, in structuralist terms, like man-made flowers: they are divided into 'species', of which the distinctive feature is the country of origin, while within each species there exists tantalizing variation. The stamp collector sets to work to classify them. He arranges his stamps in an album, a page for the species of each country. The stamps on each page 'rhyme' with each other, while they contrast with those on other pages.

But Pavlov was right: stamp collecting is a worthless activity. As we have moved through my examples, from an infant learning to recognize the objects in the world about him, to a child learning to name pictures in a book, to a man sticking stamps in an album, we have moved further and further from activities which have any obvious biological function. They are all, I submit, examples of the propensity to classify, but with each example the classification seems to have less and less direct survival value.

We should not be surprised. Earlier, I compared the pleasure men get from classification with the pleasure they get from sexual activity. Now, though sex has a clear biological function, it goes without saying that not every particular example of sexual activity has in fact to be biologically relevant to be enjoyable. Indeed, much sexual activity takes place at times when the woman, for natural or artificial reasons, is most unlikely to conceive. And so too the process of classification may give pleasure in its own right even when divorced from its proper biological context. Once Nature had set up men's brains the way she has, certain 'unintended' consequences followed—and we are in several ways the beneficiaries. So let me turn, at last, to *beauty*—to examples of rhyme and contrast which people deem aesthetically attractive. I want first to consider not 'works of art' but certain natural phenomena which men call beautiful and yet which have no 'natural' value to us.

Among the wealth of examples of beauty in nature, I shall choose the case of flowers. Flowers have an almost universal appeal, to men of all cultures, all classes, and all ages. We grow them in gardens, decorate our houses and our bodies with them, and above all value them as features of the natural landscape. They are regarded indeed as paragons of natural beauty, and I believe it is no accident that they are so admired, for in at least three ways flowers are the embodiment of 'visual rhyme'.

Consider first the static form of a simple flower such as a buttercup or daisy. The flower-head consists of a set of petals arranged in radial symmetry around a cluster of stamens, and the flower-head is carried on a stalk which bears a set of leaves. Petals, stamens, and leaves form three sets of contrasting rhyming elements: each petal differs in detail from the other members of its class yet shares their distinctive shape and colour, and the same is true for the stamens and the leaves; the features that serve to unite each set serve at the same time to separate one set from another. Secondly, consider the flower's *kinetic* form. The living flower is in a continual state of growth, changing its form from day to day. The transformations which occur as the flower buds, blossoms and decays give rise to a temporal structure in which each successive form rhymes with the preceding one. Thirdly, consider groups of flowers. Typically each flowering plant bears several blooms, and plants of the same species

6 Aconyte. Organic 'rhyme' instantiated in the unfolding shoot of an aconyte.

7 Girl. Photo P. Goodliffe.

tend to grow in close proximity, so that we are presented with a variety of related blooms on show together. But, more than this, groups of flowers of *different* species commonly grow alongside one another—daisies and buttercups beside each other in the field, violets and primroses together in the hedgerow. Thus while the flowers of one species rhyme with each other the rhyme is given added poignancy by the contrasting rhymes of different species. It is this last aspect that perhaps more than

anything makes flowers so special to us. The flowers of different species are of necessity perceptually distinct in colour, form and smell in order that they may command the loyalty of pollinating insects. Men neither eat their pollen nor collect their nectar, yet flowers provide us with a kind of nourishment— food for our minds, ideally suited to satisfy our hunger for classification.

But flowers have no monopoly of natural beauty. In fact almost wherever we come across organic forms we discover the structure of visual rhyme. Long before architects invented the *module*, Nature employed a similar design principle, basing her living creations on the principle of replication—at one level replication of structural elements within a single body, and at another replication of the body of the organism as a whole. But, at either level, the replicas are seldom, if ever, perfect copies: in the leaves of a tree, the spots of a leopard, the bodies of a flight of geese, we are presented with sets of 'variations on a theme'. And it is not only among living things we find such structures, for inanimate objects too tend to be shaped by physical forces into 'modular' forms—mountain peaks, pebbles on a beach, clouds, raindrops, ocean waves—each alike but different from the others. Thus, through its varied but coherent structure, a natural landscape can match the rhythmic beauty of a Gothic church. Or of a musical symphony.

Men may find beauty in many different guises. Before I turn to art let me say something of 'intellectual beauty', the beauty men find in academic scholarship. 'Pure science' is for most of its practitioners an aesthetic activity. The scientist's aim is to impose a new order on natural phenomena by uniting seemingly unrelated events under a common law. Artists have often misunderstood the nature of science. A romantic complained in a poem that Newton 'unweaved the rainbow.' But Newton's achievement was near enough itself to poetry: he showed how the rainbow 'rhymed' with the solar spectrum which he cast with a prism on his study wall.

At an extreme among scholars, pure mathematicians find their own kind of beauty in the relations among abstract numerical ideas. We—non-mathematicians—may sometimes catch the flavour of their abstract structures when we are shown the magical properties of certain ordinary numbers. I remember when as a child of eight years I was introduced by my grandfather to the number 142857. If this number is added to itself seven times in succession the following series is generated:

142857 285714 428571 571428 714285 857142 999999

Six 'rhyming' numbers, and then the sudden unexpected contrast! Imagine my awe when ten years later I found a proof that this is the *only* number which has such properties.

Children, monkeys, gardeners, stamp collectors, mathematicians—all, I think, are engaged in essentially similar aesthetic enterprises. 'Obscurity,' wrote Hume, 'is painful to the mind as well as to the eye' and it should come as no surprise to know that the late professor of Formal Logic at Cambridge University was also a prodigious collector of stamps and butterflies. But he was not, it must be said, an artist. Where does art fit in to this account of beauty?

I find it hard to talk about visual art without the help of visual illustrations, and I will make my comments brief. Until the beginning of this century most paintings were only half-concerned with beauty, their other role being generally to tell a story by means of representation, expression, symbolism and so on. Only with the advent of pure abstractionism did the goal of some artists come to be the creation of great works which were 'merely' beautiful. If we consider the finest examples of modern abstract art, exemplified for me by the works of Vasarely and of Calder, it is I think easy (perhaps too easy) to see how their structure is essentially that of a 'visual poem' built up on the basis of rhyme and

8 Gazelle. A herd of Thompson's Gazelle: to us perhaps no more than a beautiful image of rhyming animals, but to the gazelle itself—and to the cheetah its enemy—an object lesson in taxonomy?

9 'SHOKK' Victor Vasarely, 1977.

contrast between visual elements. Recently some artists have returned to the use of representational elements as the material for creating purely abstract structures. Suzi Gablik's painted collages—at first sight a crazy scrapbook of animal images—are a bold attempt in this direction, and I should like to quote from a letter in which she describes her method:

'These images work rather like a kaleidoscope, an instrument which contains bits and pieces by means of which structural patterns are realized . . . What is produced is a net of relationships . . . The images come to function both as systems of abstract relations and as objects of contemplation. These abstract relations are definable by the number and nature of the axes employed; for example, the fragments have to be alike in various respects, such as size, shape, brightness or colouring, or to partake of a common quality, like having spots or stripes or

all being smooth or all with wings or all ten foot high . . . It is a way of relating different but interwoven scales and dimensions.'

Ruskin wrote of pictures: 'You must consider the whole as a prolonged musical composition.' Among the arts music has traditionally been the medium for the purest expression of structural relations. And 'rhyme', in the form of thematic variation, emerges as the fundamental principle—the stock-in-trade of nearly every musical composer. The composer presents us with, say, a simple melody, repeats it a few times and then launches into a series of variations, playing it on a different instrument, with different emphasis or in a different key, until eventually he returns to the original. But repetition of the same theme, albeit with variations, becomes in the long run relatively dull. As in poetry—as in every other 'taxonomic' activity—*contrast* is needed to bring home the unity of the rhyming elements, and the composer typically introduces a contrasting theme with its own variations. Thus we get in a

10 'Tropisms' Suzi Gablik, 1970.

simple piece such as a Chopin nocturne the following structure: two distinct themes, *A* and *B*, arranged in the following way: *A A B A B A*. Taking the nocturne in E flat as an example, the first tune is repeated twice so that the main key and the main subject matter may be well established in the memory of the hearer. Then comes the second tune which is in the most nearly related key (so that the effect of the contrast is not lost because of too great dissimilarity). Then the two tunes alternate, while at each repetition small changes are introduced, in the form for instance of decorative arabesques in the righthand part. In more complex pieces still, such as Beethoven sonatas, we get the composer introducing a 'development' section where the motifs of the first theme are picked up and rearranged until just at the point where the hearer may be in danger of losing track of what is going on order is restored by the 'recapitulation' of the first theme pure and simple.

'Sonata form' is to my mind a perfect example of an instructive and challenging exercise in classification. If I were an educational psychologist concerned with developing teaching machines for use in schools I would not, as the American behaviourists have done, base my machines on principles derived from experiments on how pigeons perform in Skinner boxes, but instead would turn directly to the hallowed principles of musical design.

It is time to conclude this somewhat discursive essay. Our book is concerned with humane architecture and the aesthetics of the built environment. What I have tried to do here is to discuss the fundamental issue in aesthetics: the question *why* people care about their sensory surroundings. Though I have hardly touched on the central subject matter of the book, I hope that the architects and planners who read it will have found some areas at least in which my ideas 'rhyme' with theirs. Man-made cities present a panorama to our senses more complex by far than any of the examples I have chosen to discuss. Yet, houses, shops, gardens, alleys—they too may be seen as forming a nexus of relations which men in their instinctive quest for order are challenged to uncover. If the city land-scape is to be beautiful, then the classificatory puzzle must be neither too difficult nor too easy to solve.

There is one way especially in which cities have the possibility of exciting men's delight—their potential for *systematic change*. I have written above of the problem of classification primarily as that of grouping together several different but related objects. But there exists an even prior problem: that of recognizing the identity of a *single* object through time. A child, for instance, must recognize its mother: but from moment to moment the mother never looks the same—her dress, her expression, her movements continually recreate her before the child's eyes. Experience must tell us what kinds of visual transformation each particular object may undergo. And so we seek positive evidence of systematic change and take pleasure not only in examples, of *syn*chronic 'rhyme' between related objects but also of the *dia*chronic 'rhyme' that exists between a single object and its previous self—the rhyme of the flower with the bud, the rhyme of the recurring musical phrase.

11 Buildings with shadows. Photo P. Goodliffe.

12a-b St. Giles, Oxford. Photo P. Goodliffe.

Natural landscapes may exhibit the beauty of rhyme and contrast simply in their static structure. But to people who *live* in the landscape—as men live in cities—the dynamic structure, the diachronic rhymes, add a new dimension to aesthetic pleasure. They see the same landscape in a state of flux. But, through every change, the landscape retains its identity and each transformation gives them new insight into its essential character.

The dynamics of the natural landscape can be considered on at least three time scales. (1) *Weather*: the coming of storms, wind, rain, fog, sunshine, blue skies, silver clouds—every change in the weather gives the landscape new expression, new shades, new shapes . . . (2) *Night and day*: the daily cycle of the sun and moon creates a rhythm of changing light—shadows advance and retreat, sweeping the ground like the hour-hand of a clock; the mountainside which was dark against the dawn sky catches the last rays of the evening sun . . . (3) *Seasons*: the cycle of summer and winter is reflected in the growth and decay of the earth's vegetation, transforming the landscape in colour and form—leaves appear on the trees, flourish, yellow and decay, corn fields ripen and are harvested. . . . The motions of weather and daylight themselves lie embedded within the motion of the seasons, giving the annual cycle an inner unity.

Cities too have a dynamic structure, more complex still than that of nature. Modern planning often plays down or obliterates the city's dynamics, attempting to cosset its citizens in a changeless protective shell. But people invite and welcome change. The face of the city should be made as expressive and responsive as the face of the forest or the mountainside. How else are people to discover the character of the place they live in?

The influences of daylight, weather and season provide a rich source of 'unprogrammed intervention'—and invention—in the urban landscape. But in the city there are other dynamic possibilities which do not exist at all in nature. For while forests and mountains have to wait for the coming of weather and seasons to transform them, the city as a social milieu can create its own endogenous rhythms. Already, the world over, people impose a non-natural cycle on their lives, the cycle of the working week, which can and should be reflected in the urban landscape. And then there are street fairs, carnivals, and political demonstrations which for a few days each year give a new look to familiar streets and buildings.

Midsummer Common, close to the centre of the City of Cambridge, is by turn a fairground, cow pasture, a circus ring, a running track, a place through which people bicycle to work and later in the day walk their dogs and push their prams. In such ways the people of cities create their own weather and their own seasons.

It is beyond my brief to argue from theory to the practice of planning or architecture. But if I were asked for a prescription for where architects and planners should go to learn their trade, it would be this: Go out to nature and learn from experience what natural structures men find beautiful, because it is among such structures that men's aesthetic sensitivity evolved. Then return to the drawing board and attempt to emulate these structures in the design of your city streets and buildings.

If I seem to be arguing for an aesthetics of 'naturalism', it is not the naïve naturalism which would have each element mimic a natural object. We do not want cities tarted up to look like alpine meadows; we want cities in which the relations—temporal and spatial—between the artificial elements exhibit the felicitous rhymes of natural beauty.

Further reading

P. P. G. Bateson, 'Internal influences on early learning in birds' in R. A. Hinde and J. Stevenson-Hinde (ed.), *Constraints on Learning* (Academic Press, London, 1973), pp. 101–116.

C. Bell, *Art* (Chatto and Windus, London, 1913).

W. Empson, *Seven Types of Ambiguity* (Chatto and Windus, London, 1930).

M. Hadfield, *The Gardener's Companion* (Dent, London, 1936).

J. H. Herbart, *Practical Philosophy* 1808.

G. M. Hopkins, 1865, 'On the origin of beauty: a platonic dialogue', in H. House and G. Storey (ed.), *G. M. Hopkins: Journals and Papers* (Oxford University Press, London, 1959).

C. Humphrey, 'Some ideas of Saussure applied to Buryat magical drawings' in E. Ardener (ed.), *Social Anthropology and Language* (Tavistock Publications, London, 1971), pp. 271–290.

N. K. Humphrey, C. McManus, 'Status and the left cheek', *New Scientist*, 59, 427–439, 1973.

J. Kagan, 'Attention and psychological change in the young child', *Science*, 1970, no. 170, 826–830.

C. Levi-Strauss, *Structural Anthropology* (Basic Books, New York, 1963).

D. C. McLelland, J. W. Atkinson, R. A. Clark, E. L. Lowell, *The Achievement Motive* (Appleton-Century, New York, 1953).

K. Pahlen, *Music of the World: A History* (Spring Books, London, 1963).

I. P. Pavlov, 'The reflex of purpose', in *Lectures on Conditioned Reflexes, vol 1* (Lawrence and Wishart, London, 1963).

T. Reid, *Essays on the intellectual Powers of Man*, 1785.

A. N. Whitehead, *An Enquiry concerning the Principles of Natural Knowledge* (Cambridge University Press, Cambridge, 1919).

R. Wilbur, 'Poetry and the landscape', in G. Kepes (ed.), *The New Landscape in Art and Science* (Paul Theobald, Chicago, 1950) pp. 86–9.

Urban Aesthetics
Peter F. Smith

Currently there is considerable interest in the idea that we come into the world already equipped with an elaborate set of mental programmes which establish probabilities as to the way we shall react within given environmental situations.

In the previous essay in this book, Nicholas Humphrey proposed that aesthetic awareness constitutes such an intuitive mental programme which developed by normal selection mechanisms because of its survival value. He suggests that one of the programmes associated with the classification facility of the brain forms the foundation for aesthetic perception. In this general principle, he is supported by D. E. Berlyne, who believes that 'the brain could well be favourable to certain patterns quite apart from their role in everyday experience'. More recently, G. Sommerhoff, a neurophysiologist, has maintained that 'advanced organisms have become responsive to the information profile of the sensory inflow, and . . . this may be the biological basis of man's aesthetic sensibilities'.

It seems then that we can assume the existence of programmes within the brain which enable us to evaluate an 'information profile' for its own sake, quite apart from its potential usefulness. What originated as a classification capacity has evolved into aesthetic awareness, something which possibly has *indirect* survival value.

In the view of Edward O. Wilson the repertoire of mental programmes is very much associated with the limbic brain, evolutionarily the most primitive collection of systems on the cortical ladder. This is the area of the brain responsible for the emotions, and so many of those programmes will have an inbuilt emotional link.

Intuitive aesthetic perception
The intuitive capacity for aesthetic appreciation has at least four distinct components which transcend time and culture. Whilst cultural factors will have a profound influence upon the manifestations of these components, the fundamental mechanisms seem to be universal within what we may guardedly term 'advanced' cultures. They may be considered as four aesthetic programmes written by the genes

and adapted to environmental circumstances. They are: (1) a sense of pattern; (2) appreciation of rhythm; (3) recognition of balance; (4) sensitivity to harmonic relationships.

Rhyme and pattern
In relating the aesthetic response to the classification facility operated by organisms with advanced nervous systems, Nicholas Humphrey indicates that there is strong evidence that animals derive pleasure from indulging in the classification process. Consequently they actively seek to exercise this facility. 'Comparative psychologists have found that, in almost every species studied, animals will work to be exposed to novel sensory stimuli. Indeed, "stimulus novelty" is the most universal reinforce of behaviour which is known.' All higher species have a psychological appetite for both familiarity and novelty. To be of interest an object must have a degree of 'stimulus discrepancy'. But classification schemata or models are extended by small 'catastrophes' rather than fractured by the large ones which occur if the novelty quotient is excessive. Obviously, this has survival value. When an object manifests both familiarity and novelty it is described by Humphrey as possessing the quality of 'rhyme'.

Rhyme presupposes the simultaneous existence of complexity and pattern, with the latter becoming dominant, but not in a way that is obvious. The pattern that relates to rhyme does not comprise simple repetition, as in fabrics and wallpaper, but may be regarded as a system in which there may be no point-to-point correspondence but nevertheless substantial affinity. It is a question more of metaphor than of simile.

Over the course of evolution, Man has developed a capacity to detect points of affinity in stimulus presentations with a high rate of complexity. This ability, which is a vital component of the classification facility, mostly operates unconsciously.

Pattern recognition is a mental capacity which can be vigorously exercized in towns and cities. A city which one might say is dedicated to the principle of rhyming pattern is Amsterdam. In its

Medieval and Renaissance centre there is virtual standardization of building plots, producing close uniformity in the unit size of buildings. Brick is the ubiquitous building material. Most houses are five or six storeys high and wide enough to accommodate three windows. A single window is placed in the gable. Windows are divided by white glazing bars and usually contained within a white surround.

All this seems to suggest high uniformity and inevitable monotony. The reverse is true. Rarely do windows occur on the same level between buildings. There are subtle variations in the rhythm and proportion of windows. Whole styles can change, as between the Medieval and Renaissance examples. But where each house most assertively expresses its independence is in the termination to the gable. The most characteristic medieval kind is the stepped gable. In the Renaissance era architects terminated their buildings with all the extravagance of the Baroque builders of Bavaria. The strict discipline of plot size and fenestration marvellously disintegrates where the building meets the sky. So Amsterdam is a case of what Gerard Manley Hopkins called 'likeness tempered with difference' extended over a city.

Wherever a vernacular style pervades a town, a style derived from both traditional crafts and local materials, the presence of pattern and rhyme is inevitable. It achieves poetic heights equally in a French village of the Pays Basque, an Italian hill town such as Assisi, or a village in the English

1 *Left:* The City of Amsterdam.

2 *Above:* The *Vieux Carré* or French quarter of New Orleans, a pure gem of rhyming urbanism. The simple architecture is veiled by the most ornate wrought-iron balconies, often screening the building from ground to eaves. Every home is different, both in the detail of the ironwork and the extent to which natural foliage 'rhymes' with these leaves of iron.

75

Cotswolds. Vernacular builders seemed to possess a marvellous intuitive sense of rhyme which seems to be beyond the reach of the sophisticated urban planners and architects who raise great monuments to Mammon like down-town Houston, Texas.

The experience of pattern so far described occurs over time. The sense of order gradually emerges as one passes through the streets of the town (to use Humphrey's term, this is diachronic rhyme). There is another way in which pattern exerts its influence. One of the delights of visiting historic cities is the discovery of views in which the various elements combine to produce a perfect still composition. They are often described as 'picturesque' because they mimic the contrived balance and pattern of a painting (synchronic rhyme).

One such scene is the view across the harbour towards the Medieval houses of Honfleur in Normandy. At first it seems to be a case of amicable anarchy, but then gradually an awareness of pattern supersedes complexity. Certainly all the houses are of different overall height, consequently storey heights also differ. Hardly any two plot widths are the same. Yet there is one overriding feature which immediately suppresses this heterogeneity. Not only roofs but also nearly all the walls are clad in slate, imposing upon the scene a high level of uniformity of colour and texture.

The variations in plot width are contained within limits that suggest likeness rather than difference, and within each façade the ratio of window to wall is fairly constant; so is the proportion within the sub-divisions of the windows themselves. Rhyme has overtaken complexity.

On another level of perception there are four integrated patterns which may register within the brain as features contributing to likeness. Unless we have an analytical disposition, this pattern recognition will tend to occur some distance behind the forefront of consciousness. At roof level there is a pattern of lines sloping from right to left. The interval is irregular, but there again there is more to

link them into a pattern than to suggest that they are random phenomena. The same can be said about the vertical divisions between plots. In the style of the Middle Ages, each floor tends to overhang the floor below it, if only by a token amount. This produces a clear pattern of short horizontal lines accentuated by shadow. Finally, the arrangement of windows is such as to establish a strong pattern of small rectangles. In contrast to the rigid pattern of modern fenestration, just the right balance seems to have been struck here between autonomy and subordination to the whole.

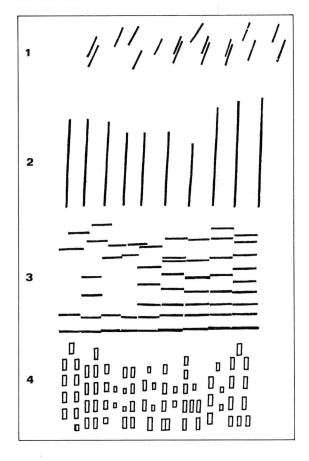

3 *Left:* Honfleur, Normandy.

4 Rhythmic patterns, Honfleur, Normandy.

Rhythm

There is a difference between rhythm and rhyme. The former relies for its impact on strict repetition. It has long been acknowledged that the brain derives particular pleasure from rhythmic presentations varying from the simple binary kind to the complex repeated sub-systems which are evident in poetry, music and architecture.

Once again there is probably a biological basis to this 'rhythm-demand'. Life is bounded on all sides by rhythms of varying frequency. It is a source of security to Man that he is bound up in this intricate system of interlocking rhythms, ranging from his own biorhythms to those which regulate the heavens.

At the same time, there is an obvious advantage in being able to recognize subtle variations in rhythm or beat. Such variations can indicate the presence of a threat, as, for example, when the normal rhythm of weather patterns is interrupted by an intense calm which presages a storm. The rhythm-demand also has a routine advantage in terms of memory and recall. It is easier to remember information such as a telephone number when it is organized into a metric sequence.

Rhythm in architecture

There is no doubt that we are emotionally stirred by the great colonnade of a Gothic cathedral or the giant pillars of Karnak. Renaissance architects fully exploited strong, simple rhythm in the wider realm of urbanism. The approach to St Peter's, Rome, was immeasurably enhanced by Bernini's giant double-columned hemispheres enclosing the Piazza. Their rhythm adds fuel to expectation. The Wood brothers transformed the city of Bath with such masterpieces as the Royal Crescent, with its rapid rhythm of half-round columns giving the long facade the pulse of life. However, rhythm can operate to bring order to a scene in much more subtle ways.

Most towns and cities are unified by commensurate rhythms at various frequencies, and this is a prime factor contributing to the characteristic sometimes referred to as 'grain'.

In the case of Amsterdam, rhythm and rhyme are closely allied. The principal beat is struck by the individual house unit. That is the prime pulse of the city, accentuated by the flourish of the gable or eaves termination. Within that basic beat there is the higher frequency of the windows, establishing a rhythm of thirds on the horizontal plane and fifths or sixths vertically. Perhaps an even more fundamental rhythm is established by the positioning of the canals. Buildings, water and bridges form an articulated whole into which subordinate rhythms fit with remarkable consistency.

Yet the charm of Amsterdam lies in the fact that these rhythms rarely establish a strict tempo: there are countless irregularities. It seems that the mind derives much greater pleasure from extrapolating rhythm from situations in which likeness is tempered with difference, than from visual presentations in which there is no relief from the tyranny of accuracy. Rhyme overtakes rhythm.

Balance

Balance is one of the easiest situations to conceive and one of the hardest to define. Because of its conceptual obviousness, it tends to be taken for granted. It is a commonplace of everyday experience, and structural balance, of course, a prerequisite of all physical activity. Similarly, the homeostatic mechanisms of the brain work to establish balance throughout the organism, regulating temperature, heart-rate and the need for sustenance.

What is perhaps more remarkable is the fact that the human brain is able to perceive balance in, for example, visual situations which are not obviously symmetrical. It seems capable of working by analogy with the physical world in ascribing the quality of balance to a purely visual milieu. But even more significant is the fact that there can be wide agreement about the highly complex organizations of colours, textures, and shapes, which cohere into a state of balance. It follows that there is broad agreement about the various 'weights' or values which are ascribed to particular areas of colour, texture, shape or volume. In other words, the brain appears to interpret visual data according to a kind of code which emerges from the characteristics of neuronal behaviour.

The *Gestalt* psychologists are right to affirm that the human brain does have a preference for patterns which ultimately balance out. Perhaps this is because balance is the most obvious form of order, and certainly a prime task of the brain in its transactions with the sensory world is to discover patterns of order which reduce the gross level of complexity presented by the environment. So, the highly sophisticated skill of perceiving balance within what may initially seem a complex, random assembly of pieces of information, may owe its origin to the fact that like pattern-recognition it has survival value by lowering attentional requirements.

What is it that characterizes *aesthetic* balance? R. Arnheim has described aesthetic balance as 'a state of distribution in which everything has come to a stand-still . . . No change seems possible, and the whole assumes the character of necessity in all its parts.' The use of the word 'balance' implies a metaphoric leap from the sphere of biology to that of physics. Arnheim confirms this by suggesting that patterns are tested for balance by ascribing weight to their elements according to their size and inter-relationships. Figures of speech support Arnheim's proposition. It is common to speak of the 'weight' of an element in a building or a painting. Some features are 'strong', others 'weak'; some 'light', others 'heavy'. Certain arrangements of line and shape suggest 'movement', whilst others are 'stable' or 'static'.

So, a visual *gestalt* is tested for balance by energizing its components so that they are regarded as forces acting within a system, or weights subject to gravitational pull.

In an architectural context, the components perceived as contributing to balance may include colour, texture, tone, as well as mass, intricacy and inferred weight. Even symbolism may be responsible for setting up a force-field which may significantly affect the 'force-system' established by purely visual inter-relations of phenomena.

When balance is immediately perceived, this suggests that the sensory presentation is relatively 'pure', which is another way of saying that it is low in complexity. In Palladio's celebrated Villa Capra (or Rotonda), the concept is deceptively simple. The relatively few geometrical elements are composed into a totality which is immediately perceived as perfect: nothing could be altered without destroying the harmony of the whole.

Balance can also, however, be recognized in scenes which at first seem to be quite arbitrarily composed. One of the great attractions of visiting historic towns lies in the discovery of views in which everything seems to cohere to produce perfect balance. An important aspect of the appeal of such discoveries is the surprise element. Complexity suddenly gives way to that particular kind of aesthetic order in which everything seems to be held in the grip of a powerful gravitational force. The little Breton town of Jossilin will serve as an example. It offers numerous views which fall into the category of the 'picturesque', meaning that they achieve balance or harmony.

In one such view attention is drawn to the various elements which make up the scene. Within the brain, a classification activity is initiated, prompted by the need to organize data according to how they relate to past experiences. At this stage of perception, the attention is concentrated on the various bits of information in the picture. Each parcel of information has an element of independence, and in the analogy with the physical world may be said to have its own centre of gravity.

If the scene is exploded so that these identifiable elements are separated from their context, they may be depicted as having a centre of gravity and consequently a force-field (fig. 5–6). The strength of a particular force-field is measured in terms of gross complexity. Complexity is another word for information. Each element in the picture is a semi-independent package of information, made up of visual intricacy and of saturation of colour, texture and area. Gross complexity is a term we may use to describe complexity multiplied by area.

The force-field that is set up may be compared to a system of planets. This analogy helps us to

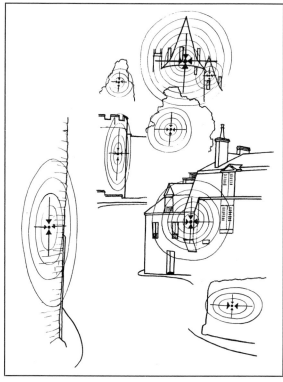

visualize what Arnheim means when he talks about mental 'pushes and pulls' ... If the scene is re-assembled, it is evident that each item, with its force-field, is exerting an influence upon its neighbours. Since the whole thing stays stable, then all the various force-fields must ultimately contribute to a *resultant* centre of gravity. When this is somewhere near the centre of the system, then the whole scene is perceived by the mind as manifesting the quality of balance. The innate preference for balance exhibited by the brain will cause adjustments to be made where necessary in the interests of equilibrium. Values will be manipulated to create a zero force-system—in other words, the brain cheats.

Another factor influencing our assessment of such scenes is symbolism. This is a most important subject (especially in relation to historic towns), which throws a bias into the aesthetic response.

5 *Left:* Jossilin, Brittany.

6 *Above:* 'Planetary diagram', Jossilin, Brittany.

The scene of Honfleur was only partially analyzed earlier. It was used to show how the principle of rhyme can operate in a townscape. However, the dominant feature of the scene is the slender spire or flèche of the town church. What this does is to act as a kind of polarizing force. It establishes a powerful centre of gravity which subjugates everything else within its field of force. It establishes balance by monopolistic principles. Whole cities are like this, for example Florence. Wherever you are in this city, the great dome of the Cathedral is never far from view. It is a splendidly tyrannical object.

The concept of balance is equally applicable where there is a dialogue between opposites, such as between the old and the new. At Queens' College, Cambridge, a new building designed by Powell and Moya is situated in the Grove, which is separated by the River Cam from the historic buildings of the college. The building is entirely contemporary, and yet in no way detracts from the scene. Indeed, it proves that an uncompromisingly new building can enhance a milieu which is predominantly historical. The reasons why it does this are numerous. In the first place the Cripps Building, as it is called, is an elegant design, employing the sharp contrasts of tone characteristic of these architects. The elements comprising the façade are well proportioned. At the same time, they are assembled into a composition which achieves fine proportion and perfect scale in relation to the other buildings of the college.

The circular columniation of the perimeter structure is a strong aesthetic component and establishes a kind of metaphophoric relationship with the exposed timber-framing of the President's Lodge, which is Tudor. Thus there is intrinsic aesthetic quality as well as a subtle point of correspondence between new and old. However, what elevates the scene in my opinion to the level of great architecture is the fact that the new strikes a *balance* with the old. It does this on the basis of *equivalent complexity*.

The Cripps Building certainly exhibits complexity on the level of novelty. At the same time it is a sophisticated design in terms of the interplay of elements: there is complexity of organization and of visual incident. The impact of this two-edged complexity is softened by the setting. The profusion of trees in the Grove injects a strong element of familiarity into the scene, reminiscent of the genius of the Greeks for establishing a dialectic between architecture and nature.

The historic architecture of the college manifests complexity exclusively on the level of visual incident. Few other corners of Cambridge achieve the rate of visual events displayed by the President's Lodge. Powell and Moya have succeeded in sharpening our perception of the old 'Romantic' buildings by placing a disciplined Classical design nearby. The river provides just the right amount of separation. The distance is critical: it facilitates the necessary mental 'arching' across time and space, enabling two very different kinds of complexity to be related, thus facilitating the perception of a balance of opposites.

7 President's Lodge and Cripps Building, Queens' College, Cambridge.

Except perhaps for the idiosyncratic creations of Site Inc. of New York, the building which has most violated people's architectural expectations within living memory is the Centre Georges Pompidou, Paris. Proudly vaunting its sophisticated structural skeleton and innumerable brightly painted pipes and ducts like some colossal machine, its 'surprisingness' is absolute. Yet even this bold leap towards the machine Baroque can become aesthetically powerful in a dialectic with the simple and sometimes venerable buildings of the Beaubourg. Somehow they are able to absorb the shock waves. It is the ultimate in oppositeness which, by some miracle, works—perhaps by constituting equivalent complexity to the whole of the rest of Paris!

8–9 Centre Pompidou, Paris.

Harmony

The last intuitive aesthetic capacity of the brain is the ability to respond to harmony. It is a condition of harmony that there be at least two entities which are not identical, and between which there is sufficient difference to dispel uncertainty, but not so much as to cause excessive dominance. One of the most enduring relationships which is regarded as aesthetically satisfying is the golden mean or divine proportion. Mathematically it is expressed as $1:1+(\sqrt{\frac{5-1}{2}}\ )$. It has dominated art and architecture, and has accordingly been subject to innumerable psychological tests.[10]

The golden mean or ratio relates to the Fibonacci series in which each term is the sum of the two preceding terms: 1, 1, 2, 3, 5, 8, 13, etc. As the values in the series get higher, the greater the approximation to the golden ratio, 1:1·61803. This Fibonacci series occurs frequently in the branching of plants and the organization of spirals in seashells and other natural forms. Therefore its prominence as an aesthetic preference may well be due in part to its wide availability in nature. It is even possible that the normative harmonic status of the golden ratio and the related Fibonacci series stems from the biological architecture of the cortical system.

10 Hilversum City Hall.

11 Convent of St. Marie de la Tourette.

According to certain theorists of the Modern Movement, the new architecture of the twentieth century was to be above such decadent things as aesthetics. One of the most celebrated buildings of the inter-war years is an enduring contradiction of this argument. This is Dudok's town-hall for the city of Hilversum, Holland. The different-sized cuboids of the Hilversum design interlock to produce harmony of a rare quality. The slender tower serves to pull the visual centre of gravity sufficiently off-centre to constitute harmony rather than symmetrical balance. What is satisfying here is the tension created by a displacement that is great enough to be clearly discernible, but not so great as to cause overturning.

In the discussion of balance it was suggested that the interaction between the elements of a scene can produce a gravitational focus which is literally at the centre of the scene. At other times it is possible for the centre of gravity to be off-centre by an amount which conforms to a harmonic mean.

A dramatic view of the central tower of Lincoln Cathedral is given as one begins to ascend the ancient approach called The Strait. Visually and symbolically the tower is a powerful element. In the metaphoric terms of field theory, it generates a powerful force-field which draws everything into its orbit. The tower is off-centre, and so the centre of gravity is pulled over to the left of the picture. It is also raised above the centre in the horizontal plane. The result is a composition in which the relative areas of complexity produce a ratio roughly corresponding to the golden section in both the horizontal and vertical dimensions.

So, scenes like Honfleur and Lincoln owe their aesthetic excellence to the fact that they constitute an orchestration of rhythm and balance, rhyme and harmony built up from numerous matrices ranging from basic features like lines and edges, to symbolism.

Pleasure and emotion

So far, this has been an attempt to describe the intuitive aesthetic value system. But such a description does not account for the way we 'feel' about beauty. Aesthetic perception and feeling are inseparable, since the obvious thing about aesthetic experience is that it is a source of pleasure. This immediately implies the involvement of the emotions.

It is now widely accepted that the basis of aesthetic experience stems from the interaction between chance and order, complexity and redundancy. Complexity comprises anything which causes arousal through some kind of mis-match with the existing organization of information in the brain. Arousal involves the activation of the 'orienting reflex' which comprises a wide range of physical changes necessary to enable us to cope with the threat inherent in uncertainty. This ties in with Nicholas Humphrey's indication that all higher

12. The Strait, Lincoln.

species of animal derive pleasure from encountering moderate novelty, to the extent that they will deliberately search for it. This pleasure associated with the experience of moderate novelty has been related to a particular class of emotions associated with the sympathetic division of the nervous system. This class of emotion is directly linked to the generalized condition of arousal. It promotes the numerous physical changes which have the effect of 'toning up' the organism. There is inherent pleasure in the experience of arousal, which is called by psychologists the 'primary reward system', and by the rest of us 'excitement'.

Whilst this aspect of perception is concerned with the classification routine (that is, the equating of data with existing schemas or models, usually in verbally designated categories), another mental mode is involved in searching for redundancy or patterns of affinity on the phenomenological level. The pattern recognition routine tends to be a slower process than its classification counterpart. However, when an awareness of pattern or balance becomes dominant over the awareness of complexity or disorder, then a marked and sudden psychological change occurs involving a dramatic emotional switch. The recognition of pattern or system excites another class of emotion which has the effect of lowering arousal and counteracting the physiological changes activated by the arousal emotions. This supervention by de-arousal emotion has been termed the 'secondary reward system'[14] and the suggestion is that it is related to the parasympathetic division of the nervous system.

But in a situation containing aesthetic reward potential, the reduction of complexity by the recognition of pattern, rhythm, balance or harmony causes a reversal of emotion. De-arousal emotion supplants arousal emotion, and so the aesthetic sequence passes into the 'secondary reward' phase. It is interesting that the most recent psychological descriptions of aesthetic experience reinforce the philosophical definitions of the last two centuries which defined aesthetic pleasure as the perception of order within complexity.

This can be summed up by a diagram:

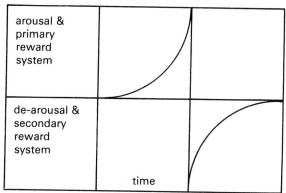

arousal & primary reward system	
de-arousal & secondary reward system	time

13 Diagram.

Marghanita Laski calls this emotional crossover 'ecstatic' experience, the sort of phenomenon that may be regarded as a kind of controlled catastrophe.

The pleasure derived from the classification process itself represents a lower-key version of the transition from complexity to less complexity, as novelty is seen to have points of contact with familiarity—differences yielding to partial likeness. So the classification procedure may be considered to represent the continuous binary rhythm of arousal and de-arousal—a sequence of primary and secondary rewards. Humphrey is right, therefore, in believing that the classification facility is at the heart of the aesthetic response.

The limbic value system
Whilst the aesthetic response just described involves an alliance between the emotions and the 'higher' brain, there is a final category of aesthetic experience which tends to be undervalued because its appeal is deemed to be on a primitive or vulgar level.

Since the publication of the Papez-MacLean theory of brain structure and activity, it has been increasingly accepted that the so-called 'primitive' structures in the mid-brain and brain-stem areas can make a detailed response to outside stimuli without the fact being consciously perceived. What this means is that the limbic brain is equipped with its own repertoire of programmes, some of which constitute what might be called a proto-

aesthetic value system which works in parallel with higher aesthetic perception. Within this value system, pleasure is derived from things which have a touch of the exotic. The limbic brain has a well-developed appetite for sensory stimulation at or near saturation level. This may be expressed as complexity of incident or saturation in the sense of intensity of colour or sound.

At the same time, the limbic brain is particularly receptive to strong serial rhythm, either as beat, or the repetition of simple metric 'phrases'. The great arches of the Pont du Gard, or its modern equivalent at Morlaix, Brittany, nourish this appetite for

14 Morlaix, Brittany.

gigantic beat rhythm. Indeed, the limbic value system embraces gigantism. Since the great ziggurats of the Mesopotamian civilization, man has taken particular delight in building to a scale larger than life. The same motivation is behind the Pyramids, Liverpool Cathedral and the Sears Tower, Chicago.

At certain times in history, the limbic value system achieved a monopoly in art and architecture. One notable instance occurred in the eighteenth century throughout the southern Austro-German: as a style it is identified as Baroque-rococo. According to Philip Drew we are due for such a development in contemporary architecture.

15 Sears Tower.

It may be argued that what he calls 'machine Baroque' has already arrived, pulsating in the centre of Paris—the Centre Pompidou.

There is no doubt that towns and cities are greatly enlivened by injections of the somewhat licentious sensory events that appeal to the limbic brain. In particular, the traditional market-place makes a most important contribution in this realm of value. Where there are pavement cafés and an infinite variety of *ad hoc* contributions to the environment, this value system may exist in a dialectic relationship with higher aesthetics. The whole of the place du Tertre in Montmartre, Paris is given over to café tables and artists perpetrating an agreeable myth. It is a maelstrom of activity. But everything is contained within a frame of simple domestic buildings. In the background is the oriental dome of Sacré Cœur, a constant reminder of the eternal amid the temporal. Saturation complexity, in terms of visual incident, a concentration of people, and a rich mixture of sounds and smells, is contained within a sober frame, with a highly charged symbolic artefact presiding benignly over the whole scene.

In the United States limbic motivation has exceeded all bounds in places like Las Vegas. Even externally sober tower blocks like Water Tower Place, Chicago, become palaces of gold and glitter inside. Glass-sided lift shafts and cars complete the image, making every upward ride a kind of apotheosis. However, places which have the most profound appeal are frequently those in which there is an alliance between the higher intuitive aesthetic values and those stemming mainly from the limbic brain. Without injections of controlled vulgarity, the built environment might be a sophisticated work of art, but intolerable to inhabit.

The immediate reaction to the theoretical model outlined above may be that it is too simple and does not take into account the shifts which are constantly occurring in the hierarchy of values within individuals and whole cultures. There is such a thing as taste and fashion which, historically, have followed a well-defined cycle. The cycle achieves its dynamic owing to an appetite for higher levels of complexity. More and more tension is injected into art, until there is a reaction, and a rediscovery and reinterpretation of the norm or datum of aesthetics.

Symbolism also can throw a bias into all aesthetic systems. It can reinforce aesthetic perception or it can cause a blockage. There are numerous examples of how prejudice grounded in symbolism can result in a suspension of critical rigour.

This condensed model represents an attempt to describe a normative aesthetic value system from which taste and fashion, symbolism and social attitudes cause deviations. There has to be a datum. The argument being proposed is that the datum for aesthetic perception is constant, being the product of certain characteristics of the central nervous system and the natural environment. Furthermore, in a world veering rapidly towards values related solely to the logic of science and technology, the aesthetic value system might have greater survival value than we think.

Architecture and Emotions
Rikard Küller

'Emotion': motion, to move: the word signifies much more than passive experience. To the psychologist it implies a complex state of the human organism, involving not only feelings such as sadness, awe, fear, rage, surprise, joy, but also bodily changes of various kinds, as well as impulses towards all forms of behaviour. Do architecture and more generally the built environment provoke emotions? I am quite certain that they do. However, these are not the strong emotions that are easy to notice and identify, but rather the delicate result of a persistent everyday influence, which is probably of far greater impact than we might at first thought or be willing to acknowledge. This essay will be devoted to a discussion of emotions and their place within a theory of architectural aesthetics.

The work that occupied me in the late 1960s and early seventies aimed at finding a system for describing architecture and the built environment in perceptual terms.* Several independent studies were carried out in which groups of subjects rated various environments on adjective scales. Using about 250 different adjectives on a wide range of environments and employing subjects of different age, sex and occupation it was possible to show by means of a statistical technique called 'factor analysis' that each of the adjectives related to one or more of the following eight dimensions: pleasantness, complexity, unity, enclosedness, potency, social status, affection and lastly, originality.[8, 9, 10] These eight perceptual qualities are now being used as a means to characterizing architecture and the built environment and I will make use of them here as a convenient frame for my discussion of architecture and the emotions. As concerns emotions I will adhere to a tradition within psychology where the aim is to find basic emotional dimensions. My choice of terminology is founded on a series of experiments which began at the start of the seventies. Subjects were asked to rate their feelings in both real-life and imagined situations and the results showed that a four-dimensional sphere is demanded to account for the various emotions which humans experience.

* My research work referred to in this essay is supported by the Swedish Council for Building Research.

The four dimensions will be referred to throughout the text in terms of activation, attention, evaluation and control.

Pleasantness

There have been experimental attempts to identify and study different factors which are believed to influence the pleasantness of architectural space. In 1969, at the first architectural psychology conference in Britain, a paper entitled 'The assessment of room friendliness' was presented. The author had studied various aspects of room interiors and found that seating arrangements, slope of roof and window size were all of some importance. Subsequently one of my colleagues in Lund, Gunnar J. Sorte, carried out a more systematic analysis of the pleasantness of artifacts in the built environment. Sorte's analysis refers to eleven perceptual characteristics: mass, scale, form, colour, brightness, texture, structure, articulation, age, meaning and 'value', which is his word for the generalized idea of pleasantness. The material based on judgments of more than hundred subjects makes it possible, among other things, to study how pleasantness depends upon the other categories in the list.[23]

As a rule, pleasantness is judged to be positively influenced by rounded-off forms, negatively by square forms. Elements of colour generally seem to have a positive effect, while the absence of colour is considered to be negative. With regard to structure, a wealth of detail and variation is appreciated while uniformity is not. A certain degree of articulation is also valued, especially when it goes beyond purely functional demands. Those artifacts which seem genuine, well designed, lasting and meaningful are judged as pleasant, while those which are experienced as poorly planned, temporary, without meaning, are judged as unpleasant. Finally, while certain artifacts are considered to be pleasant because they are antique or simply because they have a sentimental value, others are appreciated for being new, modern, unused. The quoted results allegedly give a simplified picture of a very complex evaluation process; still the concensus among the subjects was very high and covered a wide range of artifacts.

Among the many attempts to predict pleasantness, the importance of colour seems to have been studied more thoroughly than any other single relationship. In 1941 the psychologist Hans J. Eysenck compiled over 20,000 colour preference ratings previously carried out in diverse experiments and concluded that people preferred colours in the following order: blue, red, green, violet, orange, and yellow.[3] However, owing to the lack of control of various colour characteristics, there were many inconsistencies in the original studies, and it has since been shown that any hue can be made more or less preferable by simply manipulating lightness and chromatic strength. A second objection which can be raised against these early studies is that the colours were applied to pieces of paper and the like. In colour studies carried out at our laboratory, employing drawings of interiors as well as full-scale model rooms, neither hue, lightness nor chromatic strength could be shown to affect the pleasantness of the room in any consistent way.[1, 7] The question, 'Is there a general order of colour preference for architectural spaces?' can therefore be answered in the negative. This does not mean that people will not be able to agree about what is a pleasant colour scheme and what is not (actually people do agree to a surprisingly large extent): the difficulty lies with predicting the reaction from a few simple colour variables.

Other attempts at predicting pleasantness make use of key concepts such as harmony, rhythm, complexity, uncertainty, mystery, etc, and often imply a search for the appropriate or optimal stimulus situation, like in the theories elaborated here in the essays by Nicholas Humphrey (pages 59–73) and Peter Smith (pages 74–86). Many of these attempts are based on physiological considerations. Daniel E. Berlyne suggested in 1971 that a moderate increase of low arousal, as well as a reduction of high arousal, will be experienced as pleasant.[2] A year later Lennart Levi presented a

1a-b Of these two buildings one was rated in an experiment as much more pleasant than the other. They also differ as to characteristics like form, colour, structure, articulation and age.

somewhat different model based on the 'stress' concept introduced by Hans Selye.[16] According to this model an increase in stress level might be experienced as either pleasant or unpleasant. Although the two models are not fully consistent with each other, both point to the interesting fact that a change of physiological arousal level often is accompanied by a change in pleasantness. This change is thought to be mediated by specific 'reward and aversion' centres in the brain.

However, these findings in themselves do not explain what it actually is that we like or dislike in our environment—or why. To understand the underlying significance of pleasantness, we must consider the fundamental biological urge to survive, grow and multiply. In order to accomplish this, all higher animals must possess some kind of system by means of which they will be able to detect, classify, evaluate and take appropriate action against certain elements in the environment that impinge upon them. Seen in this perspective, pleasantness may be considered as a projection onto the environment of an evaluation process (based on three crude values: good, harmless and bad) refined into what is commonly known as the hedonic or *evaluative* emotional dimension.

Let me take as an example Sorte's discovery that rounded-off forms are generally considered to be more pleasant than square forms. It is easy to identify here some experiences which help to explain this evaluation—the round breast of the mother, the round shape of the feeding spoon; edges are rounded off by the carpenter, while the armourer makes weapons that are sharp or pointed; and in nature the sharp and pointed might be deadly dangerous. Harry F. Harlow in his experiments on social deprivation found that baby apes would not accept a mother substitute made of metal wire, although it offered milk, but preferred a soft, rounded but milkless, rag doll.[4] Thus, emotions—whether of personal, cultural or biological origin—decidedly play an important part in the evaluation of the environment, by a process of symbolic projection.

However, one cannot expect any one-to-one relationship between emotions on the one side and the perceived qualities of the environment on the other. You might, for instance, consider your living room to be very pleasant. Sometimes, when you look around it, you might feel pleased or happy. At other times you might hardly notice the room. But even at times of sadness or depression you are not likely to find the room unpleasant. While emotions might shift quite rapidly, the qualities projected onto the environment remain much more stable. Even so, there is a mutual influence. More than twenty years ago, A. H. Maslow and Norbett L. Mintz in a classic study showed that the character of the environment had an effect on how people are perceived.[17] Subjects who spent 10–15 minutes rating a series of facial photographs in a beautiful room rated the faces as having significantly more energy and well-being than did subjects tested in either an average or an ugly room. There is also some evidence from studies carried out in Lund, in which our subjects were permitted to look at photographs of various environments and were asked to say how they thought they would feel in them. After looking at one set of landscapes and one set of living-room interiors, the subjects suggested that the more pleasant environment would contribute to an increase in calmness and security as well as to a reduction of aggressiveness—in other words, they were given a high hedonic evaluation. Also, the subjects believed that the more pleasant interiors would make them feel more agile, independent, talkative, extrovert and sociable, feelings which are all related to another of the main emotional dimensions, which I will refer to as the dimension of *control*.

In this context I also want to mention a study of the emotional impact of natural versus urban scenes recently carried out at our department by a guest researcher.[24] These contrasting environments were presented as colour slides under strictly controlled conditions. To measure emotions not only verbal rating scales were used but also physiological registration of brain and heart activity. The nature scenes were generally considered more pleasant than the urban scenes, and—more interesting from our point of view—they also seemed to have a positive effect on the hedonic emotions, while the urban pictures had a markedly negative effect. Moreover, the physiological results suggested that direct viewing of nature scenes might have a relaxing effect under certain circumstances.

In trying to create a pleasant environment, one would naturally avoid certain inappropriate conditions, for example very intense stimulation near the threshold of pain. However, time and again one is surprised to find that typically 'wrong' situations can provide maximum pleasantness. Why is a Finnish sauna so delicious, and why are discotheques appealing to young people? This difficulty of accounting for the attraction of certain conditions, as well as the intangible nature of beauty, have led some specialists to regard pleasantness as a purely idiosyncratic quality: 'there is no disputing tastes'. Some architects even seem to regard their business as pure art, well beyond the understanding of the common man. Related to this is the fact that architects do not seem to experience the built environment from the same starting-point as people in general. Results from some of my own studies indicated a considerable discrepancy between architects and laymen when they were asked to rate environments for pleasantness. Some architects have tried to hand their business over to the social scientists. 'The built environment', so they say, 'is neither pleasant nor unpleasant in itself, it all depends on how it is used and by whom'. I will return to this matter later on when discussing the problem of crowding. The point to make here is that the perceived quality of pleasantness is too closely related to the built environment for architects to be excused for side-stepping the issue in any of these ways.

Complexity and Unity
Complexity might best be understood in terms of variation or, more specifically, intensity, contrast and abundance. All the different components that we are able to distinguish will contribute to the complexity of the environment whether they be of a visual, auditive or tactile nature. Let me take colour as an example. Chromatic strength is one of the factors which will contribute most to the complexity of an environment. This is true not only for the strong reds but also for the yellow, blue and green hues. However, physiological measurements have indicated that the red colour provides higher arousal than green and blue. (Actually, in some studies intense colours of green and blue have even had an arousal reducing effect.) Therefore, it is no coincidence that red is a very popular colour in restaurants and theatres—the purpose being to maintain the arousal level of the public on a fairly high level.

The degree of unity of an environment is a matter of how well all the various parts fit together into a coherent and functional unit, for example, how well attuned are the shape and colour of the furnishings to the room as a whole. The search for unity is an ancient preoccupation. Pythagoras, Plato and Vitruvius found it in harmonics and in the proportions of the human body. Those who wish for psychological analysis of unity, however, will have to turn to the *Gestalt* psychologists, Kurt Koffka, Wolfgang Köhler and Max Wertheimer, who formulated the relationship between part and whole in a number of grouping principles.[5] By applying these *Gestalt* principles the unity of an environment can be strengthened or weakened. The experiment on colouring of interiors mentioned earlier can be taken to illustrate this. Degree of unity was found to decrease when many different colours appeared in the same room, or in a monochromatic room when the colour strength of either walls or furnishings was intensified: both of these are straightforward examples of the *Gestalt* principle of similarity. It is often possible to find a specific reason why a certain detail fit poorly into the environment. It might have the 'wrong' colour, function, form or size, or even be experienced as misplaced. However, if the incongruent detail has the character of a temporary arrangement, the unity of the totality will not necessarily be affected at all.

There is evidence to show that although the degree of unity in architectural space ought to be fairly high, it must not be permitted to be excessive. The relationship between unity and complexity seems to be the decisive factor here. If complexity is

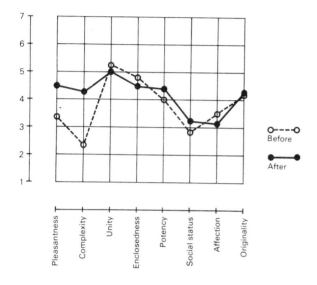

far exceeded by unity, the result is a dull and monotonous environment; whereas if the scale tips the other way, the environment may appear too chaotic. Let me give two examples. In the late sixties a housing area was built on the northern outskirts of Lund consisting of two-storey buildings of concrete and wood. The woodwork was originally painted in a brownish-grey tone, but in the early seventies this had mostly faded away and it was suggested by the architect that the buildings be repainted in dark red with a black cornice and the front doors in a rather strong green or blue. After a few blocks had been repainted a comparative study was carried out. As can be seen from the illustration, the new colour design raised complexity as well as pleasantness. One might interpret the increase in the latter quality as a result of an improved balance between complexity and unity. Evidence pointing in the same

2 The repainted buildings shown in the illustration were ranked much higher in complexity and pleasantness.

direction was obtained in an analysis of twenty-seven housing areas built in the sixties and seventies in the southern part of Sweden. The five areas examined by an experimental group to be least pleasant also showed a considerable lack of balance between complexity and unity.

Such conclusions have to be seen in a physiological context, as explicable by reference to understimulation and overstimulation of the brain. In 1949 G. Moruzzi and H. W. Magoun were able to demonstrate that every ascending nerve impulse on its way up through the brain stem first affects an area, the so-called 'reticular formation', which in turn influences the arousal level of the total nervous system including 'the emotional and intellectual' areas of the brain.[20] The average arousal level over a prolonged period of time is called tonic arousal level; it can be low (as in sleep or drowsiness), normal (as in most everyday activities), or high (as in excitation or stress). These different levels are known to correspond to feelings of being more or less alert, awake, drowsy or sleepy—sensations which belong to another basic dimension of emotions which I will call *activation*. It is known that different individuals have varying arousal requirements, that the activity which the individual is performing itself contributes further arousal (this varies widely depending on the nature of the activity in question), and that the built and social environment both add to arousal.

I have already mentioned that the complexity of an environment seems to influence emotional control (page 90). To test this assumption further I compared an office abounding in colour and pattern (high complexity and low unity) to another office very grey and dull. Subjects who stayed in the rooms for a few hours not only had a much higher physiological arousal level in the colourful room, but also felt much more introverted in that room than in the grey one, as reflected by their replies on rating scales: the chaotic visual impact made them feel strangely silent and subdued. The experiment therefore underlined the impression that a change in the complexity of the built environment can be accompanied by a change in emotional control.

If a moderate degree of visual overstimulation can produce such noticeable effects, what happens if additional factors work in the same direction—a noisy acoustic environment, a hectic task, an upsetting social situation? Stress research has helped to identify some typical effects of overstimulation. There are changes in breathing rate and pulse rate, blood pressure and blood flow, internal secretion and muscle tension, as well as an increased susceptibility to infection, coronary disease and ulcers. Furthermore, psychiatric disorders and social reactions of varying sorts have been diagnosed. For instance, a study dealing with the effects of noise showed that helpfulness towards others diminished considerably in noisy environments. In two separate experiments, one carried out in a waiting room, the other on a street, subjects exposed to 85 decibels of 'white' noise were less likely than those in lower noise conditions to offer assistance to a person in urgent need of help.[18]

How severe might be the effects of the other extreme—understimulation—was realized during the Korean conflict when prisoners of war had to endure isolation for prolonged periods. The impact on their personality was so striking that a new expression was coined: 'brain-washing'. Motivated by this, a group of researchers in Montreal began to study sensory deprivation, and their lead was soon followed by others. By means of elaborate arrangements (for example, a person was enveloped in wadding and his eyes and ears covered or he was placed in a dark, sound-proof, room, or even submersed in a large container of water at body temperature to create a dark, soundless, weightless condition), the experimenters were able to register very marked changes.[22]

After a period of sleep or boredom, isolated persons generally show symptoms of excessive emotional response. They become irritated, have difficulty in thinking clearly, and loose their power of concentration; they become increasingly susceptible to propaganda; they suffer reduced precision in locomotion and dexterity, disturbed colour vision, get physiological alterations of brain wave frequency, odd sensations of their own bodies and

3 For several decades there has been amongst architects a tendency to play down complexity in favour of unity—the sterile outcome of this can be found all over the world today.

in certain cases, hallucinations. A number of writers have suggested that some of these deprivation symptoms may also occur in sterile urban environments. Consider a standardized and excessively uniform housing area whose appearance is characterized by a minimum of complexity. Add to this an inadequacy of meaningful activities and of social affiliation. As a friend of mine, a professor of neurophysiology in Lund, put it: 'Perhaps these environments will cause deficiencies in the brains of our children, "holes" that will never be possible to fill in.'

Open and closed spaces

Enclosedness implies a sense of enclosure—the very feeling of being in a room. This quality implies that one has a clear impression of the dynamics of the room, its centre, its extent and its boundaries. It is, however, a mistake to believe that the walls and ceiling completely determine the degree of experienced enclosure. Place yourself on a large stone in a field and get some local children to seat themselves around you. Read a story aloud. You will find yourself in a 'room' with the stone as its central point and its boundaries determined by the strength of your voice. When evening draws in you light a small fire next to the stone and as darkness descends the feeling of enclosure increases. The crucial factor, apparently, is not walls or ceiling, but the presence of a focal point and a feeling of togetherness.

In most indoor rooms, however, the positions of doors and windows, curtains, carpets, lamps and pictures, will be relatively fixed. The arrangements of each of these will affect the enclosedness perceived, as will the character of the surrounding surfaces. Large openings reduce the impression of enclosure, and so do light walls, floors and ceilings. Thus, if the walls of a rectangular room are painted with the long sides dark and the short sides light, it seems even longer; whereas if the short sides are dark and the long sides light, it seems more like a square. The general rule is that light surfaces repel each other while dark surfaces attract each other. Also, if the furnishings have strong colours they will stand out against the background of the walls, and because of the resulting increase in contrast, the room is likely to appear less enclosed. Generally, a room with well-suited furniture is experienced as less enclosed than both a completely empty room and an over-furnished room. Other factors of importance are the proportions of the room and its acoustic characteristics.[6]

We now come to the question of whether there is any relationship between enclosedness and emotions. With the exception of agoraphobic and claustrophobic reactions, it is difficult to trace any connections although much speculation has been offered from an evolutionary point of view along the following lines. Our ancestors for a long time lived along the border area between savanna and forest and in times of danger took refuge in pits or caves and later in fortresses or towns surrounded by protective moats and walls: hence, enclosed spaces provide us with a feeling of security. To me this reasoning does not seem valid. There are numerous examples of tribes which for long periods lived in deserts or on plains, owing their survival to their great mobility over vast land areas. Nevertheless I think it is possible to arrive at a tentative theoretical understanding of the relationship between enclosedness and emotions.

In its interaction with the environment the organism tries to detect, classify and evaluate significant patterns but this capacity is limited. By definition, undivided attention can only be given to one pattern at a time. Thus, if the flow of impressions becomes too rapid we must protect ourselves against the danger of overstimulation. This may be attempted, not always successfully, by a redistribution of attention. There are also external means of filtering undesired stimulation: for example by orienting oneself away from or by increasing the physical distance to the stimulation; or by using an elaborate system of barriers or walls. Enclosedness is therefore a means of filtering impressions of the environment, of raising or lowering one's arousal level. When one feels rested and in full control then one is apt to open up the filter more than if one feels tired and introverted.

This theory might be applied also in the present research and discussions on social crowding. Crowding here will be taken to mean a social situation which, mainly through density or proximity of people, will cause emotional activation and a rise in tonic arousal level.[15] There is much evidence that the presence of other people in the immediate vicinity tends to increase arousal. Excessive aggression, social disorganization and even massive death rates were all found to be effects of crowding in animal colonies. Studies on humans support the hypothesis that prolonged crowding can produce psychological and physiological stress. Most people avoid excessive crowding. Experiments have shown that as people approach each other they tend to orient away and use less eye contact to compensate for the increasing closeness. As a rule, we avoid seating arrangements where there is a risk of eye-contact with strangers.

Of course, a densely peopled situation will sometimes be found to be amenable, as on the dance-floor or at a fair. In a room full of friends, the increase in arousal will not be stressful at all. The view taken by many writers that crowding is merely a question of available space therefore does not hold. In addition to factors such as density and proximity, eye-contact, facial expression and posture, we have to consider interpersonal relations such as friendliness in order to be able to understand the meaning of crowding. Also, I will venture the hypothesis that whether or not a person will like a situation that might be described by some as crowded, will depend on his level of emotional control. However, all other conditions being equal, the probability of crowding is likely to increase in direct proportion to the enclosedness of the space itself. Thus, enclosedness is a matter of not only what is kept out but also what is kept within. The cave might become a home but also a trap, the open field a hopeless emptiness or a welcome road to escape.

Potency
Although describing an essential aspect of architecture, potency is less well understood within the framework of psychology. The expression of inherent power, of potential force, encountered in monumental architecture is accomplished not only through its large scale or mass but also through coarse forms, crude materials, rough textures and dark colours. The Great Pyramid at Gizeh is the most highly potent building I can think of. However, many examples of buildings high in potency can also be found in most urban environments. In

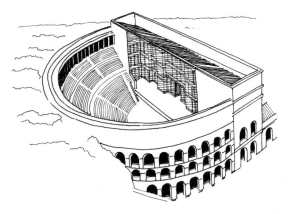

4 Like most antique theatres the one in Orange in the southeastern part of France has a well accentuated focal point.

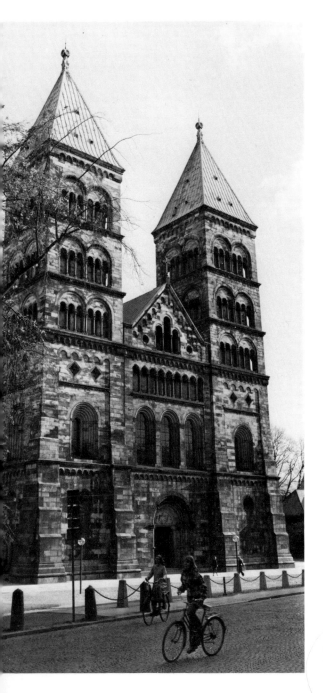

5 The cathedral situated in the centre of Lund presents a magnificent spectacle to the visitor; does it also convey a message of power?

popular belief powerful and dominating buildings are considered to lend authority to those in charge of them, while the occasional visitor might feel impressed, submissive or even guilty. Court houses and church buildings often seem to have this effect. Is it for instance the sublime function of cathedrals to make the regular visitor feel proud to be part of such a grand congregation but to fill the outsider with awe? However, I know of no research which has set out to confirm or contradict this hypothesis, in which many architects seem to have believed.

Earlier on I discussed the emotional dimension of control, relating it to feelings ranging from independent and extroverted to silent and subdued. Can it be that there is a direct, close link between these feelings and the perceived quality of potency? In this connection I want to mention an idea expressed by Murray S. Miron and Charles E. Osgood; the latter has been for many years working on semantic analysis in a more general context than I myself. These writers consider potency as an expression of the amount of physiological effort it will take for the individual to come to terms with the stimulus situation.[19] Thus, a building of high potency would be—initially—more difficult to incorporate in a physiological sense—or in emotional terms to control mentally. Allegedly this is at present nothing more than a hypothesis, but an interesting one because of its far reaching implications. It would mean for instance that the typical high rise building merely through its visual characteristics might make it more difficult for people to establish emotional control over their environment.

Social status and the urge to conform
Social status denotes an evaluation of the built environment in socio-economic terms. Social status has often been used by planners and architects to differentiate space in elaborate ways, for instance in the lay-out of towns and in theatre auditoria. The

public co-operates in this by showing a strong preference for the expensive and exclusive, rather than the cheap and simple. In the choice of a home, or an area in which to be housed, social status is of great consequence. In buildings the choice of materials and colour scheme is the most obvious consideration in this respect; high status being reflected in the quality of the woodwork, metalwork and brickwork; dark colours giving a more expensive look, while strong colours mostly will look cheap. Also, the very fact of employing an architect in itself carries a social status message. Today the most typical examples of high-status buildings are embassies, banks, galleries, theatres and private villas.

I know of no experimental studies that throw light on the emotional significance of social status in the built environment. However, there is no doubt that social classification and discrimination relate to basic human needs: as Nicholas Humphrey points out, they serve the organism in its attempts to organize its environment and thus have a definite survival value. But there is a counter-tendency that confuses the picture somewhat. Although individuals often strive to obtain higher status, and

6 Some years ago, when the municipal theatre in Malmö, abounding in white marble, was partly coated with corrugated asbestos sheeting, this led to serious protests from the citizens because of the cheapness of the material.

whole classes of people struggle to rise socio-economically, there is a force of the same magnitude whose effect is to sustain the status quo: this is the urge to conform. Conformity, more often than not also means security, to be one of a group, to share ideas and ideals, outwardly expressed in styles of hair, dress, car, house and lifestyle generally. It is a great drawback to planning that so little is known about how these two antithetical forces operate.

Affection and originality
Affection, the next quality in my list, implies a kind of recognition, an impression of familiarity—not necessarily because we have been in a particular place before, but perhaps as a result of our biological and cultural inheritance. For instance, in the Swedish landscape any meadow with its typical flowers and birches, surrounded by mixed forest, is likely to rouse in me fond and tender feelings, even if

it is my first visit there. In the same way, in an experiment, an old farm house painted in red ochre, a small whitewashed country church and a piece of cultivated landscape were rated very high in affection although the subjects had never seen the environments to which they were responding. In an urban environment, affection attaches mostly to places that are left reasonably untouched for some length of time. Here again, familiarity in the strict literal sense need not play a part. A tourist visiting an old town for the first time will react in a way that is indebted to comparable encounters on previous travels. Affection will immediately be felt. Biologically speaking, there seems to be a wide register of readily identifiable environments, suggesting perhaps in Jungian terms, the archetypes stored up in the collective unconscious.

As well as this kind of immediate recognition there is also a process of continuous familiarization. There are the environments we were born into, grew up in, in some cases spent the whole of our lives in. People not only get used to new things, but also might develop, after some time, an affection for them. A place might rate high in affection only after a person has used it a while, filled it with personal belongings, put his mark on it. In a sense, affection always implies that we have made the place our own, that we have appropriated it, and find it well-adjusted to our personality.

The importance of this dimension for urban design was clearly demonstrated in a study at Lund of seventeen housing areas, all of them less than six years old. It was found that areas ranking high in affection were much more readily recognized from photographs and correctly placed in their respective

7 The old city of Malmö has an atmosphere typical of old cities all over Europe. Its wealth of detail and the variation in design and colour makes it appealing and attractive even on a rainy day.

geographical location. The familiar design obviously helped people to memorize the houses and put them in the proper places.

To some extent we are prepared to accept changes, to develop an affection for new things. The same old place might become boring and from time to time many of us will set out to seek the new, excited by the thought of travel, and the prospect of moving on. However, when it is a matter of altering an existing environment, there is a limit to what we can tolerate. When the old surroundings disappear too quickly and too extensively, and when the replacement is too different from what people are used to, there is likely to be a strong reaction. This is not necessarily because the old was good and the new is bad: quite the opposite might actually be true, which leads planners and politicians to assume that people are irrational.

Originality, meaning 'fresh and unusual' as well as 'initial, first', is something of a counterbalance to affection. However, it is not the opposite of this quality. An original piece of architecture, which will be original even after the passage of time, may come to provoke an expression of affection; and conversely, of course, total lack of originality is no guarantee that affection will be felt. For these reasons, I have avoided the terms 'novelty and familiarity', for these would have suggested a continuum, in which a building would start off as novel and end up as familiar.

Few attempts have been made to establish experimentally what contributes to an impression of originality. In the studies on colours of interiors we found that using strong colours on the walls led to ratings of high originality. A reasonable and simple explanation for this is that people do not normally expect wall surfaces to be painted in intense colours. The unexpected as well as the unusual is therefore a contributory factor.

To understand better the mechanisms behind affection and originality I must bring in two concepts from psychology: orientation and habituation. Any moderate change in the environment is likely to attract a person's attention. He will turn his eyes, head or body towards it for the purpose of

evaluation: is it good, bad or harmless? The significance of this mechanism is well understood. In 1927 Ivan Petrovich Pavlov gave the following description.[21]

'It is the reflex which brings about the immediate response in man and animals of the lightest changes in the world around them, so that they immediately orientate their appropriate receptor organ in accordance with the perceptible quality in the agent bringing about the change, making full investigation of it. The biological significance of this reflex is obvious. If the animal were not provided with such a reflex its life would hang at every moment by a thread.'

After this initial orientation reaction, one of several different things can occur. If the object of attention is difficult to perceive or to classify, there might follow a prolonged period of exploration, but eventually an evaluation is likely to occur on a conscious or subconscious level. If the assessment is 'good', it will be followed by an approach, physically or mentally. If it is 'bad' the reaction will be

8 The high originality which characterizes many modern buildings will, in the long run, not be able to serve as a substitute for an elaborate articulation. The church is from the southern part of Malmö.

withdrawal, which again might take a physical or mental form. A third possibility is the double evaluation 'good and bad' usually known as conflict. However, in most cases the evaluation will be 'harmless, of no significance', and the subject will turn away and shortly forget about the experience. All that remains in this event will be a lasting tendency to disregard, to look away from, whatever caused the initial orientation reaction. This tendency has been termed habituation.

On the physiological level, the orientation reaction will always be accompanied by a temporary increase of arousal—a so-called 'phasic arousal' reaction—which is likely to be sustained and finally canalized if orientation leads to exploration, conflict, approach or withdrawal. Frequently the phasic arousal reaction will be accompanied by mental feelings of curiosity, interest and the like. On the other hand, when habituation occurs, there is no increase in arousal and no feeling of interest.

This range of feelings and bodily changes corresponds, in my view to a fourth dimension of emotions which I will call the dimension of *attention*, by means of which we are now in a better position to discuss the impact of affection and originality. In a place of high originality numerous strong orientation reactions will initially occur, but owing to habituation they will eventually level off. Now if originality is the only quality present to any considerable degree the place will be evaluated as harmless and there will be nothing left to attend to, but if there is 'something more', i.e. something that we recognize because of its biological, cultural or personal significance, the place will continue to hold our interest. Thus, affection will serve to sustain emotional attention. In a place of high affection— the landscape of the native country, the old town centre with its typical buildings, the familiar room filled with personal belongings—there will always be things to recognize.

Conclusion

Only 15 years ago very little work had been done in the field of architectural psychology. Today it looks very much like any other scientific discipline and the problem of tomorrow will be that there are too many facts and that the theories are not good enough. This being the situation I think it is important to make priorities. I hope I have been able to put over something of the importance of the relation between architecture and the emotions as a topic for further exploration. But this is far from enough. To understand the interplay between man and his environment we will have to apply a much wider approach including the social, cultural and biological setting. We will have on our hands a highly complex model where we must be able to trace the details without loosing sense of the totality. This is an enormous task but there is progress under way. I believe that it is only within an ecological framework that it will be possible to get a proper understanding of the subtle impact of architecture and the built environment.[11, 12, 13, 14]

I have in this essay discussed eight perceptual qualities pertaining to architecture and to the built environment generally, and tried to show how these are in different ways related to four basic emotional dimensions, activation, attention, evaluation, and control, sometimes fairly directly, at other times through a complex interplay. It is clear beyond doubt that the built environment has far reaching consequences for the human emotions either we prefer to regard them as mental feelings or physiological processes. Many of these effects are now generally accepted and well known, others are only partly understood or completely unrecognized. In addition to the facts based on experimental studies I have put forward a number of hypotheses in the hope of stimulating experiment.

Notes to the text
[1] C.-A. Acking & R. Küller, 'The perception of an interior as a function of its colour', *Ergonomics*, 1972 vol. 15, no 6, 645–654.
[2] D. E. Berlyne, *Aesthetics and psychobiology* (Appleton Century Crofts, New York, 1971) pp. 206–20.
[3] H. J. Eysenck, 'A critical and experimental study of colour preferences', *American Journal of Psychology*, 54, 385–394, 1941.
[4] H. F. Harlow & M. K. Harlow, 'Social deprivation in monkeys', *Scientific American*, 1962, 207, no 5, 136–46.
[5] D. Kretch & R. S. Crutchfield, *Elements of psychology* (Alfred A. Knopf, New York, 1958).
[6] R. Küller, *Rumsperception* (L. T. H. Lund, 1971).

[7] R. Küller, 'The perception of an interior as a function of its colour'. In B. Honikman (ed.), Proceedings of the Architectural Psychology Conference at Kingston, Kingston Polytechnic & RIBA Publications, London, 1971.

[8] R. Küller, 'A semantic model for describing perceived environment'. National Swedish Institute for Building Research, Document D12, Stockholm, 1971.

[9] R. Küller, 'Beyond semantic measurement', in R. Küller (ed.) 1973, *Architectural Psychology*. Proceedings of the Lund Conference, Studenlitteratur, Lund & Dowden, Hutchinson & Ross, Stroudburg, 1971.

[10] R. Küller, 'Semantisk miljobeskrivning. Psykologiforlaget, Stockholm, 1950.

[11] R. Küller, 'En samfunnsorientert teori for sampspillet mellom menneskene og omgivelsene' Det fysiske miljo og mennesket, Seminar vid NTH, Inst psykologi og sosialforskning, Inst by og regionplanleggning, 1976, Universitet i Trondheim, Trondheim.

[12] R. Küller, 'The use of space—some psychological and philosophical aspects' in P. Korosec-Serfaty (ed.), Appropriation of space. Proceedings of the Strasbourg Conference, CIACO, Louvain-la-Neuve, 1976.

[13] R. Küller, 'Psychophysiological conditions in theatre construction' in Arnott *et al* (eds.), *Theatre Space* (Prestel Verlag, Munchen, 1977).

[14] R. Küller, 'Fartygsmiljons aktiveringsgrad—en omgivnings—psykologisk analys. L.T.H., Lund, 1978.

[15] R. Küller, 'Social and the complexity of the built environment—A theoretical and experimental framework' in M. R. Gurkaynak & W. E. LeCompte (eds.) (in press), *Human Consequences of Crowding* (Plenum Publishing Corporation, New York.)

[16] L. Levi (ed.) 'Stress and Distress Response of Psychosocial Stimuli'. Supplement no 528 to Acta Medica Scandinavia, 1972, vol. 91.

[17] A. H. Maslow & N. L. Mintz, 'Effects of asthetic surroundings I. Initial short-term effects of three asthetic conditions upon 'energy' and 'well-being' in faces'. *J. of Psychol.*, 1956, 41. 247–54.

[18] K. E. Mathews & L. K. Canon, 'Environmental noise level as a determinant of helping behaviour'. *J. Per. Soc. Psychol.*, 1975, 23, 571–77.

[19] M. S. Miron & C. E. Osgood, 'Language and Behaviour: The Multivariate Structure of Qualification' in R. B. Cattell (ed.), *Handbook of Multivariate Experimental Psychology* (Rand McNally & Co, Chicago, 1966).

[20] G. Moruzzi & H. W. Magoun, 'Brain stem reticular formation and activation of the EEG. Electroenceph'. *Clin. Neurophysiol.*, 1949, vol. 1.

[21] I. P. Pavlov, 'Conditioned reflexes' (Clarendon Press, Oxford, 1927).

[22] P. Solomon, P. E. Kubzansky, P. H. Liederman, H. J. Mendelson, R. Trumbull & D. Wexler, (eds.), *Sensory Deprivation*. A symposium held at Harvard Medical School, Harvard Univ. Press, Cambridge, Mass, 1961.

[23] G. J. Sorte, Forthcoming dissertation, L.T.H., Lund.

[24] R. Ulrich, *Psycho-physiological effects of nature versus urban scenes* (Byggdok, Stockholm, 1978).

Humanity in the Built Environment
Carl-Axel Acking

We are living in a society which has often shown signs of cynicism, even if for the most part unconsciously. Oscar Wilde once described a cynic as 'one who knows the price of everything and the value of nothing'. But some of us were aroused from our complacency by Rachel Carson's ecological book, *Silent Spring*. We began to realize that the birds were no longer singing and that we had disturbed life in nature. Something happened which is reminiscent of the discovery made by a Molière character: that he is speaking prose and has been doing so his whole life without even noticing it. Suddenly we understood that we had been treating our surroundings carelessly. In the following years we began to be interested in the preservation of the environment: our air, our water, our soil. The whole of nature was in need of protection. We at last began to show some interest in ecological problems, and more recently in problems of human ecology as well. As a consequence, we also began to evaluate the influence of architecture and planning upon the mind.

In the following pages I would like to explore the diverse ways in which we started to look at our environment, and to provide an analytical aetiology of the problems that beset us. Later on I will attempt to bring these various elements into perspective and offer some directives for humanity in the built environment.

In his book *The Human Zoo* Desmond Morris has pointed out that man as a species has a particularly acute need for stimuli from his surroundings and that this biologically determined need has been one of the most important preconditions for the development of those features which we think of as characteristically human. The low levels of brain activity produced by understimulation or partial sensory deprivation, which was first studied under the direction of D. O. Hebb at the University of Montreal in the 1950s, have been shown to be just as directly damaging to the central nervous system as the tension brought about by overstimulation.

Our central nervous system must receive a continuous flow of sensations in order to function properly. A steady flow of signals must be transmitted to the brain from the body itself—from its muscles, joints and internal organs—and from sensory organs in the form of visual, auditory, olfactory and tactile impressions. The eyes must receive a constant 'background static' of images, including lines and angles created by surfaces and bodies, contrasts, figures, colours, motions and points at rest. The ears must be provided not only with information from the internal organs (the buzzing from the respiratory tract and the sinuses), but also, under normal environmental conditions, background noises such as the wind rustling through the treetops, the chirping of the birds, falling rain, and the sounds of people's voices. Deprived of this static, which is not transmitting any specific information, our central nervous system cannot function normally. Considered from this point of view, the built environment acquires a special importance. According to the Swedish neurologist Professor David H. Ingvar, it is arguable that the oversimplified, paltry architecture of our modern cities is actively harmful, and in part a cause of the environmental neuroses from which city-dwellers are at present suffering.

Such statements can hardly be proved. We still cannot measure with any precision how visual or auditory experiences of the built environment affect individual nervous systems, or groups of nervous systems. We cannot compare the flow of sensory information for someone living in a large, sterile high-rise block of flats, with that for someone lucky enough to live in a richly varied seventeenth-century house in the 'old town' section of Stockholm. It is even less possible for us to measure the long-term consequences of variations in this 'background static'. Of course sociologists can provide us with certain indications, by indirect methods such as surveys of enjoyment and attitudes. If one counts divorces, empty wine bottles, broken windows and hours spent at the welfare bureau, a pattern of connections does seem to emerge. However, the links are not clearly defined, and no causal relationships can firmly be established. Professor Ingvar implies this, while maintaining that because of lack of concrete evidence, one is forced to make do with extrapolating from present-day knowledge about the brain. The danger is that we will hyper-critically repudiate what we instinctively feel to be true: that a wealth of variation in sensory input is a necessity of life, and that we should strive to increase this wealth in the built environment in order to ensure the well-being of everyone who lives in it.

Unfortunately, the richness of living among tightly arranged, low and varyingly shaped homes has been replaced by emptiness; and small dimensions have given way to huge, inhuman proportions. The possibilities of social contact have become fewer, and social life has therefore become a watered-down experience as Stanley Milgram (1970) has pointed out. Passiveness has taken the place of activity. The chance to meet other people on our own familiar ground and to see them performing their everyday activities is stimulating. It provides us with information about society and its members, and about the people who are our neighbours. It is particularly important for the social development of the children that they are able to observe their social surroundings and become familiar with them.

In earlier agricultural societies as well as in those dominated by crafts and guilds, places of living and of work were usually co-ordinated and the distribution of wares was less complicated than now. A significant feature of industrial society is a differentiation between where people live and where they work. This fact, among others, has contributed to the socio-psychological problems that have such an influence today on societal planning and construction.

The lack of day-care centres and play schools does not make things easier, and for many families causes severe problems. It is ironic that the aged, who could have time enough at least to help mind the children, are concentrated by society's well-intentioned measures in special institutions, where they become inactive and get on each others nerves.

The broken tradition of the craftsman in building has not yet been replaced by comparable and convincing industrial methods. Not even in the economic sense are new methods always superior.

1 'It is difficult to compare the flow of sensory information for someone living in a large, sterile high rise block of flats. . . .' Birmingham, England. Photo P. Goodliffe.

Of course, the problems are not as simple as they are presented here. The political and socio-economic realities are also part of the picture.

Just as in other forms of art, the art of building contains much which has little to do with the intellect, but rather is perceived by the senses. It is just this which contributes to our feelings of comfort or discomfort, pleasure or displeasure, in the built environment. A sensitive and thoughtful treatment of sensory characteristics is an important ingredient for the user of architecture, who not only sees the front of a building as an illustration, but literally enters into it, takes possession of it and lives behind it.

I would rather speak of emotional experiences and reactions than of aesthetic values, because the words 'aesthetics' and 'aesthetic values' are so easily misunderstood. The eighteenth-century German philosopher A. G. Baumgarten has provided us with good reasons for such care in our use of language. He was probably one of the first to make the word 'aesthetics' synonymous with the study of that which is beautiful. The poet and philosopher Schiller was further responsible for allowing the use of the word 'aesthetic' instead of beautiful to spread and acquire tradition. I think it is important for us to abandon a use of the word which implies a value judgement, and return to an earlier usage by which it referred only to objects and events which produce sensations.

Sensory perception is a source of great pleasure as well as an infinitely rich source of information. An infant, for example, is joyous when one hand is able to catch the other. Later on, the child thinks it can pull down the moon. The discovery of the third dimension creates endless new problems, but the child is partly compensated for the fact that the visual world is difficult to grasp by increased experience within other areas of the senses. The child soon learns which characteristics various materials possess. Such sensory qualities as hard, soft, light, porous, slippery, coarse, and the like, become striking, even exciting.

Similarly, just as the blind person in an auditory and tactile way receives information about spatial conditions, the sighted person receives information about the size, distance and character of the various street localities in which he operates through hearing and feeling, in addition to his visual perception. In his book *Experiencing Architecture* (London, 1959), the Danish Professor Steen Eiler Rasmussen describes in one place how the size and boundaries of a market space behind us are conveyed on an autumn day by the rustle of leaves which the wind carries from the fronts of buildings and whirls about our legs.

A more subtle description of the richness of auditory information is provided by another Dane, the composer Carl Nielsen, in his book *Living Music*. Here, he compares the pause in music with what happens when we walk near a stream and cross over a bridge, and the rippling of the stream fades, disappears under the bridge, and finally comes back when the bridge is crossed.

That we do not merely use our eyes when we

2 Designing for the blind. The choice of materials, both for internal and external space is an important consideration for designers involving all our senses. For the blind, areas are not only for tactile orientation but also for acoustic orientation.

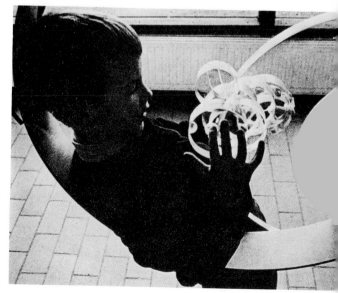

perceive the built environment has long been clear to everyone, but the experience gained from a recent series of research projects concerning the visually handicapped has to a great degree increased my sensitivity to and knowledge about the importance of the other senses for architects, planners and other environmental designers.

For the blind, areas are areas not only for tactile orientation but also for acoustic orientation. Further research into the needs of the visually handicapped in the design of the environment will extend existing knowledge of how it is possible, by simple means, not only to provide non-visual information for the poorly-sighted but also to enrich the environmental perception of those with normal sight, just as Frank Lloyd Wright, Basil Spence and Charles Moore did. One of the suggestions I can think of as a result of our studies is the introduction of different olfactory codes for different central underground stations in a city. Even people deeply involved in reading newspapers will be able to smell the fragrance of the right station.

I maintain that we have great difficulty today in assigning perceptual significance to the various structures surrounding us, and in interpreting their content. One could present the hypothesis that up until now we have employed what is nowadays called 'semiotics' by C. S. Pierce and 'semiology' by the Swiss philosopher F. Saussure, i.e. an interpretation of our visual impressions which guides us, leads us and aids us in orientation. If we accept that such a semiotic process has been at work, which we more or less consciously have been using, we can also suppose that in today's world, because of industrialized construction, grandness of scale, and so many other factors, the old semiotics are no longer in force. One may then ask the question: do we not need to create a new semiotics which we can make use of in order to find our way through this world?

This problem has intrigued many in recent times, for undoubtedly it is very pressing. Among those who have applied themselves to it is Umberto Eco, author of the book *The Absent Structure*, which covers semiotics in general and contains a chapter

3 We need to develop the new science of semiotics which we can make use of in order to find our way through this world.

specifically on architectural semiotics. This science, which allows one to decipher and interpret the signs and symbols which our buildings and their organization express, has been taken from the medical theory of symptoms. In philosophy, semiotics was introduced as far back as the 1600s by John Locke, as the science of the signs and symbols which man utilizes in order to communicate the significance of objects. During the 1960s there was a strong increase of interest in the general theory of signs, as we can see from the great volume of literature on the subject which has been published in recent years. Works focusing on semiotics have appeared in both the United States and Europe, and the establishment of the international scientific journal,

Semiotica, which was begun in 1969, indicates that semiotics is widely accepted as a legitimate area of enquiry. The language of architecture, just like that of the films, computers, road signs, and the written and spoken word bears a message; and this belongs to the field of semiotics. According to Susanne K. Langer, there is a great difference between a sign and a symbol. A sign can be understood as being a signal. A signal causes us to make a decision about what is meant. The meaning of a symbol, on the other hand, can be understood directly. Among other things, it is the capacity to use symbols which separates man from other living beings. Most words are more than signals. They are used to name objects, not to direct one's nose, eyes or ears towards them. Words of this type are not symptomatic of the presence of objects, they are symbols; that is, they represent or play the part of objects. A dog, however, hears the name, raises his ears and looks for the person. The transition from a word's signalling function to its symbolic function, according to Langer, is gradual, a result of social organization, an instrument which proves itself indispensable the moment it is discovered and which develops itself through successful use. The symbol-creating function is one of mankind's primary activities; the universality and fluidity of human speech implies that. The transformation of experiences into symbols is a fundamental process of the human mind. This is implicit in speech, which is one of our most important means of expression. But we are so used to being strongly influenced by the symbolic function of words that we consider them to be the *only* important means of expression, and take it for granted that all other symbolic activities must be either practical, or else irrational, playful or ineffective. Actually, language is the natural outlet for only one type of symbolic process. At another level of consciousness, events occur in the human mind, transformations of experience which terminate in a completely different way. They conclude in actions which need neither be practical nor impart information, though they *can* be both active and social. Langer alludes in this connection to actions of the kind which we call 'ritual'.

While the study of semiotics was being taken further elsewhere in Europe, our own research group at Lund set itself to investigate the way we describe, verbally, buildings. We used semantic differential measurement, treated the results with factor analysis and found several important factors that people use in describing the connotative meanings we give to our built environment.* Other investigators carrying out comparable studies in Holland and the U.S.A. found similar factors.

It is interesting (although incidental) to note Langer's point that whatever it is that is expressed in music has been considered exclusive and particular to this art form, and inexpressible in any other idiom. We have studied various emotions which have arisen in listeners during the performance of music. Words which correspond to these emotions are, for example, 'melancholic', 'grave', 'restful', 'happy', 'irritated', and so forth; they all seem to belong to the enjoyment evaluation factor which we have developed, which we have termed 'pleasantness'.**

The French philosopher Roland Barthes writes that at the very moment that a society recognizes its own existence, every undertaking alters to become a sign of itself. And in his introduction to semantic research Umberto Eco says that the architectonic code gives birth to an iconic code. Using a spoon to carry food to the mouth is just one fulfilment of its function. The spoon promotes a certain way of eating and characterizes this eating. The object communicates its function even if it is unused. This, I believe, is an interesting idea that could be usefully pursued in architecture. In Genoa, Martin Krampen, the Professor of Communications, has experimented in this area by asking subjects to identify arbitrarily chosen buildings and then to state what criteria they have used in identification. A variation on this approach is to get the subjects to evaluate a

* See the piece by Rikard Küller, pp. 87–100.

** It seems to be the case that our analysis of adjectives covering the visual area is partly applicable in the auditory area as well. This idea is supported as Langer suggests, by our pilot studies on the spatial perceptions of visually handicapped people to which I have already referred.

series of sketches which merely describe the volume or contour of a building and to transform them into more detailed descriptions. Applying this method, Krampen wishes to determine which criteria are vital in providing the building with a character corresponding to its function. If architecture, now and in the future, is to be a medium for easing communication and orientation in our complicated society, and not merely a technically functional manifestation, more intensive research is required by architects and psychologists working together. Beyond this, and based on the findings of such research, there is a need for education in applied aesthetics in architecture.

When the parishioners of the little village of Ronchamp decided to build a pilgrimage chapel on the mountain, they chose an architect who they knew had created some of the most striking buildings of the time, but who until then had not built any churches: Le Corbusier. They expected him to solve this traditional task in the perspective of our own age. Perhaps they were merely speculating in notoriety and wanted to make their village world-renowned; if this was their aim, they succeeded. However, perhaps their intentions were somewhat deeper; perhaps they wanted a building of unusual significance for their services. They succeeded in this too. For a pilgrims' chapel and a house of God for a Catholic parish, there are no fixed sacral building forms. But genuine tradition, based on liturgical requirements, can be fulfilled in various ways, and in Ronchamp it is the Calvinist, Le Corbusier, who has shown the way. For those who comprehend the visual idiom of our time, and for the primitive, pious parishioners who, while they may not understand this idiom, are not impeded in their response by an excess of dogmatic and historic learning, this building sings God's praises and provides a devotional experience which is genuine and mighty.

It is a frequent experience that so many stimulating and beautiful illustrations in architectural journals represent a view other than that which we see with our own eyes. The camera does not always tell the whole truth. When one is confronted with the physical reality, it sometimes seems less interesting than a photograph, but often the opposite occurs. Architecture is not experienced merely as a fixed image but as something which is visually perceived as dynamic, as the observer moves in relation to it, and which at the same time speaks to more senses than vision. This means that an architectural description, like that of any work of art, will be as incomplete as the description of the fragrance of a rose. I will therefore refrain from further attempts at using mere words to provide an image of the chapel in Ronchamp.

Of course, a present-day church does not necessarily have to be designed in a way which deviates from earlier styles. It can be maintained that tradition in ecclesiastical architecture is pronounced and should not be broken with. If one builds with accepted materials and craftsman-like methods, there is reason to allow this to be expressed even in the design. Our period, however, uses additional materials and different building methods, which in the hands of a truly talented architect can give to the results a richer and freer, or more imaginatively stimulating character, which perhaps will respond better to the ideas of the coming generation. That people will develop an altered outlook in our own lifetimes is surely quite clear. The rapid mobility, through modern systems of transport and communication, which characterizes our time—automobiles, aircraft, films and television are the obvious examples—has added new dimensions to our viewing of images. Time and space have become more closely united in our interpretation of representations. Perspective vision, which was typical for Renaissance Man, has been replaced by beyond-the-horizon vision, which in turn is giving way to kaleidoscopic vision, with its fast-shifting images and a flexible relationship between surface and depth.

In the chapel in Ronchamp, for the first time we become familiar with a church which was intended by its originator to transcend present-day forms of expression and to present reality as others will come to see it in the future.

For centuries, architects applying sensitivity and intuition have succeeded in engaging mankind in

4a-b Nôtre Dame Du Haut, Ronchamp designed by Le Corbusier. Two drawings by Paul Hodgkinson, Oxford.

their spatial creations. By allowing men to take possession of their works, by allowing them to move freely within them and, through this, introducing the dynamic moment into a room which itself is static, the architect is able to generate a particular mood, which is precisely the one that is appropriate and desired. Through insight, introspection and artistic creative processes, spatial creation of this kind has taken place, with the drawing board and the architectural model as its basic tools. We can spontaneously feel the impact of a piece of architecture without having to deploy scientific methods specially devised for measuring it. However, if we wish to know in greater detail about what it is that influences us psychologically, we can be sure today of more than we could ten years ago.

5 Airport pavilion by Eero Saarinen. Motion—The mirror image of time—is of great importance in connection with how an architectural effort is perceived.

Man's own motion adds the crucial dynamic moment to architecture.

Our spatial behaviour is very dependent on how the environment is shaped and though often, one fails to reflect that the architect has a role which is similar to the conductor of an orchestra, with the slight difference that those who are unconsciously conducted by the architect are anonymous to him.

It follows that as the architecture gets worse, the number of signs and directions increases. Eero Saarinens airport pavilion at Kennedy Airport is an example of good architecture in function leading people in the right way with practically no signs at all.

Cooperation between creative designers and vigorous scientific investigators has provided us with the means of starting to obtain knowledge about the psychological influence on us of the planned environment.

Attempts at such spatial approach to design in recent times have not always been considered successful and as a result of this justified feeling aid has been summoned from other sources. Motivated by a social conscience, rather like a doctor on duty, the painter and the visual artist have rushed out to save the life of a doomed room. Full of enthusiasm, and with all the earnestness of social crusaders, they have changed underground stations into fairytale caves and Evangelical Lutheran churches into pantheistical forest cottages, with a flourish which would have heartened old Swedenborg, but which for a coming generation must seem extraordinarily surprising.

However, in a transport installation such as an underground station or an airport, a person under modern-day stresses is probably more receptive to objective information than to the ever-so sophisticated fine arts. That this objective information can be provided to a high degree through spatial design is demonstrated by examples such as the TWA building created by Eero Saarinen at Kennedy Airport in New York. This remarkable building is an organically realized spatial structure in which the architect provides not merely guidance and support but at the same time sets up a rhythm, which can almost be seen as a poetic work, whereby the lightness and dynamics of air travel are mirrored in surrounding cavities of concrete and glass. A minimal number of signs is needed here, as one is led the right way without them.

From what I have just said about the visual artist's participation in spatial design, one might get the idea that I am generally negative towards it. This is definitely not the case, but I do not believe in his contributions as compensation for an absence of architectural spatial design. On the other hand, they can be valid as enrichment in particular cases.

In his *Eupalinos*, which is a dialogue between Socrates and Phaedra, Paul Valéry lets us know that there are:
'Mute buildings
Buildings that speak.
And buildings that sing.'

The first he despises. The second he appreciates if they speak clearly and describe their function, for example, as either a market hall or hall of justice.

Concerning the rare buildings which sing, it seems that they have qualities that we cannot grasp by simple phrases. As with the fragrance of the rose, we can only understand with our senses. Nevertheless, we can proceed on the assumption that these buildings and these rooms are built using genuine materials and veracious principles of constructions.

At some universities there is the chance of studying poetry and even creative writing. But it is unlikely that students go on to become poets because they have attended. We educate architects— but what they go on to do is produce an intelligent interpretation of a building programme which can be practically and technically satisfying. It seldom becomes poetry. The poetic side of architecture does not easily find expression in the materialistic, mercantile, bureaucratic and at times falsifying machinery of which today's society consists.

One of Sweden's oldest companies uses full-page advertisements to advertise plastic-coated metal sheets with illusionary surface coatings, which can conjure up desks of 'oak' sheet-metal, chairs with 'textile' plate work, bathrooms with 'rosewood' sheet-metal walls, and medicine cabinets coated in 'leather' sheet-metal. The poor woodpecker who adorns the advertisement has bent his beak in trying to attack the rosewood panel.

In Sweden, practical functional demands and social ethos, together with the development of industrialized construction methods during the past fifty years, have been the characteristic concerns of the building sector. Economic and technical forces within building production and the rigid goal-formulations of a growing bureaucracy, coupled with arsenals of building norms and detailed standard requirements, have greatly fettered both architects and planners. Only people with the strongest architectural convictions have managed to obtain sympathy for their attempts to provide particular character, variation and humanly comprehensible scale to structures, buildings or town-planning, and even then only in exceptional cases.

In solving the spatial problems of urban planning, in both the public and private environments, we have almost weaned ourselves off making higher demands, and instead merely try to satisfy purely practical and technical requirements.

The Swedish poet Ekelof says in his poetry: What I have written—is written between the lines. That which, despite everything, is written between the lines in the present-day art of architecture, is usually erased at the blueprint stage by efficient representatives of examining bodies and the procedures of the authorities, who do not accept poetry.

My late colleague and friend, 'M.E.M.', who was one of the greatest illustrators in Sweden and who had a rich humour, depicts a phenomenon which is a common experience for an architect of our day. He describes the mayor of a city council as delivering the following speech: 'Mister poet, in accordance with the Council's decision, your poem is accepted with the revisions and amendments specified in the enclosed writ.'

In recent years, the reactions of the mass media to the sterile, inhuman character of many of our housing areas and the frightening unhomely atmosphere of our schools, hospitals and other public institutions have aroused a new interest in environmental spatial design and the problems it attempts to cope with. But it is clear that such reactions can easily cause the pendulum to swing the opposite way, and instead of over-simplified skyscrapers we may run the risk of a corresponding tiresomeness in identically repeated rows of one-storey houses, which furthermore destroy land and nature. This danger has been noted, and in a well-meant attempt to achieve desirable spatial variation in the town imagery of some recent housing areas, nostalgic emotions have led to synthetic imitation of styles characteristic of earlier social periods. This has even been taken as far as glueing on plastic window bars. Naturally, such an attitude will produce no singing houses—and no singing spatial combinations. If they did sing, it would be in *falsetto*.

Only in very rare cases can we find spatial creations from our own age which provide us with the sort of emotional experience which earlier epochs provided, and still provide. Perhaps a few believe that architecture created even in our age has a role beyond the purely practical and technical, and thus still belongs to the fine arts.

What we can learn from earlier generations is, essentially, simplicity and truthful expression with regard to form, material and construction. In my opinion this aspect of architectural culture is not so much a question of aesthetics as of ethics. It seems important to make this point because ethics, just like semiotics, is something which hardly exists in architecture today.

In the preceding pages I have tried to provide an analytical aetiology of the current state of affairs in the art of architecture. One may have read between the lines several ways by which I believe we could contribute to making our environments more humane. I will not attempt to offer some further, explicit suggestions, with examples of how we could achieve some of these directives.

In contrast to a reductionist theory which states that the whole is merely the sum of its parts, *Gestalt* psychologists proposed the whole is something more than this sum. I hope that architects will show in their work that this is so, even if their ability to do so is often limited. Two prerequisites for achieving these aims are: first, a deep understanding of the objects; and second, a careful study of the parts and their relationship to the whole. To answer these needs the architect will have to show respect for and be able to collaborate with other specialists. Small standardized elements can be combined in different ways to give variety to our buildings in their overall effect. This lesson can be learned from nature in the way, for example, a tree's smallest part, the leaf is repeated in the total composition.* The well-known

* See the piece by Nicholas Humphrey, pp. 59–74.

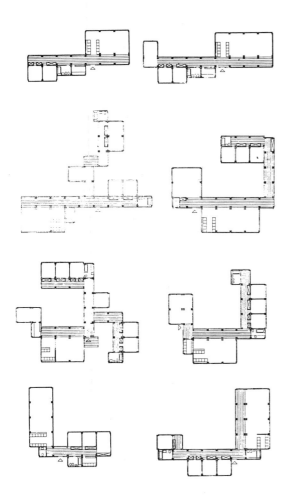

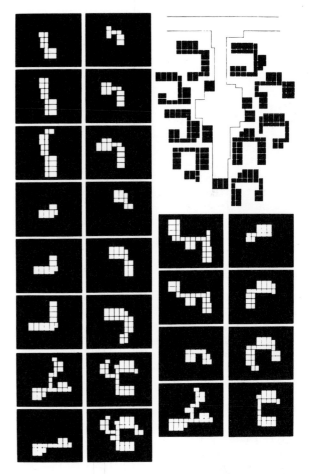

6a *Above:* The additive method employed by architect Jørn Utzon. Through the use of standardized parts in both furniture design and the buildings themselves, a varied and interesting end-product has been achieved.

6b *Above right:* There with variations. An additive method of housing built by industrial techniques. Architect Jørn Utzon.

architect Jørn Utzon, who was responsible for the Sydney Opera House and in 1978 was awarded the Royal Gold Medal from the Royal Institute of British Architects, has given us quite a few examples, including housing areas, school buildings and other constructions, in which this additive method has been employed. Through the use of standardized parts, in both furniture design and the buildings themselves, a varied and interesting end-product has been achieved. These projects, which exhibit a high degree of freedom on the part of the designer, are characterized by the organic qualities of the finished work. Surprisingly, this additive

7 Sidney Opera House by Jørn Utzon.

method has also been used in the monumental opera house in Sydney, in which the shells have been built up with standardized elements generated by the surface area of a sphere. The opera house is an example of how an exciting sculptural effect (in the building seen as a whole) can be achieved by a limited number of different parts.

The lack of time allocated for planning and design is one of the reasons I would give for the neglect of the 'human factor'. Others are largeness of scale, uniformity, absence of character in the design and failure to identify. For generations architects have been trying to create order and clarity using expressive and varied design. Lately, however, technical-economic and solely functional aspects have been allowed to dominate, and a grasp on the total effect has been lost. One way I would like to suggest of escaping from this dilemma is to establish, through research, how industrial machinery should be constructed in order to contribute to the fulfilment of the human need for variety and for a comprehensible scale. A more imaginative use of industrial and mechanized technology is necessary, which may be achieved by creative research.

The present-day emphasis on flexibility is probably a reason for the lack of character in modern architecture. The important thing is not so much the need for semiotic truth—the simple demand that form should follow function, or even that it should give a poetic expression of a building's character. What is far more vital is to fulfil the requirement for individual character and identifiability in order to simplify orientation and add to our experience. In every kind of art we like to find expressions of caprice as well as order. Why not in architecture?

On the same level as music, painting and sculpture, architecture is regarded as an art. But in architecture there is an additional utility aspect. We can more or less choose what we wish to experience in sculpture and painting, but we can't escape from architecture. It is all the more necessary then that architecture should be experienced through all our senses. The essential means in painting are colour and form, in sculpture mass and form. Mass, form, colour, but above all space are the means in architecture. Movement is essential in experiencing architecture and can be seen as the mirror of time. Rapid movement and the increased importance of the written message characterize the dynamics of modern society. But the visual quality in most of our cities remains of a very low standard.

We ought to show a little more consideration for our combined knowledge about Man, his needs and his reactions when faced with different situations and events. When we plan and construct we have a tendency to proceed from a short sighted viewpoint, and to choose the easiest calculations using a formula that incorporates the given numerical values x and y which are convenient for our purposes, while often ignoring factor z, the human factor. Perhaps we would not have been forced to pay some of the social costs if we had built differently. Among the decision-makers there is a strong tendency to take into account the economic, the technical and the practically functional in a project, but expressions of human emotional experiences are given less consideration, a tendency which I blame upon our inability to quantify the latter scientific units. However, I have now considerable hope in new evaluation methods and general research in architectural psychology. I now turn to the question of architectural education. I would defend present-day architectural teaching methods against the criticism that the students are only trained for today's problems and only about present building techniques. I would argue that training aims to establish a working methodology with an interplay between analytical and synthetic creative work. By this mode of working not only may future technical problems be solved but new functional needs will be answered as well. Even human needs of an emotional character should figure on the design agenda. The architect's methodology is to a great extent an interplay between individual parts and the whole. This cannot be taught theoretically but has to be gained by intensive training, and practice in spatial thinking and successful communication. I will not try to offer a full description of creativity. The creative person is said to be non-conformistic, self sufficient, introvert, radical and perhaps intolerant. I believe that these personality traits have hampered creative people from reaching positions of responsibility in our society. The predominance of the *receptive* talent in creativity is a possible reason for the low priority given to aesthetics in practical architectural decision-making.

In fostering the architectural student's creativity, his sketchwork is an important medium for 'internal' communication—that is, the creative process, within his own mind. In order to communicate with those for whom he builds—authorities, and the like—other methods are needed, such as perspectives and models, and why not use movies, taken within small-scale models?

8 In professions engaged in the planning and design of the environment there is need for facilities which can demonstrate its appearance before it is built. The simulator at Lund is one of such methods which enable the subject who looks in a TV screen to see in a realistic way the view inside and outside the model at eye level. By varying the speed of the moving camera he can achieve a movement corresponding to walking, cycling or travelling by car.

I would like to conclude by stressing three factors that are vital for the creation of human environments. First, interdisciplinary research into human relationships with the physical environment must be further encouraged, and a closer collaboration developed between the field of psychology and that of architecture. Secondly, there must be an increase in user participation: this source of opinion, together with the results of research, should be the basis for formulating in detail the human needs that must be expressed in any programme for a site. Thirdly, consideration should be given to co-ordinating the details with the unity, the parts with the whole, by all those professionally concerned with creating towns and buildings; and such people should be especially trained in this approach.

When these objectives are fulfilled, perhaps we can take the first steps in seeing the whole as greater than the sum of its parts. In the terms of the dialogue between Socrates and Phaedra, we will have no mute buildings, and more buildings that speak clearly to us; we will even have more buildings that can sing to us. Architecture will then be poetry.

Further reading

C.-A. Acking, 'Evaluation of Planned Environment', *Document D7:1974*.

C.-A. Acking, *National Swedish Building Research*. 'Reduced visual Ability and Environmental Experience'. S67 National Swedish Institute for Building Research.

C.-A. Acking, 'Environmental Simulating Methods and Public Communication'. *Document D8:1976*.

C.-A. Acking, Bygg Manskligt, Askild & Karnekull, Stockholm.

C.-A. Acking & R. Küller, 'Perception of the Human Environment'. In Honikman, B. (ed.), Proceedings of the Architectural Psychol, Conference at Kingston Polytechnic. (RIBA Publications, London, 1971).

C.-A. Acking & R. Küller, 'The Perception of an Interior as a Function of its Colour'. *Ergonomics* 1972 vol. 15, no 6, p. 645–654.

C.-A. Acking & R. Küller, 'Presentation and Judgement of Planned Environment and the Hypothesis of Arousal'. In Preiser W. F. E. (ed.), Environmental Design Research, Proceedings EDRA Four. Dowden, Hutchinson & Ross. Stroudburg, Pennsylvania, 1973.

C.-A. Acking & G. Sorte, 'How do we verbalize what we see?' *Landscape Architecture*, 1973, vol. 64, 1, USA.

C.-A. Acking & R. Küller, 'Interior space and colour', In T. Porter & B. Mikellides, (ed.), *Colour for Architecture* (Studio Vista, London, 1976).

E. T. Hall, *The Hidden Dimension* Doubleday, New York, 1966), pp. 143–4.

Human Energy
Charles Moore

'Energy' in our society is generally seen as a number of suspicious phenomena, perhaps misleading, probably vaguely occult. The u.s. Food and Drug Administration is said to be preparing a suit against certain advertisers of cranberries, who claim that their berry contains more 'food energy' than other fruits, which turns out to mean simply that it contains more calories. In other uses, energy is seen as emanating from the fingers of saints in quantities sufficient to be piled up on the photographic plates of Eastern European photographers. My argument, too, is based on energy, of a slightly different sort: that is, the energy human beings have to devote to the act of dwelling, in our houses and our cities and countryside. Our buildings, I have come to believe, if they are to succeed, must be able to receive a great deal of that energy and store it, and even repay it with interest. Only then will their inhabitants feel at home, connected in space and time to the planet and the past, 'centered' as dancers say, not only with their imaginations, but with their whole bodies.

Making such places, clearly, isn't easy. They occur certainly with appalling infrequency on our planet at the present time. The hope of the participatory planners of the 1960s that a liberated populace, large with a sense of Place, would give birth to inhabitable spaces with the designer as a kind of midwife has not been realized, so far as I know; there is a requirement for an expert. Architecture without members of our own professional societies is readily conceivable; but architecture without expertise is not. From prehistoric times there have been specialists in the siting and construction of dwellings, including the Chinese *feng shui*, who seem from our distant culture to have been mapping the currents of energy in the earth with the same search (and need) for precision that has animated the acupuncturists' search for currents in the human body.

But experts and exertise don't create spaces without inhabitants and the act of inhabiting is a difficult one (at least in our time) requiring extensive investment on the part of the inhabitant, in time, energy, and care. To make his investment, the dweller has to be interested. Mies van der Rohe's famous statement, 'I don't want to be interesting, I want to be good,' needs for us architects, I believe, to be turned around: 'I don't want to be good, in allegiance to some abstract system, or doctrine: I want to be interesting, to shape buildings that will engage people, and encourage their investment of their energy to dwell.'

To be interesting, it seems to me, one (and one's buildings) must be immediately accessible and comprehensible, and even pleasant, but they should, as well, reward further familiarity. It wouldn't do to be able to say, as people did once of an American presidential candidate, 'deep down, he's shallow'. Because the building has to repay not only immediate but continuing care, with layers of revelations. The architect's task, I'm fond of saying, is not so much to compose shapes and spaces in allegiance to some canons of proportion and form as to choreograph the familiar and the surprising, to reach the inhabitants with what is familiar to them, what feels easy, not threatening and not strange, and then to pepper the comfortable with the surprise that will maintain their interest and excitement, and open up new insights even into the familiar, which is in danger without that opening of going stale and unnoticed.

What is most familiar, of course, is what lies around us, loosely labelled the vernacular. The term, I'm afraid, confuses: it immediately conjures up in the minds of art historians and many others, images of the elegant cubist assemblages of the Greek islands or Mexico, beautiful compositions made by villagers in strict response to familiar conditions of site and society, with a stringently limited palette of materials and a (for us) thrilling level of agreement about colour and shape and scale. The contemporary North American vernacular, on the other hand, the one that concerns me here, is very different from that, on just about every count: it is not traditional, in the way the Greek island village is, its ways of doing things handed down through generations, hence understood, or at least assumed, by almost everybody. It is the work of a nation composed of people who, at one time or another, in greater or less degree, have eschewed tradition, to strike out on their own. The distinctions between rich and poor have not vanished on our shores but they are unclear and any possible hierarchy is full of inversions—cf. the contemporary joke about the doctor (American doctors are thought to have excellent incomes) who calls the plumber, then complains about the bill, saying 'That is more per hour than I make', to which the plumber replies 'I made less too when I was a doctor'. And, with a few regional exceptions, there just aren't any peasants, people so close to some piece of land that they understand its moods and requirements while they are at the same time free of any pretensions that would stand in the way of their response to the physical conditions.

Most Americans are (and I say it with some pride) indeed pretentious and eclectic to a fault, and, I think, to a considerable virtue. We are mobile, and pick up our impressions from (and even relate to) places far distant from each other. The number of farmers in Fargo, North Dakota, who go to Florida for the winter is astonishing, and travelling to distant places during vacations is by now a standard activity of Americans, as of Western Europeans. American intellectuals wince at the possibility (which they generally hotly deny) that our normal mode of existing is as tourists but, it seems to me, tourists we basically are. We collect the exotic to us, and we take ourselves off to unfamiliar situations. My own great-grandfather, a farm boy in southern Michigan a century and a half ago, on land then very recently wrested from the Indians, kept his farm notes in Latin and his personal diaries in Greek, and Thomas Jefferson had, a few decades before, proposed that the architecture of the ancient

1 Thomas Jefferson's house Monticello has so captured the American imagination that it is on the five-cent piece.

Greek and Roman republics be reproduced in order to help his own new republic attain stature through its buildings. We still seek to make our own the manner of building of distant places. When Santa Barbara, California, experienced a devastating earthquake in 1925, its citizens determined to build the city back according to a shared image of 'Spanish'. They even created an elaborate mythical history for themselves, including spirited Mexican festivals (to which they barely remembered to invite the city's Mexican population). And in the process, they achieved for themselves one of the country's most attractive cities.

Some of our most lively and convincing places, in fact, are fantasies, Williamsburgs or Disneylands. We have created, in this century, so many places to

live in which the imagination cannot dwell that we flock, as tourists, to those places where it can. The stones in the Roman Forum have doubtless been there longer than the stones of Disneyland, but the stones of the Forum have been rearranged, and we are as much tourists one place as the other, though none the worse off for that.

So, as befits us, North America's vernacular architecture is composed not often of the autochthonous toil of peasants, but generally of the ingenuity of the pioneer, homesick or adventurous, or both, casting his net a great distance through time and space, catching exoticisms and incongruities as well as (infrequent) moments of the sublime. The work is animated by considerable care, and attention, and love which has usually been

2 Opulence has its virtues, even in a tiny city hall at Gilroy, California.

3 A more widely familiar format is used for a handsome house in New England, with intimations of the shipbuilder's art.

4 Even hollow mountains exhibit some architectural quality, witness the Matterhorn at Disneyland.

5 H. H. Richardson said the commissions he would most like would be a Mississippi River steamboat or a grain elevator.

lost on critics looking for something else, and it provides a rich source for the designer who is willing to admit buildings speaking in many voices, at many levels of importance. This, of course, represents a switch.

For a long time, trained architects have required of themselves that they be Original, and of their buildings that they be Important. The former has created neighborhoods without unity or texture, where every building calls for separate attention, like giraffes and rhinoceri at the zoo. The latter, a

denial of freedom of speech to buildings, has made them tongue-tied, unable to speak for fear of not speaking Importantly, and consequently not very interesting to the people who are trying to inhabit them. If, I believe, their architects relaxed a little, and let their buildings be gentle or whimsical or shyly charming or ingratiating or surprising or rowdy or funny, or even a little weird, fringe sometimes and not always central, then people's interest in them might increase. This is not, I believe, in conflict with the belief which I also hold, that

6 A small house in Southern California recalls the archetypes of C. A. Jung.

7 We assume a certain naïveté among those who do not believe in the full efficacy of the arch, but this makes a telling combination.

8 The powers of all the classical talismans are deployed in the façade of this litttle house in Guanajuato, Mexico.

easy. It is aided by some allies that we have, which reflect our shape (like statues or chimneys) or demonstrate our care (like flowers, and gardens) or move and change and are lively (like natural light can be). These allies in habitation, if their efficacy is not dimmed by mindless repetition, can stand in for us, to suggest inhabitability, and even mimic it, in ways parallel to the practice among primitive peoples of sympathetic magic. If places are specifically invested with attention, they can suggest human presence even in its absence: a door elaborated suggests the importance of human entry; a window seat or a bay window or a balcony allows the imagination to people the place, and eases us into the possibility that we might people it ourselves.

All this is based on the proposition that there is a great deal of energy available to bring buildings alive by inhabiting them; that it exists in the hands (and hearts) of people who might do the inhabiting, in far greater portion than it exists in the hands of architects (though there have to be architects of some sort to give shape to buildings); that inhabiting is an act which has been so often frustrated that it requires all the assistance we can give it, but is altogether worth the trouble, since buildings which are capable of absorbing human energy in great enough amount are able to pay back the inhabitants, with interest.

Now energy, as I began by noting, is suspicious and mysterious stuff, and a view of architecture based on it, while it is, I believe, correct, is not 'rational'. My own experience of architecture, and the experience of people I know, does not accord with any of the available 'rational' theories of architecture. They all seem to be extrapolated from some other discipline, like linguistics, in ways parallel to 'rational' Renaissance extrapolations from Aristotle. The opposite of 'rational' is not 'irrational' of course, but 'sensible', and Galileo's act of dropping balls of unequal weight off the leaning tower of Pisa, noting that they fell at about the same speed was a 'sensible' act which eventually confounded the 'rational' position, which was (at least at that time) wrong. Our own instruments to parallel Galileo's dropped balls might, it seems to

dwellings should be the center of the world for their inhabitants. *That* cause is clearly much better served by exalting in differences: humankind would not be very well served if every man expected to marry a famous beauty, and suffered lasting disappointment when he did not. And surely we can exult in the differences that come our way, without gracelessly straining after Originality.

But even with freedom of speech for buildings, the act of dwelling is, for many people, not at all

9 Unabashed graphics make this store-front in New Mexico brightly expressive.

10 A more modest house in Louisiana employs classical forms in a way locally familiar.

me, even be postcards. For years, architects have been building buildings which have been accepted, for lack of better, as living places; but you wouldn't want to visit there. When people *do* visit a place they like, and feel some connection with and are inhabiting it (usually as tourists) they often send postcards to friends and relatives to announce their arrival, and their pleasure. This is a hard test to quantify, and impossible to administer, but I like it because it so compromises the position of architects who create Original High Art which they believe to be unrelated to human experience and in no need of being inhabited. It's sensible to care what people want.

A Conflict between Art and Life?

Robert Maguire

'Where we [the architectural practice of Robert Maguire and Keith Murray] have got to—and this is not a theory of architecture, still less a philosophy, but it is at least a satisfying structure which enables us to get on and do things—is a kind of reversal of traditional modern-architectural attitudes by setting aside at the beginning intentions or ambitions about creating architecture as such, and just starting off with the intention of serving life through buildings (or even through no buildings, if that would serve life better).

To serve life: that sounds a bit pretentious, but I mean it at a rather simple level, in the sense of making things which help people in their lives as individuals or as communities, rather than placing burdens upon them; and I include in that emotional burdens placed as the price of physical convenience.

This is, for us, a satisfying framework within which to work. First, because most of the projects which we have been engaged in are at the bottom end of the cost scale and the approach suits such work very well: and second because in common with an increasing number of architects and other people we feel some emotional difficulty with the idea of building at a high level of artistic pretension in the world where it is only too obvious that many people haven't either the food or shelter to keep themselves going. So we see our job as craft rather than as fine art and the aim of most of what we do as the achievement of a high standard of ordinariness.'[1]

Since saying those words at the RIBA Annual Conference in 1976, I have become increasingly aware that many architects believe that there is a fundamental choice of values which the architect has to make—between the values of art and the values of life—and that every now and again he is obliged, as an artist, to stand up for the values of art and (regrettably but excusably) to compromise the values of life. Put thus bluntly, this belief may be unrecognizable to many who show by their attitudes and actions that they hold it, and may even provoke horror or derision. For, paradoxically, one of the effects of late Modern Movement orthodoxy is the establishment of a conviction that whenever

the architect *thinks* he has created art, it necessarily follows that he has served life. Yet this conviction, which ordinary people's experience on a massive scale shows to be false, can be held by the architect side by side with the belief in the necessity of a fundamental choice of values, and also side by side with a genuine liberal humanitarianism. We are a confused profession, profoundly and exceptionally well-intentioned, yet guilty-feeling and defensive about our effects; and a large measure of our confusion is, I believe, due to the fact that few of us now wish to venture as far as saying in just what the art of architecture lies, and how the 'doing' of it relates to a concern for the lives of people. My purpose in this paper is to make an attempt at this.

The recent past

I feel it may be helpful first to look at some of the reasons for the present difficulty of discussion. They have their roots—as do so many of the problems facing architects—in architectural education. In the years immediately following World War II, the overwhelming majority of schools of architecture were teaching various versions of a peculiarly British form of Beaux Arts design. The art of architecture was seen to consist in the achievement of certain well-codified aesthetic attributes— Balance, Proportion, Rhythm, Scale and so on. The manner of this teaching ensured constant reference to the Classical tradition, but its substance did not necessarily imply that; so that while it certainly tended to engender NeoClassical styles it was also possible (though rare) to use it simply with the intention of stimulating students to a greater visual awareness. Nevertheless, as it was concerned solely with visual attributes for their own sake, it fostered a style-based view of architecture: artistry and stylistic fluency were seen to be synonymous.

The criteria which accompanied the late Modern Movement orthodoxy which steadily ousted this state of affairs after the success of the South Bank Exhibition of 1951 were very different in nature. Where the Beaux Arts approach had proposed attributes, the new order proposed whole concepts and—ultimately more damaging—precepts. Art

1a–b Stag Hill Court student housing at the University of Surrey, Guildford, 1967–70 (architects: Robert Maguire & Keith Murray). Housing 430 students, Stag Hill Court was a response to a very open initial brief from the University: to find an uninstitutional way of housing students, within severe limitations of cost and site. Clients and architects were concerned with the tendency to isolation in a disconcertingly large minority of students in technological universities. The basic unit of the scheme is a ten-person house (in 1967, when the scheme was designed, such relatively small groupings were rare). But the social effectiveness of the Court probably lies in the identity given to each house by emphasis on its individual front door—which, however, is glazed to avoid a feeling of exclusion—the internal layout of rooms to avoid any semblance of a corridor, and the very large common, kitchen-dining-sitting room shared by each group of ten. The 'garret' shape of the rooms is also important, as is the system of putting the houses together on the sloping site to give a series of tight alleyways and courtyards. There is a stronger feeling of place—'our place'—here than anywhere else in the University.

was to be achieved through *relevance to the age*. Hence, the importance of the word 'modern'. Relevance to the age—modernity—was only to be achieved through honesty and truth to that series of externalized concepts which are now so familiar to us: the nature of materials, the expression of structure, and the external expression of the uses of a building seen as patterns of activity or process.[2] The notable omission from this list is the inner life and feeling of Man; insofar as these were acknowledged they were to be *acted on* by the ensuing architecture rather than considered as needing to be served by it.

It is surprising that in our age with its increased knowledge and widespread understanding of the workings of the human mind, the strong moral imperative of these precepts should not quickly have been seen as leading almost inevitably to a massive inhibition of the architect's creativity, and also to a narrow conformity, born of the fear that if he were not seen to be modern, he would have failed

2 Houses for married students at St Stephen's House, Oxford, 1974–77 (architects: Robert Maguire & Keith Murray). This small group of nine houses is situated in the back garden of a Victorian house belonging to the college, itself a student residence. The site is in a Conservation Area and one of the problems the architects faced was to keep down the scale of actually quite high buildings.

The houses are for married student couples whose length of stay is up to three years. Most are 'mature' students and have their own furniture. The usual alternative accommodation during their stay in Oxford would be a furnished bed-sitting-room with shared cooking and bathing facilities. In the face of this situation the college decided to build, even though the accommodation could only be two-thirds of government-recommended Parker Morris space standards. There is a kitchen-dining-sitting-room, on each ground floor, and a double bedroom with shower/w.c. in the roof space over.

The success of the scheme has called some doubt on the Parker Morris standards as far as minimum 'starter homes' are concerned. The standards are so demanding that it is uneconomical to provide such homes; consequently young married couples are constrained to occupy bed-sitters or live with in-laws. Would not something less than perfection be preferable to nothing?

3a–c All Saints' Church, Crewe, 1962–66 (architects: Robert Maguire & Keith Murray). This is an Anglican parish church and hall built to replace a much-loved but outworn 'tin church' in a low-income-group area of an industrial town. It serves an established local community with a very strong sense of identity, and the acknowledged success of the building (liturgically, socially and pastorally) is probably due to the considerable rapport developed between this community and the architects over a fairly long preliminary discussion period.

Internally, the church could be said to be typical of the kind of plan the architects were evolving in the sixties to meet a new understanding in the Churches of the liturgy, but it reflects even more the feelings of a particular group of people in a particular place about what a church meant to them. Externally the same may be said: the building is important in the street scene but does not overpower the 'railway terraces' of Crewe. The vicarage is played down by losing it under the extended roof wing of the hall; a vicarage needs to be a fairly large house but its very size may alienate the vicar from the people of the parish.

as an artist. Undoubtedly, in practice, being modern has been linked to the adoption of a particular set of visual images, i.e. a style: and Modern Movement orthodoxy is as essentially a style-based view of architecture as the modern NeoClassicism it replaced.

This is reflected in the schools by the fact that, since the imperative precepts cannot be taught as leading inexorably to the style (or set of styles) they are supposed to have engendered, they are acquired by the student largely through their operation in continuous *retrospective* criticism (and therefore through development of skill in retrospective justification—a deplorable feature not only of architectural schools but also of discussion in the architectural press).

But those designing buildings—students or practising architects—ultimately do have the problem, simply stated, of what to make their buildings look like (we can perhaps now admit that it is remarkable how wide the range of possibilities actually is), and since it is generally felt that this must have something to do with art, there is a constant casting-around for the evidently artistic, resulting in a parade of—again stylistic—fashion. The most influential phenomenon here has been the adoption of an 'artistic stance' by some architects of capability, characterized by traditional forms of artist's arrogance in personal behaviour, and often brilliantly handled but mannered distortions of Modern Movement imagery in their work. This has given an impression that the archetype of architecture as art is the individual building seen as a jewel, in isolation, and above all as a manifestation of style.

It may be said that the confused field has led to a general abandonment of teaching and to a great extent of discussion of what it is about architecture that makes it art. On the other hand we are not short of statements about the application of methodology and technology to design, and although these statements are often in conflict with one another and frequently represent whole approaches which are irreconcilable, their very subject matter resonates with that apparent 'relevance to the age' which seems to reassure the modern architect (but

increasingly less so, the modern architectural student) that he is still, in some vague way, an artist. I believe that this is a situation which has arisen by default, that it is extremely destructive of values which many who have succumbed to it nevertheless hold dear, and that it is one root cause of the alarm presently shown by the public concerning much of our activity as a profession.*

There are, however, theorists who appear sincerely to believe that the assiduous application of researched knowledge and of technological know-how through a comprehensive working method could eventually produce an architecture which is totally relevant in all its aspects, and that therefore the nearer one can get to this ideal, the better. It is unclear whether the results of such a programme are seen in any sense as art, or whether that consideration has got lost. It seems likely that the category is still allowed, and since the programme itself is a development of (or perhaps an extreme distortion of) certain approaches implicit in Modern Movement orthodoxy, it also seems likely that the achievement of art is taken as automatic, since one of the total relevances would be 'relevance to the age'. While I respect the sincerity of these theorists, I believe that the approach is misguided because, in its extreme mistrust of what is traditionally known as intuition, it rejects *understanding* in favour, exclusively, of explicit *knowledge* and assumes that all relevant factors can and will be knowable. I would run the risk of saying that this is evident nonsense, but for the fact that some people seem seriously to believe it. Their hypothesis is in any case quite unproven, since no single building of distinction has yet arrived through this approach.

I propose, therefore, that despite our reluctance to clarify the matter, there is an 'art' aspect of architecture *to achieve which the architect engages in certain kinds of activity*, however little he knows it or wishes to acknowledge it. Every architect must surely admit that occasionally he fiddles with the

---

* I know from now frequent experience of misinterpretation that at this point it is necessary to state that I am not opposed to the application of methodology or technology to design, but am simply pointing out an acute imbalance which needs redressing.

4a–b New cloister and church at St Mary's Abbey, West Malling, Kent, 1962–66 (architects: Robert Maguire & Keith Murray). St Mary's is the home of a community of Anglican Benedictine nuns, who live an 'enclosed' life of prayer, committed to one place. That place was an ancient but largely ruined abbey and a later country house, but it lacked that central place of quietness-in-activity which the cloister as a form has provided for contemplatives in so many other ages and cultures.

The new cloister is a simple structure but also has a kind of complexity. In 1967 the *Architectural Review* took the architects to task for using leaded lights ('tea-shoppe glazing') in the pivoting casements, and implied that plate glass would have been more appropriate as exploiting modern technological possibilities and reflecting the spirit of the age. It is perhaps difficult for the modern architect or critic, nurtured on such essentially abstract assumptions, to allow that an old technique with its superficially 'dated' appearance may be appropriate to a very specific emotional need. The nun lives her whole life with this place; she does not need the immediate revelation afforded by plate glass. The complexity of the cloister structure and glazing is knowable rather than mysterious, yet responds constantly to different lights and seasons.

5a–b St Paul's with St Luke's Primary School, Bow Common, London 1970–71 (architects: Robert Maguire & Keith Murray). This is a school for children from 4 to 11 years in one of London's poorest districts.

Educational allowances remain fixed for long periods, and as the cost of building rises, the size of the schools grows smaller. Yet, for the success of progressive methods of teaching, space is needed more than anything else. By 1970 the size of schools had become so small that teaching (or more to the point, learning) was suffering greatly.

The school at Bow Common provided 30% more teaching space for the same money, by using an industrial or agricultural shed as the basic structure. The designers set out to transform this structure—by adjusting its scale to that of children, by treating such things as air ducts as objects of fun, by colour, and care generally for children's needs. The result is a children's studio-workshop; a tool for the teachers and a 'place of our own' for the children.

The children complete the transformation themselves. Their own creativity is stimulated by the possibilities of doing more to this building, which being already quite unlike anything else within their experience, gives a freedom to explore.

position or proportion of a window, for example, in order to achieve some object about which he may or may not feel he is clear, but which he knows is dependent on his sensibility.

The nature of architecture as art

Here of course I have to stand up and declare myself: how I see art. I am going to do so in the words of Susanne Langer, with whose philosophy of art I find I can go almost all the way:

'At this point I will make bold to offer a definition of art, which serves to distinguish a work of art from anything else in the world, and at the same time to show why, and how, a utilitarian object may be *also* a work of art; and how a work of so-called pure art may fail of its purpose and be simply bad, just as a shoe that cannot be worn is simply bad by failing of its purpose. . . . Here is the tentative definition. . . . Art is the creation of forms symbolic of human feeling.

The word "creation" is introduced here with full awareness of its problematical character. There is a definite reason to say a craftsman *produces* goods, but *creates* a thing of beauty. . . . An artifact as such is merely a combination of material parts, or a modification of a natural object to suit human purposes. It is not a creation, but an arrangement of given factors. A work of art, on the other hand, is more than an "arrangement" of given things—even qualitative things. Something emerges from the arrangement . . . which was not there before, and this, rather than the arranged material, is the symbol of sentience.'[3]

One point I wish to make about this view of art is that it is expressed not as an imperative ('art should be . . .') but—by implication at least—as a perception: *when forms symbolic of human feeling are created, then we have something which we recognize as art.* So for a start it entirely by-passes the question of style, leaving the field open, and relating the whole matter firmly to people. This is not to say that style is unimportant. On the contrary, the emergence of style can be seen as an indication of

maturity or of integrity in creation; a symptom rather than a prime objective.

Langer develops her definition further in relation specifically to architecture:

'As *scene* is the basic abstraction of pictorial art, and *kinetic volume* of sculpture, that of architecture is *an ethnic domain*. Actually, of course, a domain is not a "thing" among other "things"; it is the sphere of influence of a function, or functions; it may have physical effects on some geographical locality or it may not. Nomadic cultures, or cultural phenomena like the seafaring life, do not inscribe themselves on any fixed place on earth. Yet a ship, constantly changing its location, is none the less a self-contained place, and so is a Gypsy camp, an Indian camp, or a circus camp, however often it shifts its geodetic bearings. Literally, we say a camp is *in* a place; culturally it is a place. A Gypsy camp is a different place from an Indian camp, though it may be geographically where the Indian camp used to be.

A place, in this non-geographical sense, is a created thing, an ethnic domain made visible, tangible, sensible . . . architecture articulates the "ethnic domain", or virtual "place", by treatment of an actual place.'

This concept of 'ethnic domain' bears a remarkable resemblance (though approached from a different direction) to Norberg-Schulz's 'existential space'—the space Man creates to respond to his own being, in order more fully to realize his existence, since 'mere' existence is not possible for him. Langer goes on to relate this to Man in his cultural context:

'A culture is made up, factually, of the activities of human being; it is a system of interlocking and intersecting actions, a continuous functional pattern. As such it is, of course, intangible and invisible. It has physical ingredients—artifacts; also physical symptoms—the ethnic effects that are stamped on the human face, known as its "expression", and the influence of the social condition on the development, posture, and movement of the human body. But all such items are fragments that "mean" the total pattern of life only to those who are acquainted with and may be reminded of it. They are the ingredients in a culture, not its image.

The architect creates its image: a physically present human environment that expresses the characteristic rhythmic functional patterns which constitute a culture. Such patterns are the alternations of sleep and waking, venture and safety, emotion and calm, austerity and abandon; the tempo, and the smoothness or abruptness of life; the simple forms of childhood and the complexities of full moral stature, the sacramental and the capricious moods that mark a social order, and that are repeated, though with characteristic selection, by every personal life springing from that order.'

This envisages a very close affinity—a kind of mutual response—between built form and the life it serves. If we think of it as a programme for ourselves it is indeed daunting; but then we have become far too used to our moral imperatives: 'architecture should be. . .' In fact of course we are quite accustomed to recognizing this affinity in the architecture of the past and in that of cultures other than our own. It is on these grounds that we now admit a Cumbrian hill farm or a Peruvian squatter settlement into our category 'architecture' as readily as Wells Cathedral or the Palazzo Rucellai. And while we might wish to adjust Langer's wording when she says that it is the *architect* who creates this image, it may be more useful to take 'architect' to mean anyone who is creating in her sense.*

Such a view of architecture as an art presents no fundamental problem of a choice between the values of art and those of life. However, it presents other problems for the aspiring artist. How is one to know when one has produced art? What does one do to achieve it? The answers are, of course, the traditional ones: you cannot be sure, there is no security here.† There never was, and never will be, a formula for guaranteeing artistic results. What perhaps one can say is that artistic merit, and even

more so that maturity we recognize as style, is unlikely to be achieved by a preoccupation with artistic pretension or even artistic endeavour as such. The mainspring, for the architect, is evidently the life—in all its breadth and depth—of the people for whom he is building; and the way he serves that life (the processes he is involved in) will depend on the depth of his knowledge and understanding of it. Out of this, an architecture may arise—an architecture recognizable as art.

We can also pursue further these matters of knowledge, understanding and process, to try to see where, in the doing of the curious task of designing, the sensibilities and creative faculties of the architect come into play, and what their nature is. What follows is such an attempt. I am aware that it does not go very far, but it is a start; I believe that it may be a useful start on a release from the burdens of the myth that designing is an intellectual process in which data is manipulated until it evolves into a design scheme.[4]

First, I put forward the proposition that there are three 'inputs' into the design process: the *problem as given, available data* concerning it, and the *person of the designer*.

The *problem as given* consists of the people and life to be served on the one hand, and physical, economic and political facts on the other—for instance, a site, a climate, a cost limit, town-planning constraints. These things will be partly bound up in a 'brief', partly observable, and partly approachable only through living experience.

Available data consists of a possibly formidable mass of information relevant to the problem, but

* This in turn raises the very important question of the ambivalent position of the 'proper' architect as an agent in the matter: does he stand in the way of this affinity being achieved, or is he now an essential interpreter? Perhaps usually both; and one of the main tasks of an architectural education is to lessen the one and facilitate the other. The conflict will, however, always remain.

† It may well be that the attractiveness of determinist theories of architecture lies in the security they give, the hope perhaps that if one could get to the point where all the required operations were so researched and defined that they could be 'done' correctly, one could be sure of being beyond criticism.

130

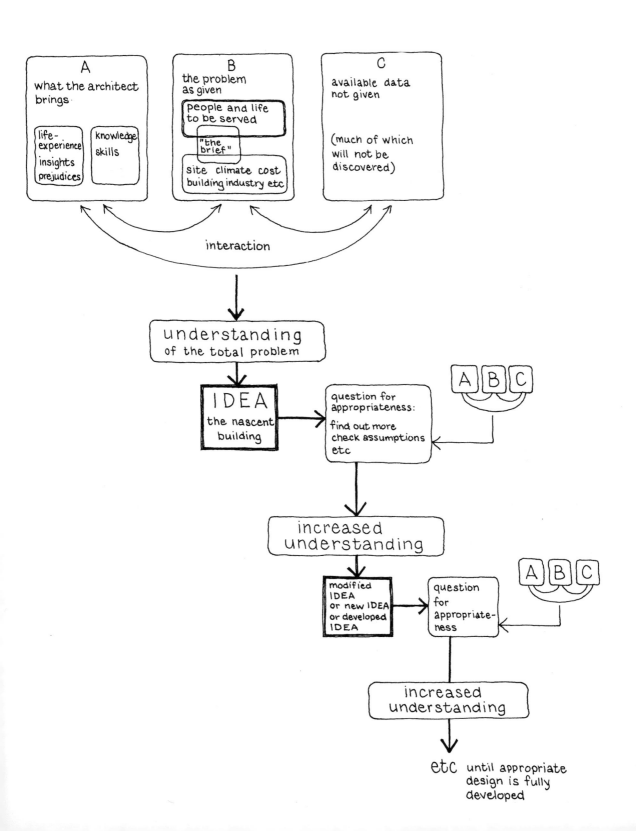

A

what the architect brings

life-experience insights prejudices

knowledge skills

B

the problem as given

people and life to be served

"the brief"

site climate cost building industry etc

C

available data not given

(much of which will not be discovered)

interaction

understanding of the total problem

IDEA the nascent building

question for appropriateness: find out more check assumptions etc

A B C

increased understanding

modified IDEA or new IDEA or developed IDEA

question for appropriateness

A B C

increased understanding

etc until appropriate design is fully developed

which would have to be hunted down and then sifted in order to become useful. Some data, for example information on the conditions under which grants are awarded for up-grading homes, or the latest government recommendations on avoiding condensation, may easily be tracked down. Other important data may escape one for ever. We live in an imperfect world.

The person of the designer is the crucial factor, because it is his faculties which work on everything else, and effect their transformation into a design. On the one hand, he comes with the usually acknowledged knowledge and skills, but he also comes with his own life experience, his developed sensibility, and his prejudices.

What I believe happens in the designing process is shown here in the diagram, which is not meant to be chronologically exact like a flow-chart.

Nor is it a methodology, but simply an interpretation of what happens in any case, whether acknowledged or not. The important points about it are, first, that an *idea* only comes through an *understanding* of the total situation, and not directly from knowledge by any process of manipulation; second, that understanding *increases* through the rejection of inappropriate ideas, which is why the diagram is a very static representation of an incredibly dynamic set of happenings, in which for example a major understanding may arrive late and cause a complete re-assessment of what has been 'established' so far; and third, the number of 'feedback' operations is usually vast, continuing until all details have been worked out.*

Some points at which the creative insights and sensibilities of the architect can come into play are:

a The architect brings into the situation his own fund of life experience with its insights which are peculiar to him as an individual, and some of

these become factors relevant to the problem automatically. On the negative side, by the same token a number of wrong assumptions will inevitably be incorporated.

b The architect needs to get close to the people, place and life to be served; to get a feeling for as well as a knowledge of these, by some means.

c All incoming information, including researched data which the architect must somehow 'decide' to seek, is questioned for reliability, adequacy, and implications. Lateral thinking sequences are often applied to develop a wide view and/or a view in depth, and can be at least as important as the deductive manipulation which is also applied.

d The factors relevant to the problem include some which are only unconsciously recognized ('felt').

e The culmination of the preparatory activity is the gaining by the architect of an *understanding* of the nature of the total problem. In achieving this, he has made probably thousands of mental connections involving his insights and sensibilities, as well as a great deal of deductive processing. And it is only by means of this understanding that the vast array of varied, variable, and often disparate data can be 'made sense of'. This understanding leads to the conceiving of an idea—the tentative solution simultaneously to meet all the factors, the nascent building.

f This understanding also involves the assigning of different values to the various factors, and especially to those which are in some conflict with each other. Some of this can be done by reference to more or less objective criteria, but much will have to depend on feeling.

g In questioning the appropriateness of his idea the architect is again relying to quite an extent on insight.

h In the later stages of development (detail) he is referring complete sub-sections of the problem to miniature versions of the same procedure.

---

* For this reason the fairly recent attempt in Britain to divide drawings into design-stage drawings and production drawings is a gross distortion of the process. 'Working drawings' were always, and so far as I know still are, the scene of detailed designing. This is untidy, and resists rational management, but is inevitable and necessary for good design.

The architect's creative faculties

Evidently a number of rather different creative faculties are needed or desirable for all this. A few which I have been able to identify are:

a An openness to life experience.
b An affinity for people over a wide range of social conditions, and a feeling for the creative possibilities inherent in ordinary human situations.
c Some ability to recognize one's own feelings and, far from rejecting them, to make them as conscious as possible.
d A capacity for lateral thinking.
e A heightened perception, linked with a spirit of enquiry about things seen (perhaps it always is).
f The facility of recall and of making connections.
g An appreciation of the way of working of visual images—'what things do'.
h An appreciation of the way in which images and feeling, and images and cultures, have related historically.
i The ability to visualize (see in the mind's eye) in three dimensions.
j A feeling for structure (both in the engineer's sense and in the conceptual sense) in forms.
k The central and indispensable power to produce an idea from an understanding of data.
   And there must be many more.

These facilities are of several different kinds; perhaps in the end, many different kinds. Some are commonplace, but no less creative for that, and some are very special to the creative artist. Some are essentially psychological states, and may vary in any one person from one time to another. Considering them, however, it seems to me that two things become quite clear. No person, however well-disposed and considerate of humanity, is likely to produce an architecture without possessing such faculties in fair measure (although many may, and

do, produce architecture because they do have them, yet are not recognizably 'architects'). And secondly, no 'architect' who does not exercise these faculties in the service of life is really practising architecture at all, although he may be practising something else, such as sculptural self-expression, quite successfully.

If one accepts these creative faculties, and others like them, as the life-blood of the architect, then the apparent conflict between art and life disappears. The architect is seen as a very particular kind of person: a person who can articulate built form so that it bears the imprint of human life and feeling.

Notes to the Text

[1] Robert Maguire, 'Something out of the Ordinary', in *Architecture: Opportunities, Achievements,* RIBA Publications London, 1977; also published under the title 'The Value of Tradition' in *The Architects' Journal*, London, 18 August 1976.
[2] David Watkin has done a thorough debunking of these concepts in his book *Morality and Architecture* (Clarendon Press, Oxford, 1977) but in doing so has thrown out the baby with the bathwater, leaving us with little else than 'taste'. It is, for example, one thing to decry the assertion that 'if it works, it will be beautiful' but quite another to deny or ignore the fact that some things (e.g. hand-tools and certain boats) *are* beautiful largely *because* they 'work' superbly. We have to observe them and think hard about why this should be so.
[3] Susanne K. Langer, *Feeling and Form* (Routledge and Kegan Paul, London, 1953).
[4] A sociologist, Robert Nisbet, makes the distinction very clearly in his book *Sociology as an Art Form* (Heinemann, London, 1976): 'The great scientists have long been aware of the basic unity of the creative act as found in the arts and in the sciences. A large and growing literature attests to the awareness. Only in the social sciences, and particularly, I regret to say, in sociology, the field in which the largest number of textbooks on 'methodology' exists, has awareness of the real nature of discovery tended to lag. Countless works in the social sciences reveal the inability of their authors to bear in mind the crucial difference between what may properly be called the *logic of discovery* and the *logic of demonstration*. The second is properly subject to rules and prescriptions; the first isn't. Of all sins against the Muse, however, the greatest is the assertion, or strong implication, in textbooks on methodology and theory construction that the first (and utterly vital) logic can somehow be summoned by obeying the rules of the second. Only intellectual drought and barrenness can result from that misconception.'

1 *Left:* Contrasts in Landskrona, Sweden. On the left is a result of the massive construction programme mounted in Sweden during the 1960s, with its unimaginative use of prefabricated and industrialized building systems. On the right is the Esperanza estate by Erskine, Rosenvold and Linnett (1968–1970) where pre-fabricated and standardized elements have also been used, but on a small scale, stressing variety and irregularities.

2 *Below:* A view of the Esperanza estate. A cycle-path and footpath lead through the area in an interesting twisting manner, with natural goals at each end and activities dotted along the route. There are also inviting 'gossip benches' and other places where unpretentious contact can be made.

3 *Opposite:* A lane leading to house entrances in Esperanza. Priority is given to public and semi-public space in preference to private gardens in an attempt to increase the contact possibilities. The garden wall has a sliding shutter by which individual preference for privacy or contact can be regulated.

Housing and Human Needs: the work of Ralph Erskine (with original sketches by Ralph Erskine)

Mats Egelius

There is a good deal of human nature in Man, and by definition always will be. However, Man often has to question the humane nature of his living environment. Some critics attribute the failures of most mass-housing to architects' ignorance of users' needs; for example, the need for contact, privacy and identification with one's home. To rectify these shortcomings, several architects, such as Christoffer Alexander, Amos Rappoport and Oscar Newman, have been exploring a social dimension of architecture. This search has been particularly vigorous not only in the U.S.A. but also in Scandinavia, where the approach has been promulgated through books by Sven Hesselgren, Carl-Axel Acking and Ingrid Gehl, as well as in the housing projects of Ralph Erskine.

After a particularly energetic social concern during the late sixties, we now see a marked retreat of architecture to formal preoccupations and 'good design'. Any suggestions that the right physical framework can create a better society, or that a humane design can be found only after a social analysis, run the risk of being labelled naive. The belief that architecture shapes human activities is unproven, but still a positive force in as much as an architect must have faith in the importance of what he is doing. In any case, everyone must at least acknowledge that the physical environment facilitates various activities even if it does not actually generate them.

It is difficult to predict social behaviour, and most social scientists refrain from committing themselves. There is also a general scepticism about the obsession with 'objective' research, and in the case

of housing there are few chances to manipulate people's environment for research purposes, as all changes must be seriously intended as improvements. Instead of being involved in petty statistical arguments, research into the living environment has to concentrate on a broad understanding of the problems and the basic needs of the users.

Contact

The desired level of stimulation from the physical and social environment varies among individuals, but stimulation, which embraces human contact, is always necessary to some degree for anyone to function normally in society. Today there is an increasing need to design for contact as family sizes dwindle. More and more people live alone, the proportion of old people increases, and more people do monotonous jobs with little collaboration. There are also the effects of an extreme differentiation of activities, with large-scale zones, leading to internally homogeneous areas for living, working, shopping, learning and entertainment, with people confined to only one activity at a time. Such a planning philosophy is characterized by few contact points, an inhumane scale, social segregation and a distorted age structure. The spatial separation also creates a demand for a vast traffic machinery, to bind together the elements previously separated.

When planning to reverse the trend, and increase contacts, one first has to take into account the physical limitation of our senses. Facial expressions, for example, are only meaningful within a distance of twenty metres. This indicates that a small scale will facilitate social contacts, which can only develop, moreover, when a sufficiently small number of people see each other often enough. This points to a need for clusters of houses, preferably of a fairly small number, say between 6 and 25, centred around some contact-creating activity, such as a playing field, launderette or communal building. Activities inside the dwellings, including living rooms and kitchens, could also be laid open to the passer-by, to draw these sections into the public zone. That the planners of most modern housing ignore social experiences in favour of physical gains is shown by the orientation towards the sun, instead of towards a square or a street. This denies the inhabitants the possibility of experiencing other people, which may take the form of a sort of passive contact in which a person receives information without reacting to it.

Instead of being dispersed, the activities in a housing project should be spatially concentrated to increase the likelihood of social interaction, which will encourage the growth of new activities. Naturally, other parts of the estate will be quieter, making it possible to choose an area to live in which has a suitable level of stimulation. This variation could be emphasized in the details of the design, with paved areas, benches and other man-made urban characteristics in the active part, while the quieter part could be simpler, its character derived from nature.

Privacy

As well as facilitating contact, housing should allow the individual to reduce and control stimuli at a level individually preferred, thus minimizing conflict and stress. To reduce the overload in information flow a filter* is needed to screen out some pieces of information, recode some into larger units, and decrease the impact of others. The overload is also decreased by physical defences such as increased distances, barriers, fences or plants.

When there is a choice, people who share the same manners, values and status cluster together in coherent sub groups to reduce the overload. This suggests need to modify the policy that advocates a total integration of different cultural groups. Instead, individuals should be encouraged to choose an environment that is familiar. However, this does not mean that the society should tolerate big differences in standards or services in different areas, or that racial minorities should be segregated into too large enclaves of the community.

The problems of designing for an adequate level of privacy and anonymity are aggravated by the considerable variation in individuals' needs, depending on age, health, social status, personality,

* See the piece by Rikard Küller, pp. 87–100.

136

4 Brittgarden in Tibro, Sweden, by Erskine, Rosenvold and Scheiwiller (1959–62). The estate is planned as a small community within a community. The multi-storey perimeter buildings to the north define the neighbourhood, and there are several low-rise clusters in so-called 'gossip groups' laid out so that the scale gradually diminishes as you move into the area. The 'identifying image' is further developed by an aesthetic of informality, signifying individualism, and a rich use of colour—the front doors are in many different colours, while the chimneys have red and green woodwork with a black trim.

etc. One way to answer the different needs is to vary the proximity of dwellings to major footpaths and other activity spots. However, the only safe solution is to allow the individual to erect his own barriers, either in a physical or symbolic sense.

The individual dwelling lay-out must also ensure privacy, peace and personal integrity, which are especially important in a time with more leisure, more noisy equipment and lightweight construction techniques. Ideally, every individual should have his or her own well-insulated room, separated from the living areas by a buffer zone. The zoning must also ensure some separation between the parents' and children's bedrooms and give protection for those studying. The system of buffer zones should be extended to noisy activities in the area, especially playgrounds and busy roads.

Identity

The need to re-establish the feeling of identity in an urban situation has arisen because of the alienation apparent in most modern housing, where the inhabitants lack the opportunity to project themselves into the physical and social environment. Many different theories have been put forward on how to recreate this identity, the most obvious being the introduction of neighbourhood units. The ideal neighbourhood has its own shops, nursery school, places of work and sports facilities. It should not be too large, perhaps a maximum of 500 residents, and should preferably be broken down into several smaller clusters, each of the latter having its own outdoor space, launderette, parking and playing facilities. When creating neighbourhoods, the pattern of social organization and management must be carefully considered. An area's identity can also be emphasized by physical design, use of colours or built-in meaning. These characteristics, however, are often impossible to lay down on paper. Instead, a flexible framework should be created with some spaces left undesigned to be moulded by the user at a later date.

5 Eaglestone, Milton Keynes, England, by Ralph Erskine with M. Linnett and K. Tham (1973–76). To keep the cost down, a set of standardized elements has been used, which also ensures that the emphasis on variety and the individuality of each dwelling does not prevent the estate from having a unified character. Eaglestone is planned in a complex manner, both in its details and in the treatment of space, with obvious resemblances to the English-style village. The physical characteristics, though not necessarily, the idealized social community, that have traditionally developed over the years are in the instant village created by careful design.

Personalization

Personalization is creating identity at a personal level, accommodating the inhabitant's own spontaneous usage in an open-ended environment. It is closely linked with territoriality, as it is an important way to establish a domain. As many Western societies have abolished the lawful right to physical defence of the home, this is mainly done with rules and symbols. The rules are obeyed when each individual dwelling is clearly expressed, perhaps by conversions, colour, decorations, fences, walls and landscaping. If the right to personalization were established, it would encourage a different character for different areas, thereby aiding orientation. Such an improvement would be especially important in the often uniform new housing schemes, for it would allow something of the desirable complexity and richness of unplanned cities to be re-captured.

Aesthetics

The inhabitants wish to adjust the environment to their own tastes, so the architect's aspiration to create estates with a strong aesthetic identity is a constant reason for conflict. However, housing must be recognized to be too complicated and dynamic to be conceived only as aesthetically beautiful in the art sense—nor can it be a sculptural object that people have to stand back from or move around to admire. A majority of new housing estates are biased in favour of the aesthetic considerations. The design is approached in a very form-orientated way, with careful proportions of masses, etc., but the scale is so distorted that the order and harmony can only be appreciated in model perspective.

Even though the artistic elements of order and harmony should perhaps not be ignored, architects must base their aesthetic on human needs. They have to see housing as a living organism, capable of coping with continuous change and assimilating innovations. Signs of human activities should be encouraged; washing or mats hung out for airing must be anticipated and should add to the design, not destroy it.

A convincing humane aesthetic, full of human detail, has been developed by the architect Ralph Erskine, British-trained but based in Sweden since the late thirties. His housing project Eaglestone, in Milton Keynes, England, exploits irregularities and variations, which might be an important factor in encouraging the users to be more active and create their own personalized environment. As in an old village, there are many very similar houses, but small variations and additions ensure a lively variety. What traditionally has developed over time is in this instant village created by careful design. The position of doors and windows varies to suit each particular situation. The external wall-cladding shows variation in colour on both wood and bricks. The entrance courts have different treatment of porches, dustbins, enclosures, gates, fences, etc., and there is an occasional bay window or balcony. Consequently, there are large areas which tenants can paint and many forms that can be modified; and the architect's *ad hoc* use of non-permanent material on a durable main structure will necessitate a continuous change.

The exciting choice of decorative elements clearly avoids the normal limitation in modern architecture of using as few materials as possible. Instead, Erskine borrows freely from various sources in a creative manner, with many old forms and symbols revitalized to give life to the scheme. The spatial arrangement is also made highly complex, providing variety and surprise even for the local inhabitant. For the visitor the surprise is certain, for Eaglestone is so rich in meaning, like a map, that you can study it for hours without getting bored. When looking at the work of Ralph Erskine, it is important to note the social meaning of his aesthetic, the way in which his style stands for individuality, vitality, and active participation. It would obviously not be useful for another architect to copy merely the forms. But what would be worth applying more widely is the approach: to see housing in social terms, to see it with the residents' eyes, and to identify with the users.

The first thing Ralph Erskine did when he undertook to design the redevelopment of Byker, Newcastle, in the north of England, was to identify the

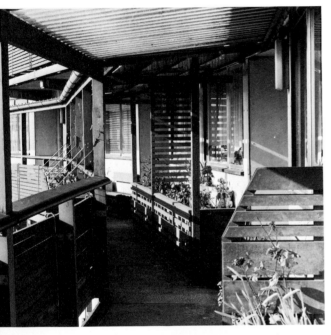

6 *Left:* Byker, Newcastle-upon-Tyne, England, by Ralph Erskine, V. Gracie, R. Tillotson, B. Ahlqvist and others (1970–81). The clear majority (80%) of the inhabitants are re-housed in high-density low-rise units, surrounded by an interminably long and rolling housing block, designed to give protection from traffic noise and to create an identity for the area.

7 *Below left:* The access-decks on the Byker Wall are kept as busy as the old streets because the entrances are close together, with the flats on two levels, going alternately up and down. The decks are narrow and frequently interrupted by conservatory-type semi-public spaces, where one can sit and admire the spectacular view and pass the time of day with the neighbours.

8 *Below:* A walkway in Byker. There are few signs of vandalism in the new areas, which might be due to the semi-private and easily supervized character of the lanes between the buildings. Another reason may be that the children, involved in their environment doing, for example, tree-planting themselves.

9 *Opposite:* Ralph Erskine's sketch of the site-office in Byker. His sketching technique gives a clear indication of the importance given to the future inhabitants, for the drawing is full of the different activities that the design makes possible—plus the ever-present trademark of a balloon optimistically rising towards the sky.

social problems involved. His eldest daughter Jane moved to the area and he made several visits in order to establish the community's relationship to itself and to the outside world. The analysis included a thorough historical study to understand the cultural and social spirit, and the use of a number of different unpretentious questionnaires.

Thereafter, the basis for collaboration with the authorities was established and Erskine's priorities concerning the client stated: first priority was to the users in Byker, second to the users from outside, and third, the client providing the money. Other initial objectives were stated in a memorandum of November 1968:

At the lowest possible cost for the residents, and in intimate contact and collaboration with them particularly, and with relevant authorities generally, to prepare a project for planning and building a complete and integrated environment for living in its widest possible sense. This would involve us in endeavouring to create positive conditions for dwelling, shopping, recreation, studying and—as far as possible—working in near contact with the home. It would involve us in considering the wishes of the people of all ages and many tastes.

We would endeavour to maintain as far as possible, valued traditions and characteristics of the neighbourhood itself and its relationships with the surrounding areas and the centre of Newcastle.

The main concern will be with those who are already resident in Byker, and the need to re-house them without breaking family ties and other valued associations or patterns of life.

We would endeavour to exploit the physical character of the site, more especially the slope towards the south, its views and sunny aspect.

Immediately after the design started, a small site office was set up in an abandoned funeral parlour, and user consultation was started. An open-door policy was adopted. Soon the residents of Byker found the way to *their* architects' inviting office,

10 The Pagens bakery in Malmo, Sweden, by Ralph Erskine, with A. Rosenvold, V. Gracie, M. Linnett and A. Nilsson (1968–69). This new building for a large bakery has three basic elements—on the ground floor, loading bays and stores serving the factory; a main office 10 metres above; and an executive suite and terraces on the roof.

11 *Near left:* The continuous open-plan office (17 × 70 metres) is reached by lift directly from the pavement. The room and furniture were designed together. The room is open (to give ease of communication) while the furniture with its integrated services gives a semi-protected personal territory. A raised back to the table partially protects and screens a sitting person without disturbing the open room, limits local sound disturbance and controls the visual effect of any untidy papers and personal paraphernalia.

which also provided a lost-and-found service, drawing classes for the children and an informal community centre. Many meetings were held in this corner-shop office, in preference to the inaccessible Town Hall, and Erskine's partner on the job, Vernon Gracie, moved into the small flat above.

Clearly, the intent of moving into old Byker was to make it possible to work in collaboration with the users of the new Byker. The location of the office was important, for the architects realized that, while they were to plan the physical framework, it was the inhabitants who would create a community. In the early stages, the user-consultation was focused on a pilot scheme on a previously-cleared site, where forty-six houses were built after extensive contact with the future residents. From the experience gained during the design many new discoveries were made: for example, the architects had not previously known about the strong local patriotism in Byker and the status hierarchy within the community. Contrary to earlier expectations, the inhabitants did not want their existing structure of houses and streets merely modernized: instead, they wanted a drastically new Byker. Nevertheless, they wished to retain many features of the old Byker, such as the corner-shops, pubs, laundries, and to save Shipley Street Baths (scheduled for demolition) and other places for meeting one another 'for a good laugh', and other activities. There was a strong body of opinion in favour of reducing the

number of flats proposed by the authorities, and heated debates took place about the traffic arrangements, amount of planting, play equipment, etc. First and foremost, the residents wanted rapid action instead of the endless promises and discussions that had been going on since the fifties. Each one wanted a dwelling (preferably a single-family house) to live in as soon as possible, and had a particular preference about its location and its planning. They all wanted to have their old neighbours around them. There was also a lot to learn from the criticisms after the completion of the pilot scheme, the major design changes it initiated was to abandon the rather drab back lane concept and the use of smooth, dark brick work (which was quickly covered with graffiti).

Now that time has passed and the new Byker is a reality, it is clear that, while the creation of an attractive physical environment has been an important aim, the educational role of the consultation has been equally important. Consultation with the residents served to clarify the theories behind planning, to question a passive life-style, and to force the participants to analyze and justify their opinions. However, before the users were able to make demands, it was important that they should be educated in all the possibilities—for insufficient knowledge of the alternatives is a serious limitation in any user-consultation dialogue. In addition, the pilot scheme was a practical teaching-tool in the education of the residents about the use of their new dwellings. This was especially important in Byker where many were unfamiliar with modern equipment and an increased living-standard. Every one of the ten thousand people that will finally be rehoused is invited to meet the architects at least once. At these meetings, some months before the move is due, facts about the new dwellings are explained, such as location, layout, cupboard spaces, size of windows etc., it is made clear that anyone has the right to demand alternative offers. These informal gatherings are important in easing the anxiety of many people who are about to move into a more or less unfamiliar environment—for the style of the new

architecture is very different from the old local red-brick back-to-backs.

Apart from the educational aspect, the main aim of any user-participation must be to find out if the inhabitants' needs are met in the suggested environment and, if not, to work out alternatives. Architects will undoubtedly design better housing under the influence of the users, and gain invaluable experience for future projects.

Building work is still going on in Byker, so it is too early to make a claim for the ultimate success of the area. However, this has not prevented a widespread coverage of the project in the media, with a careful analysis of the resettlement of an existing

community, the mixture of old and new, the village scale, the *ad hod* aesthetic and the user-participation.

After the success at Byker, Ralph Erskine has been personifying a way for architects to become useful. He has shown that there is another role for architects than to design prestigious monuments—that is, to provide accommodation for ordinary people after collaborating with them—and that the architect should serve not only one individual, or even a group of individuals, but the community as a whole.

An accessible approach is necessary to facilitate user-participation and there is no doubt that Erskine is a very accessible person. He is hospitable to everyone visiting both his office and his home, and finds it easy to relate to all sorts of people. In the office a family atmosphere is encouraged, further amplified by the close proximity that there has always been between his home and office. Few signs of hierarchy are found in the office, whose running is based on cooperation and shared responsibility, with flexible working hours, continuous discussions and an open flow of information. The work is executed through self-organized units, with shared responsibility, at least in theory, for the economy and other administrative functions. This office organization is in line with Erskine's political stand point, as it stresses the need to break down bureaucracy, and illustrates his general belief in equality. But Erskine also shares with most modern architects a reluctance to be involved in the narrower aspects of party politics or to be labelled on the political scale. He says that 'left, of course, is better than right' and is pleased that his architecture, especially outside Sweden, has often been linked to the progress of social democracy. However, the socialist view is also challenged by liberalism, or the need for individual freedom, which can be seen as an influence from his Quaker education. The fusion of these two different philosophies might appear as a contradiction, but they also bring together complementary qualities. Ultimately, the classless society, in which everyone is given an equal chance, is protected by political freedom; and conversely

individual freedom is protected by the notion that everyone has the same opportunities. This ideal collective brotherhood should be created in collaboration with nature: everyone should live in the same type of environment, using renewable resources.

The main theme through Erskine's housing philosophy is the stress on Man, and his right for a decent social and physical environment. This is at a time when modern housing has been hampered by a slavish fulfilment of a mass-produced building program and a rational technology necessitating a separation between man and nature, with the latter treated as alien. In contrast, Erskine's housing is always related to nature and the need for a balanced ecology. He is not satisfied if only a technically perfect solution is reached. Neither does he resign when confronted with the demand for standardization. Instead of monotony, the technology he has employed produces an infinite variety from a system of repetitive parts, in a style that shows an individual will to create architecture for people.

That Erskine's humane housing philosophy is also applied to the design of other building types is clearly shown in the design sketches (illustrated at the end of this essay) for an open office lay-out planned around human activities such as creative work, intimate talk, rest, meditation, intensive team work, community experiences, etc. This office, for a large bakery, Pågens, in Malmö, Sweden, has four main functions: control of orders and deliveries to and from the bakery; marketing of produce; exploration of new markets; and research and development of new products. It is a continuous open space for 45 people, glazed all around, with free-standing blocks containing lifts, stairs, toilets and restrooms. The suspended ceiling is at a height of only 2.3 metres, which makes for an intimate scale, and is relieved by sweep-up to the top of the floor-to-ceiling windows. The open room owes a certain intimacy, as well as the provision of differently sized territories, to the placing of service cores and specially designed furniture units.

In this open-plan office there is a surprisingly homely atmosphere. Generally, in the design of

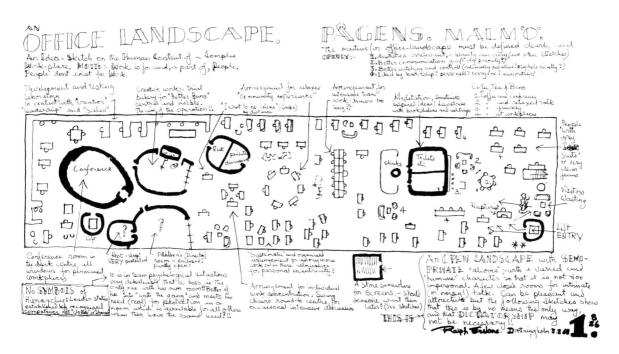

12a–f Ralph Erskine's design sketches for an open-plan office in Pagens. The original comments, in an uninhibited Anglo-Swedish form, have been revised by Erskine for this publication, to constitute a concrete contribution in the debate for a more humane working environment, showing how individual and general human needs can be satisfied in a large organization.

offices, there is much to be learnt by studying homes, which have traditionally been moulded by users' needs to a much greater extent than commercial or industrial buildings, where the organization, economy, and often a particular process, govern the form. Many successful conversions of dwellings to offices prove the point, and it is no coincidence that the Architectural Association's premises in Georgian houses at Bedford Square, London, function better than the vast majority of purpose-built schools of architecture.

The belief that humans are social, active and creative creatures must be the basis for any design, whether for offices, hospitals, industrial blocks, or buildings for educational purposes. The list of basic

human needs above should be used as a check-list in the design not only of housing, but of other building types as well.

One type of environment which has constantly been neglected from this point of view is our vast industrial estates, which fulfil few of the basic human needs. Although there is a general agreement to try and decrease both accident figures and the amount of hard, uncomfortable work, as well as to create a better indoor climate (through improved lighting and heating, cleaner air, etc.) there is a negative development in the less physical aspects of industrial life—more stress, monotonous jobs, stricter supervision and limited responsibility. If we look at just one of the basic needs previously discussed, contact, we see that there is a lot of unnecessary isolation in industry because of noise, lay-out (the machines in long rows, arranged so that the operators are kept apart from each other), form of payment (piece-work), stress created by the continuous production line, and so on. To improve conditions we should plan for a low noise-level,

IT "CHANGES"

Equally attractive visually!
More satisfaction? No friction?

PÅGENS. MALMÖ.

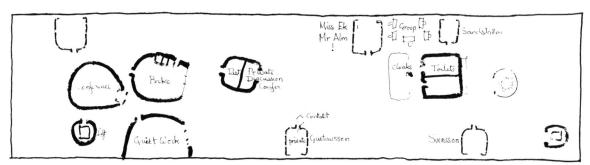

* Open office but a few have other "needs" which are respected
* Im 80m high screens with a door. Acoustic and visual separation
  for personal experience of integrity, concentration etc. Private terrain.
  Please Knock! Come In!!
* Can happen anywhere in the plan aesthetically. (NB function aspects!)

Disadvantages:- less spontaneous and rapid communication
Advantages:- Free choice, personal satisfaction, varying
space experiences, varying "community", "semi-privacy", "privacy"

Ralph Erskine D'holm 3.2.68 **2.** S26

IT SPREADS

PÅGENS. MALMÖ.

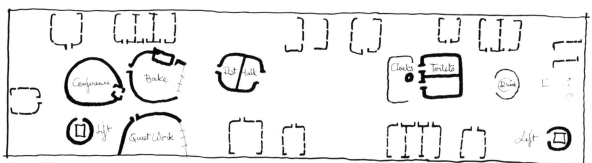

God Bless variation in people and rooms 000

Ralph Erskine D'holm 3.2.68 **3.** S26

146

MANY POSSIBILITIES   PÅGENS. MALMÖ

WHY EITHER Office Landscape OR Small rooms office?

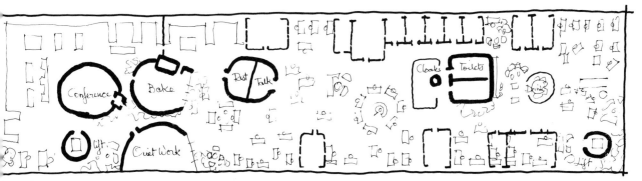

Also this goes extremely well as an interior. I could for example
make it just as nice as 1. 2. or 3.   Only different!
Why "lead" so much?
Up for individuals in a freer collective and perhaps the common task would go even better?
                Optimistic? Realistic?

Ralph Erskine D'holm 3.2.68   **4.** S26

IT HAS
BECOME A SMALLROOM OFFICE!

BUT CAN CHANGE BACK ANY TIME AS FUNCTION
FASHION OR EXPERIENCE INDICATES!
AN ARCHITECT COULD ALWAYS HELP.

PÅGENS. MALMÖ

Perhaps an office that can change, like this is a good
thing. Instead of top-decisions, psychologists, persuasion,
PR. resistance and possible friction discussions would only
decide which way to try first.

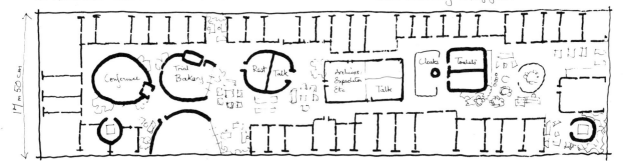

This is more difficult to make "attractive" than 1,2,3, or 4, but if people have tried the
alternatives and like this best perhaps this is the most "attractive" after all: — Architecture
is none the less "the art of the useful thing" and not "PURE ART" like sculpture!
        (Bruukskonst, Brauchskunst)
So, form and experience cannot be free from the satisfactions of good & economic use!
I did quite a nice one like this for Möller & Company in Stockholm!
FOR ALL THIS TO WORK THE BUILDING CAN'T BE TOO WIDE!

Scale 1:100

Ralph Erskine D'holm 3.2.68   **5.** S26

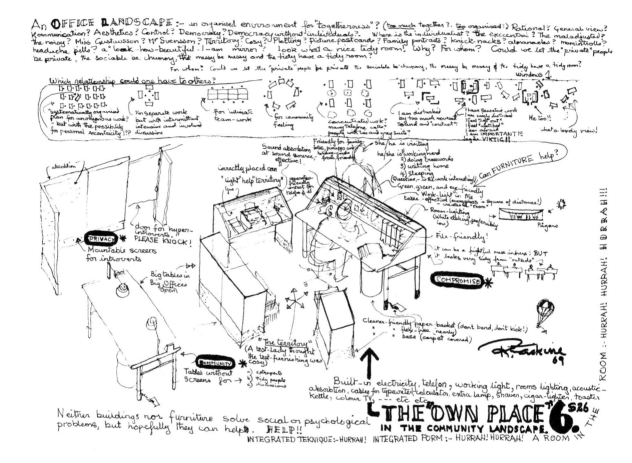

An **OFFICE LANDSCAPE**:- in organised environment for "togetherness"? (too much together?. too organised?) Rational? General view? Kommunication? Aesthetics? Control? Democrasy? Democrasy without individuals?. Where is the individualist? the excentric? The maladjusted? the noisy? Miss Gustavsson? Mr Svensson? Territory? Cosy? Plotting? Picture postcards? Family portraits? knick-nacks? almanackes? mini-trolls? headache pills? a "book - how - beautiful - I - am mirror"? look what a nice tidy room? Why? For whom? Could we let the "private" people be private, the sociable be chummy, the messy be messy and the tidy have a tidy room?

collaboration in groups, contact between work-mates and adequate break facilities.

Traditionally, however, there is little involvement by architects at all in industrial planning, and when they are consulted it is often only to decorate a process which they cannot influence. So far, the best and often the only way to improve the working environment has been to point to economic gains, for example from less absenteeism or turnover of staff. In the future, however, humane values might carry heavier weight. The process of organization and building should be carried out simultaneously,

and the consequences for the users should be taken fully into account. The architect should work through participation with a team of consultants employed directly by the users (perhaps via the trade unions). Such changes need to be implemented by political decisions. But until they are, architects must counteract the tendency to be employed only to create a facade. Architecture must embrace the whole design process, taking human needs, human activities and a human scale as its starting-point.

The Disappearing Factory: the Volvo experiment at Kalmar

Kenneth Frampton

The combination of iron, or steel, and glass to create unified, brightly illuminated interior spaces is familiar in modern architecture. What is less familiar is the early appearance of the same combination as part of a scheme to impose an unremitting rule on the patterns of human action. The function of inspection was greatly enhanced by the use of these materials. With masonry nothing like the same panorama could have been achieved. Considerations of economy and aesthetics played their part, but this eminently modern construction was justified primarily in terms of a philosophy of government, based on an idea about the way the human mind worked. It was, that is, an essay in the engineering of human behaviour through the manipulation of architectural form.

(Robin Evans, 'Regulation and Production', *Lotus 12*, Milan, 1976)

The crisis of 1968

Within three years of converting to assembly line production at their 5,000-metre long Torslanda plant built at Goteborg in 1967, Volvo found themselves plagued by chronic absenteeism and with a noticeable decline in the quality of production. The 1968 student revolt, prevalent throughout Europe, brought a good deal of this smouldering discontent to the surface and Volvo, like many other Swedish industries, was affected by a series of wild-cat strikes. At this point, the Swedish management endeavoured to establish new parameters for working hours, work rhythm and the quality of the working environment. Accordingly, a delegation from Volvo was sent to Elinor Thorsrud's Norwegian Works Research Centre in Oslo and at the end of 1969 a decision was made to delegate a certain amount of decision-making to the individual productive unit. On taking over the direction of the company in 1971, Pehr Gyllenhammar established an inter-disciplinary research team with the brief to devise a totally new productive procedure. The work of this Volvo team, eventually constituted as the so-called Ultra Group, led to the development of the Volvo automatic carrier to the design and lay-out of the new assembly plants to be built at Kalmar and Skovde.

The influence of structural changes in Swedish society

A fairly recent study on the mobility of labour in the Swedish engineering industry for the period 1969–1972 has revealed that, of 42% of the workers who left their jobs during these years, only 8% remained within the industry. The unsatisfactory quality of the engineering environment has been frequently cited by trades unions and researchers alike as the reason for this unacceptably high turnover and loss. Recently, however, other structural changes in the society have begun to exert an influence on the tendency of the labour force to remain extremely mobile. Amongst these factors, three have already had direct impact on the calibre and make-up of those working in the automobile industry: first, the 1969 Education Act that increased the minimum period of education from seven to nine years; second, the policy decision to reduce the dependency of Swedish industry on foreign labour; and third, the changing status of women in a society that began to encourage them to participate in industrial production.

Official government policy has already started to respond directly to these trends by committing itself to according a priority of employment to Swedes and to allocating no less than 70% of the industrial jobs available to women or people who are either old or handicapped. Although the desirable proportional division between these categories has yet to be decided, the inevitable entry of large numbers of women into industry must have an impact not only on the quality of the working environment (particularly in respect of its cleanliness, noise, etc.), but also on the determination of the hours to be worked. The working shift has been reduced to six hours so that household management can be sustained in conjunction with industrial production. A further reason for the institution of the six-hour-shift arises ironically, at least in the case of automobile production, out of the automobile itself—a tool which has effectively extended commutation time to and from work. Should commutation also come to be regarded as 'working' time as the unions argue it should, then only a reduction in 'shift length' would be able to compensate for the loss of 'free-time'.

At the same time, the high level of general education in a society that spontaneously realizes that without an adequate education one has little chance of adjusting to future changes in the economy, has led to a state of affairs where the number of years spent in formal education now stands at thirteen for 60% of the Volvo labour force, whereas comparable figures for 1969 show that 70% of the same labour force had only seven years of education or less. It is hardly surprising that the raising of the education level should impose conditions on the nature of production and the quality of the productive environment. There is little doubt, however, that the Volvo experiment would not have gone very far had it not been for union pressure and for the willingness of Swedish industry to operate with lower profit margins than those which generally obtain in the United States.[1]

The development of new productive procedures

Among the major incentives for the invention of new productive procedures in the Volvo concern was not only absenteeism but also a gradual decline in the overall quality of the product. Gyllenhammar, the decisive force behind the effort to restructure the Volvo work organization, was convinced from the outset that high quality could only be maintained by people who found their work to be of significance. Handing over the managerial brief to the research team for the Kalmar project, he declared:

In Kalmar we must produce a factory which, without sacrificing efficiency and economic results, provides the possibility for the employees to work in groups, to communicate freely, to carry out job rotation, to vary their rate of work, to feel identification with the products, to be aware of quality responsibility and be in a position to influence their working environment.

In addition to these criteria, which coincided with the basic union objectives, the following additional specifications were imposed by the management: (1) that the plant should have an initial capacity of 30,000 units annually, on a single day shift, with the potential for doubling this output should two shifts be introduced; (2) that the plant should be sufficiently flexible to accommodate unforeseen technical and social developments over the next twenty years; (3) that the plant should be restricted to the final assembly of painted bodies from the Torslanda plant and engines from the Skovde works; (4) that the plant should commence production in the Spring of 1974; (5) that the project should involve, including the development and testing of new machine tools, an investment of around 110,000,000 Swedish Kronor (that is, some 10% over and above what it would have cost to build a traditional on-line plant of comparable quality): (6) that all these criteria must be met in such a way was to assure reasonable levels of efficiency and profit.

Both initial research team and the second 'brainstorming' team, the Ultra Group, were asked to work with a reference group comprised of a supervisor, a foreman and two permanent workers' representatives. While the two successive research teams were equally comprised of technicians, production engineers, economists, psychologists, doctors and architects, Gyllenhammar was compelled to reject the findings of the first team as being too conservative. Within a month a somewhat reconstituted group, the Ultra Group, arrived at a solution, basing its findings on interviews with ex-Volvo workers who, above all else, declared that they would much prefer to work in teams. Two fundamental design propositions were crucial to the final development of the Kalmar system of team production. One was the tri-partite hexagonal block formation, first sketched out by the production engineer Torgny Karlsson and the architect Gerhard Goehle as a 'butterfly' factory plan; and the other was the invention of the cybernetically-controlled carrier which was, in the main, the contribution of Bertil Ahlsen, who is now in charge of the further development of this system.

3 *Below:* Plan of Kalmar, ground floor.
2 *Above:* Plan of Kalmar, first floor.

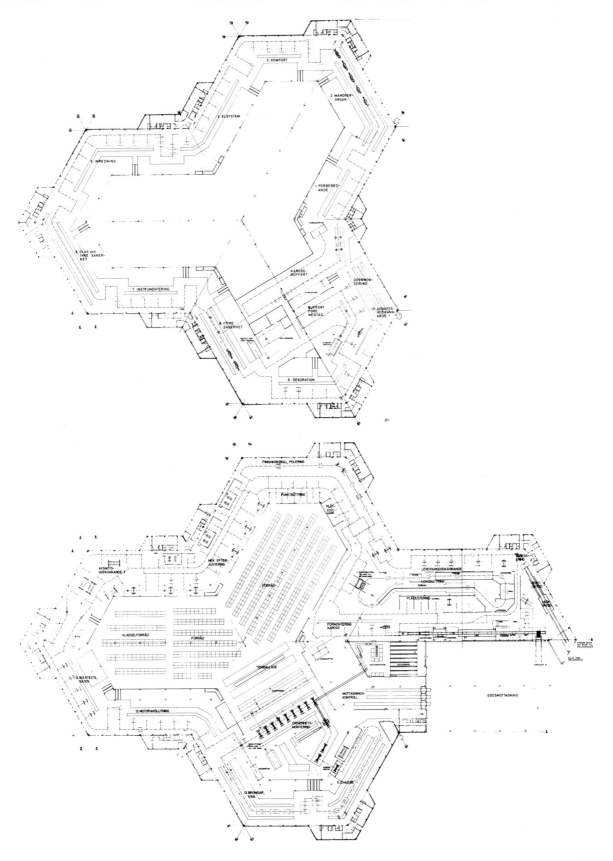

The structure, form and organization of the Kalmar plant

Within its tri-partite organization of three hexagonal blocks grouped about a triangular central core, with a complementary hexagonal block located to one side, Kalmar is organized on two levels, as a 'broken line' some one and a half miles in length. This line is structured into a sequence of regular, faceted work stations, reflecting the breaking down of the assembly process into 25 separate procedures (figs. 1–3). After having been washed and inspected, the painted body is delivered by rail from Torslanda and lifted into a mobile flat carrier (fig. 4) where it comes under the control of the central computer (fig. 1, nos. 0 and 1) which will monitor its process throughout the 25 workshop sequences. Once registered, the body is elevated to the first floor where its doors are removed, and it then passes through the various assembly teams in an anti-clockwise direction. As the body proceeds through its first-floor assembly, in which one team is responsible for the fitting of the electronics and another for the installation of the upholstery, etc., the engine, gear box, axles and exhaust systems are assembled into a complete chassis mounted on a high-level carrier on the ground floor (fig. 1, no. 28). Once the body has completed its first floor circuit it is lowered by lift to the ground floor and 'married' to the completed chassis. At this juncture, brakes and wheels are added and then the total car is returned to a low-level carrier. All that now remains is a ground-floor clockwise circuit, wherein the supplementary parts are fitted and the car passes through the final stages of adjustment, inspection, testing and sealing.

An essential feature in this system of production at two levels is the central y-shaped, ten-metre-high storage hall, housing crated components stacked in steel storage racks to the full height of the space (fig. 5). Large fork-lifts (capable of a ten-metre lift) remove these crates and deposit them against the relevant working zones. These components are then withdrawn by smaller fork-lifts belonging to each of the workshop zones and are redeposited by them at the precise points of assembly within each shop.

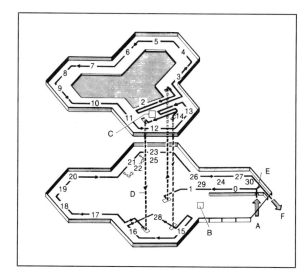

1 Pattern of production stages in the Kalmar Plant.

The complement of each workshop zone will vary from 15 to 20 people, and be further broken down into a potentially ever-changing pattern of work organization, that may assign, say, three men to assuring the continual provision and distribution of supplies, while the remaining twelve will be assigned to work in pairs, in a system of 'straight assembly', at six different carrier stations. In the system of 'straight assembly' the carrier moves from station to station at the rate set by the working team through its terminal computer. (Whereas, in 'dock assembly' the working carrier is 'docked' to one side of the straight sequence and here a team of perhaps three people will complete the entire fabrication task on one car for that particular zone and then move on to the next.)

Service elements, projecting from the main face of the building (fig. 6) and consisting of entries leading to access stairs, locker rooms, shower rooms, coffee lounges and offices, form a bridge, at every other corner, between adjacent workshops. These points house the technicians and foreman's offices, whose supervisory responsibilities include the co-ordination of the 'flow' between the two adjacent zones.

The Kalmar Carrier is aluminium-faced, steel-framed, runs on four rubber wheels and is driven by an integral electric motor fed by a battery (fig. 7). Its overall dimensions—approximately 6 by 2 metres—permit it not only to transport the unit under fabrication, but also to provide a base on which to work while the unit is in motion, at speeds varying from 3 to 30 metres per minute. The speed, timing and movement of the carrier is pre-set and then electro-magnetically controlled by a central computer, via signals transmitted through tracks set in the concrete floor. The tracks may easily be drilled out and their position and pattern re-set if a new configuration is desired. The carrier is equipped with automatic safety devices which interrupt the functioning servo-mechanism once the bumper of the carrier encounters an obstruction. It may be disconnected from automatic control and steered manually, and comes in two basic types, low and high, depending on the jig mechanisms that are built into the base. The lower-level carrier has a tilting frame capable of rotating the body of the car through ninety degrees. This device, which Volvo was the first to introduce, permits assembly work to be carried out on the underside of the car in a correct and comfortable working position (fig. 7). The high-level carrier is fitted with a four-pillar chassis jig, which can be raised and lowered for the assembly of the axle, gearbox and engine. Kalmar is at present equipped with 200 low and 38 high-level carriers. The control unit of each carrier is equipped with illuminated diodes which indicate not only whether the carrier is standing exactly over a cable but also if the cable is in operation and if the setting is manual or automatic. The same system also signals the moment at which the battery requires re-charging. Aside from all the variations that may be encoded into its movement, one of the most flexible aspects of the carrier is that basically the

4 *Above right:* In this workshop zone one car has been docked out of the straight line in order to carry out procedure of 'dock' assembly.

5 *Right:* The storage hall within the centre of the building.

153

same flat bed could be used for the assembly of any object that would roughly fit within its overall dimensions. Thus, Kalmar is by no means committed for the rest of its working life to the manufacture of automobiles.

Quality feedback control

Within the one-and-a-half-mile broken line there are four control points where the cars are checked at their respective stages against the monitored data of the central computer. As the body proceeds through the production circuit, the central memory-bank of the computer compiles the statistical errors most recently encountered in each of the sectors of the line, governed by each of the four control points. At each of these points, the controller checks for the

6 Diagrammatic model showing difference between 'dock' and straight assembly to the left. At the mid-point a 'buffer' zone of cars.

most recently recorded errors of that particular sector and searches at the same time for others. Where other faults are found, these are fed back into the computer, to contribute to the ever-changing statistical compilation of the error pattern at any particular point. Errors involving the security of the finished vehicle are given special emphasis by the computer and instant efforts are made to check an error in the production at source. In general, errors are either rectified on the spot and returned to the team or stored in the computer and rectified at the end. As far as possible, every effort is made through this system of control, which is known by the initials KVIK (KValitets Information, Kalmar), to eliminate 'built in' faults. Workshop teams may obtain feedback information, at any time, in the form of print-out, on any given car in the line. This data not only affords information as to the quality of the product at a particular stage but also monitors the current performance of the team in relation to the agreed speed of production.

Variations in the rhythm and organization of the work
The mean hourly rate of car production and hence the speed of the carrier is controlled by two variable factors: (1) the current orders for automobiles in relation to the stocks available, and (2) an agreed MTM rate of pay per productive unit per hour, established through negotiation between the management and the local union. The current speed at Kalmar is set at the moment around 15·5 cars per hour, with the carrier remaining on the average some 5 minutes at each work station or some 25–30 minutes in each shop. This rate may be increased within a particular shop from around 15·5 to 17 cars per hour in order to create a 'buffer' of completed cars for that stage, at the 'threshold' to the next shop. Any team may thereby achieve, through the creation of a buffer, a longer coffee break or, for that matter, a more varied rhythm of such breaks within its daily work schedule. No bonuses are paid over the basic MTM rate, other than the extended rest periods achieved through buffer production, or an increment paid for consistent presence within the team—an inducement clearly designed to consolidate work teams and reduce the level of absenteeism.[2] The nature and pace of the specific task within the team may be varied by the work team itself, acting collectively in any of the following ways: (1) the speed and rhythm of the work may be changed by mutual agreement; (2) an operative may change the nature of his specific task within the assembly team; (3) an operative may choose to work in a larger group (such as three) on a single car—the so-called 'dock assembly' system—in order to complete a significant section of the car and then move on, as a body, to the next car; (4) an operative may transfer from one workshop team to the next, thereby changing not only the specific task but also the assembly category (for example, by moving from the installation of electrical equipment to the fitting of upholstery).

The last of these alternatives points towards the perpetual education of the worker in the Dewey sense of the term. Theoretically, an operative can pass from workshop to workshop until he has in effect completed the entire assembly cycle and, in a certain sense, 'built the whole car'. Apart from affording an obvious route to promotion within a technical hierarchy and from approaching, in an oblique way, Gyllenhammar's idea of a team of workers being able to build an entire machine, this capacity for training and re-training within the Kalmar plant seems to be nothing less than a reflection of general awareness present throughout Swedish society; namely, that in a highly volatile techno-economy men must be prepared for continual re-training. It is now generally accepted in Sweden that at least once within his lifetime the average professional or technician will need to be partially or wholly re-educated vocationally, chiefly because of the internal restructuring or obsolescence of his initial metier.

7 Kalmar carrier.

155

Environmental quality control

The main body of the Kalmar plant consists of three hexagonal units and, for the most part, the process of assembly is carried out against the perimeter of these forms. By virtue of this location, the assembly bays are extremely well lit through continual strip windows which also afford immediate views over the surrounding landscape. In general, every effort has been made to keep the working area as unobstructed, light, quiet and well-ventilated as possible, and to this end the concrete factory floor has been kept flat and well-illuminated by shadow-free artificial light. By the same token all the pneumatic power tools are suspended on retractable arms from the ceiling. The sound generated by these tools has been reduced as much as possible; first, by running them at the lowest feasible speed, and second, by hanging absorbent acoustic bafflers from the ceilings in almost all the shops. While the noise level can still, at times, attain 85 decibels, the normal medium level throughout the plant is 65; these levels make the use of hearing protection unnecessary. Even though the air is changed at the rate of 20 cubic meters per hour per square meter (that is, around six air changes per hour), all tools producing a polluting by-product such as sanders or gasoline feeds are fitted with an instantaneous vacuum return that immediately evacuates the pollutant from the working area. Exhaust gases from cars or heavily polluting processes such as underbody-sealing and surface-finishing are immediately eliminated by powerful fans. Most of the more polluting processes are carried out in specially sealed and ventilated chambers. The standard of hygiene both within and outside the working area is scrupulously maintained by a team of continuously circulating cleaners. The same standards of hygiene and environmental control naturally extend into the three-storey personnel areas clustered at the corners around the perimeter of the building.

Representation and place in the built form

Kalmar's most representative gesture, the prominent display of the Volvo logo and a cluster of five national flags which seems to be the ubiquitous symbol of the Swedish state, serves, if nothing else, to dramatize the bland anonymity of the factory building itself (fig. 8). While this may be all that is required in this age of objective production and social welfare, the fact remains that a feeling of almost deliberate isolation, in the physical and psychological sense, pervades the entire structure and site. The bleakness of the general approach to the works can hardly be overlooked, and it is difficult to dispel the sense that one is trespassing on an area where the human species is unwelcome. This feeling is no doubt subjective, but even if one rejects as extravagant the impulse to compare Kalmar to the literally lifeless landscape of a fully automated oil refinery, one cannot but be reminded also of those windowless, introspective structures that have since become the typical building form of the American megalopolis: the factories, bowling alleys, supermarkets and stores that flank the average freeway. Flags and logo notwithstanding, the approaches to Kalmar approximate all too closely to Melvin Webber's paradigm of the 'non-place urban realm',[3] and this is distressing when one realizes that this is the landscape in which some 600 men regularly spend the best part of their working day.

The barely inflected, sandwich-like elevations are sufficient to affirm that we could not be further from Peter Behren's deification, in 1910, of the AEG Turbinenfabrik in Berlin as a 'temple' of industrial power, or from the transcendental value attached to glass, as the lucid revelation of the production process itself, that we witness in the Brinkman and Van der Vlugt, Van Nelle Factory, Rotterdam, of 1929.[4] In terms of cultural significance, Kalmar seems to lie uneasily suspended between the abstract sterility of the Torslanda complex and the more articulate aesthetic of the original Volvo works designed in separate stages by two architects, F. O. Petersen between 1944 and 1954 and Owe Svard between 1954 and 1964, whose expression seems to have been directly linked to that non-rhetorical, bland, brick aesthetic developed for the Swedish Co-operative movement under Eskil Sundahl between 1935 and 1949.

All these examples could be easily dismissed as

irrelevant aesthetic comparisons were it not for the more obvious and vital fact that, despite the saplings planted around the perimeter, insufficient effort has been made here to create an overall amenity out of the building and the site. Instead, it is evident that the best part of the investment has been consumed in providing the shelter and the instruments of production, and while such a priority is no doubt indispensable, we should bear in mind that what we are questioning here comes to a small amount of additional expenditure when compared to the basic investment of 110,000,000 Kronor. The 'anti-philanthropic' nature of the functional contract established between the unions and the management reveals itself, at this point, in all its negativity.

8 Views of the Kalmar Plant.

The poverty of the external environment at Kalmar is evident from the general blandness of the views obtaining from the shop floors and from the coffee-break rooms; the latter being not only burdened with the bleakness of the aspect but also with the physical and psychological inaccessibility of the immediate exterior space (fig. 9). The fact that neither these rooms nor the main dining space give on to terraces that are significantly related to the surrounding landscape, points to the strict limits within which the restructuring of the environment has been conceived. The hold of functionalism is so great that hedonism and production are still seen as incompatible. An equally ironic observation might also be made about the 'individual' workshop entries distributed around the perimeter, which, owing to their relative inaccessibility, seem rarely to

be used. Indeed, they appear to be almost a 'Kitsch' system of access, whose 'sign value' is meant to indicate the presence of an individual shop. The employees are not deceived, however, since naturally they all enter and leave by the main entry situated close to the road.

Thus, for all the remarkable achievements of Kalmar, three fundamental doubts remain: (1) the whole installation is only schematically related to its location and site; (2) the amenities in both visual and physical terms fail to extend beyond the hermetic skin of the production space; and (3) the building fails to represent itself in adequate terms to the society at large. In as much as Volvo planning policy is now moving towards the creation of plants comprised of free-standing workshops, this third point about representation will only become more difficult to answer.

9 Views of the Kalmar Plant.

The impact of decentralized production on physical planning

The whole tendency of the present Volvo policy—namely, the cybernetic control of decentralized production—is reflected in the physical planning of productive units at both a site and regional level. One of the most recent projects by Owe Svard, for a truck fabrication plant at Tuve, takes the almost limitless flexibility of the electro-magnetic carrier to its logical conclusion and proposes to develop the plant as a series of free-standing workshops, which will be linked solely by the magnetic track embedded into the factory site. The flow of the units in the process of being assembled would continue uninterrupted, both inside and outside, on the assumption that the problems of weather protection could either be ignored, or overcome through heating the track lanes and/or equipping the carriers with canopies. Should this project be realized in its present form it would mean an even greater

proportion of the investment allocated to the tooling itself, while the factory would be reduced to a series of free-standing sheds. This radical change in the investment pattern and the resultant physical form—that is, the 'disappearing factory—would yield a number of significant corollaries. In the first place, it would conform to the current trend to increase the proportion spent on the servicing of structures, irrespective of their particular category (a fully automated oil refinery might be, in a sense, nothing but the servicing itself). Secondly, it would automatically extend the megalopolis domain of Webber's 'non-place urban realm'—that open continuous city-scape where public institutions become increasingly difficult either to consolidate or to represent. And finally, it would amount to a breakthrough in the rationalization of factory design, as momentous for industrial production as the invention of the mobile lounge has been for the planning of airports.

At the same time, at that delicate level where the provision of collective amenity and public representation overlap, certain gains and losses would become immediately apparent and demonstrate once again our lack of adequately articulated models for building and planning, in a society that is exclusively based on a highly volatile economy. And while the reformist aims (on the frontiers of Kitsch) of 'returning' to the small decentralized workshops would be all too literally achieved, the provision of a satisfactory physical link between the respective shop floors and the collective amenity of the headquarters building would become increasingly difficult to effect. Tuve, as projected, would simply compound the already problematic nature of such links as are now ambiguously incorporated into the Skovde and Kalmar plants. These difficult site planning issues, that we habitually refer to by such ill-defined terms as 'linkage' and 'interface', return to plague us, in a concrete way, at the regional level; for abstract planning procedures, still informed by nineteenth century concepts of zoning, have succeeded in situating most of the new housing in total isolation from the places of production. As a consequence, the city of Goteborg alone has a

vacancy rate of some 4,000 empty flats. The problem increases in its complexity when one excludes, as both socially and economically undesirable, the nineteenth-century model of the 'company town', and while Tuve will depart from Volvo policy in building a sector of housing in close proximity to the plant, this will only accommodate some 25% of its total labour force.

The decentralization of production, from the delegation of work organization to the dispersal of factory infrastructure, is of course compatible with decentralization on a regional scale and with the relatively even distribution of Volvo factories throughout the Goteborg-Stockholm corridor. Of the 25 Volvo plants engaged in the production of internal combustion traction, only four factories, including Kalmar, are situated outside this megalopolitan area. And the policy of decentralization, actively pursued since the mid-1950s (with the singular exception of Torslanda) is equally compatible, ironically enough, with the various programmes for industrial decentralization to be found in the basic socialist texts, from the Marx-Engels Communist Manifesto of 1848 to Peter Kropotkin's 'Factories, Fields and Workshops' of some forty years later.[5] While this decentralization, which depended then (as it has since) on the universal distribution of electrical power, appears now to be a pre-condition for the potentially liberating force of cybernetic production, the full benefits of such liberation still stand to be outweighed by the wanton neglect of the most basic resource of all, namely the land.

This potential food-producing element, so respectfully treated by Kropotkin, seems to be the one neglected term in the present Western planning perspective, that generally tends to emphasize the productive and consumptive needs of the industrial oligopoly at the expense of the essential resources of society as a whole. Land is what constitutes the wasted intersticial matter—the so-called 'left-over space—of the modern urbanized region, that instead of being left over should really serve as the cellular organic material that significantly articulates the various aspects of the human domain.

That the need for such articulation is barely acknowledged, let alone adequately formulated tends to be borne out by the site plans for both Kalmar and Skovde.

Technology and the rationalization of work
The enforced move towards increasing the scope of worker-participation and towards shorter working hours and the decentralization of production tends as a whole towards a grass-roots re-definition of the concept of work. In this the integrated, traditional, craft-based society, torn apart by the division of labour in the eighteenth century, spontaneously begins to be reconstituted in natural opposition to the fundamental aims of capitalist production. In as much as neo-capitalism is compelled to collaborate with these tendencies (inadvertently activated through socio-economic transformations, such as the raising of educational levels and the liberation of women), the re-organization of work can only be regarded as positive. Yet while the overriding interest in productive efficiency may be forced to tolerate the creation of potential 'soviets' at shop-floor level, one should never forget that cybernetics *per se* is the language of control and that decentralization has been conducive to subtle forms of political repression.

At the same time, Volvo (and for that matter the whole of Swedish society) stands tensely balanced on the threshold of a peculiar situation, where further union gains (such as the creation of employees' funds) will only serve to drive society into a form of state capitalism in which the interests of the unions and the interests of the state will more or less coincide. Should this curious amalgam be finally achieved, the capacity of the unions to reform the working environment will no doubt become increasingly limited, and all the more so since the terms for its redefinition will be drawn, more by necessity than choice, from the fields of cybernetics, production engineering and psychological behaviourism.

In this event, all subsequent re-definition of work and the working environment will fall to the workers themselves, and even more to the political development of the society at large, beyond the immediate constraints of industrial production. Given that the historical fatality of 'divided labour' can never be redeemed by team assembly alone (for the simple reason that this finally redresses the process and not the product), then work and with it the working environment will only be adequately re-defined when the total environment that results from production is more consciously understood and collectively determined. As it is, for all the achievements of worker-participation, much that passes for participation is only the manipulation of a 'syntax' imposed from above.

It is surely no accident that the new Volvo factories at Kalmar and Skovde contain, at least in embryonic form, those distinctly separate political arenas whose discourse is divided between the two principles of rationalization identified by Jurgen Habermas in 1968 in his essay 'Technology and Science as Ideology Above all', he wrote,

'It becomes clear against this background that two concepts of rationalization must be distinguished. At the level of subsystems of purposive-rational action and scientific-technical, progress has already compelled the reorganization of social institutions and sectors and necessitates it on an even larger scale than heretofore. But this process of the development of the productive forces can be a potential for liberation if it does not replace rationalization at another level. Rationalization at the level of the institutional framework can occur only in the medium of symbolic interaction itself, that is through removing restrictions on communication.[6]'

The disproportion of emphasis accorded to these two forms of rationalization in advanced industrial society seems to find its direct reflection in the built environment, and while at Kalmar the team workshop areas function only too well for free discourse within the terms of the techno-structure, the somewhat restricted personnel or coffee-break rooms on the perimeter of the building, far from serving as adequate areas for 'symbolic interaction', are clearly only intended to function, like the saunas in the washrooms, for the instant restoration of the will to work. And it is surely no accident that these rooms are inadequately represented and that they open, not so much to pleasure gardens as to that landscape of amnesia, that empty terrain of communication that serves to separate the worker from the pleasure of his family-life. This clinical separation of the reality of work from the pleasure of life, so much of an anathema to Charles Fourier, speaks for itself. The pre-occupation of modern industry with abstract linkages, rather than concrete adjacencies, seems at this juncture to be far from accidental, for only through their being masked by the opportunism of their dislocation may the so-called 'value free' abstractions of exploitation be kept open and intact. The question is, as Jurgen Habermas has written, 'not whether we completely utilize an available or creatable potential but whether we choose what we want for the purpose of the pacification and gratification of existence. But it must be immediately noted that we are only posing this question and cannot answer it in advance. For the solution demands precisely that unrestricted communication about the goals of life activity and conduct against which advanced capitalism, structurally dependent on a depoliticized public realm, puts up a strong resistance.'[7]

I would like to acknowledge the assistance of Mary Scott of the Royal College of Art who helped to gather most of this material and was solely responsible for obtaining information about the Skovde engine works.

Notes to the text
[1] See Emma Rothschild, 'GM in Trouble 1. The Vega', *The New York Review of Books*, 25 February, 1971, p. 15. 'Foreign manufacturers produce cars cheaply . . . because they have a high level of productivity, and because they accept smaller profits than American corporations. GM makes about three times as great a profit on each vehicle it produces as its foreign competitors; a profit of $239 per vehicle for Toyota, $59 per vehicle for VW, and $57 per vehicle for Datsun/Nissan.'
[2] Absenteeism at Kalmar has fallen to about 15%—so that the present labour force is some 15% above strength. When they are all present this 'surplus' is used to maintain the plant.
[3] See Melvin Webber, *Explorations in Urban Structure* University of Pennsylvania, 1964. Webber first coined the term 'non-place urban realm' as a general paradigm for megalopolis in 1961 in the essay 'Order in Diversity: Community without Propinquity', that appears in Lowdon Wingo, Jr (ed.), *Cities and Space* (John Hopkins Press, 1963).
[4] See Le Corbusier, *The Radiant City* (Orion Press, 1964), p. 179. Le Corbusier was well aware of the representative aspects of the Van Nelle factory when he wrote: 'Everything is transparent; everyone can see and be seen as he works. . . . The manager of the factory is there in his glass office. He can be seen. And he himself, from his office, can see the whole illuminated Dutch horizon, and, in the far distance, the life of the great port. The immense refectory continues the pattern. The managers, the highest and lowest administrative grades, the workers, male and female, all eat together in the same great room, which has transparent walls opening out onto endless views of meadows. 'This ecstatic description continues, 'there is no proletariat here'. Nothing surely could be more Saint-Simonian than this, or closer to the general attitude of the Volvo management to the factory at Kalmar. What is missing, however, at Kalmar is the rhetorical expression of this fact and on the whole, whatever doubts one may entertain for Le Corbusier's idealism, this would seem to be at a loss.
[5] See Peter Kropotkin, *Factories, Fields and Workshops*, London, 1888. In his conclusion Kropotkin wrote: 'The scattering of industries over the country—so as to bring the factory admist fields, to make agriculture derive all those profits which it always finds in being combined with industry (see the Eastern States of America) and to produce a combination of industrial with agricultural work—is surely the next step to be made, as soon as a re-organization of our present conditions is possible. . . . This step is imposed by the necessity of producing for the producers themselves; it is imposed by the necessity for each healthy man and woman to spend a part of their lives in manual work in the free air; and it will be rendered the more necessary when the great social movements, which have now become unavoidable, come to disturb the present international trade, and compel each nation to revert to her own resources for her own maintenance.'
[6] Jurgen Habermas, 'Technology and Science as an Ideology', in *Towards a Rational Society* (Beacon Press, Boston, 1971), p. 118.
[7] *Idem*, pp. 119 and 120.

Architecture and Bureaucracy
Lucien Kroll

Architecture is made for man; this goes without saying, though some types of architecture follow the precept more closely than others. It is a question of balancing two tendencies, to 'command' and to 'obey'—a delicate and difficult task. When one of these two tendencies comes to dominate at the cost of the other, aberrations occur. Somewhere along the path which Man has been following from his primordial state, he established himself and gathered a family around him. Then other families settled near the first ones, apparently without any pre-determined overall plan, yet following subtle cultural and social laws, at first unspoken, but gradually formulated as the number of inhabitants grew. This development was subject to constant principles, as well as to other influences that varied according to ethnic traditions, geographical and economic circumstances, as well as other hidden factors.

At the other extreme, those in control of our settlements have often favoured the authoritarian imposition of a plan—for instance, a street grid, such as the intersection of the *decumanus* (east–west axis) and *cardo* (north–south axis) in Roman towns. Even if you start with an artificial order of this kind, irregularities arise, contingent forces, diagonals, a society which is full of contradictory but interconnected elements. Balance is thus re-established and the structure revitalized. All this is well known. Attempts to impose order artificially have been made by our contemporaries. This was foretold, prepared for and introduced by the utopianists, then joyfully made a reality, with different degrees of success, by the great administrative, bureaucratic and industrial powers. It has been pursued greedily, partly for the simple reason that the technical resources for it were available. The preferred procedure has been to raze existing buildings on the site, complete the development, and afterwards move in the inhabitants, who in the meantime have been given no opportunity to influence the structure, texture and appearance of their new environment.

These authoritarian tendencies, of course, do not exist in the built environment alone; they are symptomatic of a discernible fragmentation of society and its behaviour patterns, parallel with the specialization of labour, division of social roles, and even the division into different ways of spending time. However, it is not inevitable that technology should command in this way. The determining factor is the authoritarian structure which dwells within the conscious or unconscious mind of each of society's technocrats, though not necessarily without misgivings. The myriad dreams, aspirations, unquantifiable human needs have been banished, leaving only the purely material, easily definable needs that were mixed among them. Priority has been given exclusively to material factors which are instantly verifiable. The result is rational lay-out in large specialized zones; mechanical channels of communication; and worship, sport, education and culture carefully separated from their context in time and space. Sinister building projects in industrial areas stand empty and alien, perhaps given a sham sense of vitality by their polychrome sheet metal. We now know well enough what urban motorways involve. The authorities mutter platitudes, not knowing which way to turn. More and more, new ventures go rapidly out of date. The more functional a project, the less use it is. The absurd centralization of all decisions concerning the creation of areas to be lived in has produced disasters which stimulate us to look for new forms of organization. We feel that it may be possible to correct the equilibrium by introducing elements which have been overlooked. For instance, exciting possibilities are opened up for architects who are prepared to draw inspiration from the haphazard contributions of the local residents, and to adapt the skills of craftsmen and industrial workers in order to express those contributions.

Although they are difficult to characterize precisely, it seems to me that our motives for thinking along these lines have been primarily political; or rather, they have been 'protopolitical'. In order to create a type of politics unrealizable at present, we are trying out in advance the different methods which might one day bring about the political situation we have in mind. This is simply a question

1 'I have decided to force them to accept this civilization! The forest will be destroyed to make way for a natural park!' *Asterix*

of suggesting prototypes (whether they are accepted or rejected is not the point), and of taking note of their possibilities or drawbacks. We have never imagined that we could bring about revolution with pockets of alternative architecture, which, to make a revolutionary impact, would have to infiltrate the existing constraints. The familiar question is this: 'If tomorrow morning we woke up to find the earth taken over by the local authorities, how would that change our way of planning and constructing the built environment?' We might also ask: 'If tomorrow a factory were run by a workers' co-operative, by tomorrow evening what changes would there be in the factory's products?' It is to these questions that we are attempting to sketch in answers. These are of no value in themselves; their worth lies in the way we have come to them, and how they relate to parallel experiments. Of course, a theoretical model precedes the attempt to realize it. However, in the course of turning the model into reality, events always contrive to modify it by revealing on the one hand what cannot be done, and on the other hand possibilities hitherto unsuspected. In our field, action produced more knowledge than does contemplation, if it is integrated with the theoretical process. It is not a matter of saying, for example, 'A team of psychologists will organize resident participation, provide me with the results, and I will design the building'; nor can one say, 'The plans are completed. My builder will carry them out in the usual way.'

My first piece of work based on user participation was to transform a cow-shed for a hundred cows into craft workshops for joiners, goldsmiths and potters. I had lots of time, and was able to question *all* the people involved—workers, employees, bosses, neighbours and so on. Both the overall plan and the smallest details of the workshops were designed with the participation of the future users. Subsequently, the execution was finalized with the builders. This was the way to go about it.

On another occasion, the extension of a room required some basic decisions. Should we tear out the existing stone floor-tiles, which were no longer manufactured, and completely resurface the floor with a similar tiling? I proposed that we left the original flooring in place and that we bought new tiles of half a dozen different colours. With the floor-layers we agreed approximately on the areas to be covered by each colour and we asked the workers to decide at random the demarcation line between the different types, taking into account the quantities in stock. The workers had to turn off their transistor radio—it spoilt their concentration. Often the architect has to stand at the workman's side to tackle the problem. 'How are *we* going to solve this one?' he has to say.

It seems to us that a reverent attitude towards people and their relationships (with themselves, with each other, with space, history, society, etc) automatically prevents the sterile production of technological artefacts that are uninhabitable. This attitude, if it can be achieved, leads to active and direct communication with the only one who really matters in an architectural project: the person or persons for whom it is designed, be it house, workshop, factory, office, museum, or road. A spontaneous method of architecture, bypassing planners, still seems impossible at present; the people we design for have difficulty in conceptualizing or making associations, or transferring ideas into reality, when they are left to their own devices. Such a method has so far only produced shanty towns, either those in poverty-stricken zones surrounding vast building complexes, or the luxury type in tourist areas. It is here that contemporary popular culture is able to express without excessive constraint its sense of scale, space, proportion, form, colour, while at the same time reproducing cultural models to which people are constantly exposed. How is it possible to introduce this rich inventiveness into institutions responsible for training minds and moulding imaginations without undermining them? Or rather: how can we promote training methods and attitudes (in architecture and other fields) which are not only compatible with such inventiveness, but also tend to enrich and expand it? The answer is not to neutralize or dispense with the architect. On the contrary, we believe that the more the architect is personally involved, the more this creativity can develop and take root. We also believe that only the architect has had the right education (in the sense that he has not been overeducated) to sustain him in this attitude and equip him for the role.

The story has already been told elsewhere of the medical students of the Catholic University of Louvain, who contested the master plan of the medical faculty complex which the University was proposing to set up in Woluwé-St-Lambert, a suburb of Brussels. The grounds of their complaint were these: that the plan broke up residential, academic and entertainment facilities into completely separate areas, all designed in the same monumental style. A huge machine was about to impose an establishment attitude on the inhabitants by 'demobilizing' the political and social viewpoints which the students wanted to incorporate into their studies. After the University had refused to modify its basic plan, the students secured the right to

2 The roofs of the restaurant and the West side of the Mémé, of business students' accommodation and the welfare department.

choose the architect, so they could urge him to assure them that he would respect their own centre, their relationship with themselves, but also their relations with the neighbouring areas, above all with the part of town most accessible to them: the Kapelleveld. The students suggested us, and the University authorities had no objections, even though we were not associated with university circles: they saw in us a solution, an alibi for the severe architecture which they had already uncompromisingly decided on.

Through sketches, pamphlets, conferences, conversations, we were able to achieve a high degree of clarity about our aims and methods: the authorities approved everything enthusiastically and work commenced on the first buildings. We have the impression now that everything was based on a fundamental misunderstanding. The authorities never really believed we were going to carry out what we proposed; and regarded our consultations with students as a formality. Their cooperation with us

3 One day we said to the builders 'mix with bricks as you see fit; you start here and go at least up to there'.

4 We suggested the general form and the builder invented the shapes.

gave rise to a finished product in which they hardly recognized their more traditional intentions.

The University fails perhaps to recognize sufficiently in all this the traits of a system which unconsciously calls upon the inhabitants to obey, without concerning themselves in matters that are not part of their immediate role. Further scrutiny would reveal the image of a social law which distinguishes the Catholic University from all the people who are beyond the pale, including the students. The University, according to this principle, decided to change architects as one might change one's hairdresser. They dismissed us with the same casualness with which they had engaged us, thus admitting the failure (or the confusion) of their policy of friendly cooperation and the frustration of the plan which ostensibly expressed it.

Of course the students resisted firmly but politely the formidable cohort of more 'disciplined' architects sent in by the authorities. With the departure of their architects they saw the chances of bringing

about their sociable environment disappear. And to whose advantage?

Our own attitude was clear to all those who were involved, without exception: to the students who were going to live in the place, to the neighbours, to the University authorities (through the intermediary of their departments for construction, social planning and security), more informally to others whom we asked to play the role of inhabitant, and to the building contractors and craftsmen via their foremen, their workers, etc.

It is difficult to describe in a few words how the students acted, how we listened, interpreted, made suggestions, modifications, how we acted upon them and how they acted upon us. We have given an account elsewhere of how it was possible to work out a coherent scheme, made up of various elements, without excessively compromising the differences between the members of a team and how this could lead, through a succession of conflicts, from the written expression of intentions to an

165

architecture embodying them (or making them possible). We, of course, projected into the scheme our own intentions, our sub-culture, our professional neuroses, our inadequacies, and so on.

Our collaboration with the University officials was extraordinarily cordial for several years: by this time they were adept at diplomacy. It must also be remembered that the higher authorities had their hands completely full with the creation of a new university town—Louvain-la-Neuve—and that this ambition took up all available energy and competence. Moreover, the gigantic problems posed by the adjoining hospital and the faculties put our modest activities in the shade; thus we had several exceptionally constructive and serene years.

There was even at one point the question of designing a structure which would house the university building department: we organized groups of officials and asked them in our customary manner to work out some plans together. Many very precious insights into what to build emerged from this. To cite but one: 'So as not to let ourselves be submerged by our own bureaucracy, we would sometimes like to stop our paperwork, pick up a spade and do ten minutes' gardening: so let's have a French window.' The officials responsible for university security tried to interpret and elaborate on their own regulations with us, sometimes even on a Sunday morning. It was a honeymoon period. It did not last long enough, being undermined from two directions. In the first place the policy of consultation displeased the rector who, without warning, had decided to break up the work from 1970 and announced in writing: 'I can no longer collaborate with eccentrics and nihilistic freaks. The only hope is to start from scratch at Woluwe and Ottignies. I am closely scrutinizing the plans for public buildings. The great problem remains that of putting life into the future campuses. We must divide up the student accommodation into small areas and surround them by an effective and discrete presence of academic staff.' As a result all the buildings which had not been actually started were abandoned under various pretexts such as cost, security, comfort, which did not hold water when examined closely. In the second place a clumsy civil servant obsessed with norms had decided to bring us to heel: for several years we had to out-manoeuvre him in order to complete the buildings which had been commenced.

During the only sunny week of last March (1978) students erected a tent to hold 1,500 people and for eight days brought the space alive: theatre, songs, games, hot dogs, beer, the lot—and a retaliatory exhibition demonstrating the absurdity of the town planning policies of the authorities and the neglected state of the ghetto building-site—'a muddy area, like Verdun in 1917, its monotony broken up here and there by a building with an unfinished facade or sometimes covered up with temporary materials (tarred cardboard etc)'. The feeling of isolation is tragic.

After that, further meetings were organized: concerted action encountered bureaucratic intransigence. Now, the University wants to impose a new plan. They wish to abandon the centre originally planned as an extension of the residential area of Kapelleveld and move it back opposite the hospital (a grim prospect) to take advantage of the activity created by the patients and their visitors! In other words, 'Let's close ourselves off, we'll be better away from everyone else.'

Fortunately we wanted to see these spaces turned into neither a work of art nor an intellectual achievement, but a living process, an open-ended dynamic activity in which each generation adds a new meaning and enriches it with its contradictions. Without this attitude we would have been very vulnerable. We would have taken these brutal misunderstandings as a personal attack and reacted aggressively. Even gardens are not innocent. We observe this stop-go policy with all the more detachment because it is carried out thoroughly and energetically. How much fun we'll have watching them continue our buildings without us!

Some Projects of the Atelier d'Urbanisme et d'Architecture Lucien Kroll

The Family House at Braine l'Alleud (Belgium)
Founded by Claire Vanderam, the Family House at Braine l'Alleud attempts to help retarded and psychologically handicapped children.

The difficulties these children face are to do with their relationship with other children, with adults, and also with space. The therapy is based on a special technique of 'being present' in front of the child, of understanding and being receptive to the reactions of each child within his group. In this sense it is non-manipulative.

The building had to be modelled on this attitude and avoid all trace of severity or uniformity. It had to be an instrument, a catalyst of relationship—a *house*, not a school or a hospital. We tried to cooperate with the staff to choose whereabouts in town the house should be, but this didn't work out. For the children the house became a *home*, which they created themselves, together with the adults. In their own time they established a non-competitive, family atmosphere. Their natural curiosity led to spontaneous communication, as a means of perceiving reality. This attitude—which should be regarded as normal—became the basis for the architecture. We provided, for each group of children, a different classroom and common room; and the rooms were not arranged along a corridor, but grouped around three centres. The colours vary from one area to another, as does the height of the ceilings. The variety in structure, lighting and orientation of rooms (no two rooms face the same direction) helps the children become better adjusted to their environment. The materials, as well as the shapes of the house, are ordinary and cheap—stone blocks, cement, bricks, dyed wood. In this way we avoided imposing upon the children the excessive sophistication of modern architecture and of the sub-culture which produced it.

The Kassel Gesamt Hochschule is a project to create 100,000 square metres of university complex in an area very close to the old town centre and at present taken up by the enormous disused factory

5 What the builders created in front of the Medical Faculties at Woluwe.

buildings of Henschel. We have been called in as consultants, because we had taken part in a national competition. We feel that it is necessary to respect the character of the town, its history and geography, as well as search for an urban style of architecture which is complex, compact, varied and small-scale, in contrast with the existing industrial buildings. We also want to vary the style and form to create elements of surprise.

Our proposal is that a large percentage of the factory buildings should be retained, but that the middle should be knocked out, and a road brought through, bisecting the new school of architecture. The trees and the river near the road would be tidied up and made to look attractive. The gaps between existing buildings would be filled in with small, traditional structures, housing the university faculties, which would be designed according to how they are used rather than the subject taught in them. Various accommodation blocks and service facilities would 'squat' in readily accessible spaces. The

6 The Kassel Gesamt Hochsule, West Germany.

link with the old town would be difficult to create, because as a result of badly planned reconstruction there are not enough structures left to build on— mostly street complexes, empty spaces, cars, trams and tunnels. We have suggested that one of the spaces should be closed off with a girder retrieved from the demolition work: it could provide support for climbing plants and be a focal point for festivals, proclaiming the notion that the ancient structure lives again.

Cergy, 'Les Vignes Blanches'

We were one of the sixteen prize-winners of the 'Town Houses' competition organized by the new town of Cergy-Pontoise, to the west of Paris. We declared that the participation of the inhabitants was essential, before we could produce plans. (No participation, no plans) At numerous meetings we collected information about the feelings of groups and individuals, no matter how vague their re- actions. So far about thirty families have contri- buted to the overall plan and the design of common areas (gardens, public roads, shared facilities) and personal living areas. We have called in an organi- zation which helps the inhabitants to form a cooper- ative and ensures that the project is successfully carried out. Building starts soon.

Some participants have suggested designs which they have seen in magazines; others have created their own; others still have asked us to design for them, broadly following their own wishes. Our concern is to preserve and interpret the organic disorder of the inhabitants' conceptions, while at the same time introducing harmony through our own ideas. We have rarely felt so disoriented. We ask ourselves, 'Is it architecture?' It's certainly not the architecture we were taught.

The Factory Town of Selestat, Alsace

The brewery of Kronenbourg brought us in as consultants (along with four other architects) for a new factory of about 100,000 square metres, to be built near the small town of Selestat in Alsace. The directors wanted the spatial organization to be determined by consideration, not for the beer in its barrels and pipes, but for the employees who needed to feel at home in their place of work.

The factory was to be roughly the same size as the old town! What would be the effect of making the factory a self-contained area contiguous with the town? We pursued this line of thought and even- tually suggested avoiding the sense of an enclosed space by imposing, as far as possible, an urban grid that opened onto the countryside—a network of streets and squares on which were placed at random technical installations (where teams of workers could be seen working from the street), social and cultural facilities, and places reserved for unforeseen ventures. The different factory areas were planned, not as amorphous workshops, but in the form of 'houses' on a more approachable scale, with slanting roofs. The big factory buildings were kept in the background to form a contrast. To create a sense of history each phase was to be characterized by a different architectural form and different materials; for example, the factory refectory of the first phase would be in the traditional Alsace style.

Urban 'Rehabilitation' in Alençon

The town of Alençon possesses one of the most unfortunate low cost estates in France—Perseigne.

Built between 1963 and 1968, Perseigne disposes of 7000 inhabitants in 2,100 flats. As with many such estates, the town planning underlying it was dictated by the operations of a crane, the architecture by a model capable of replication. Perseigne suffers from all the ills which we now delight in identifying in such schemes. The new town council abandoned the transformation of the old town centre into a pedestrian shopping precinct and decided instead to find a way of 'rehabilitating' the estate.

We were entrusted with a coordinating mission, requiring close collaboration with the promoters and town planners. After listening to ideas and

7 Cergy Les Vignes Blanches.

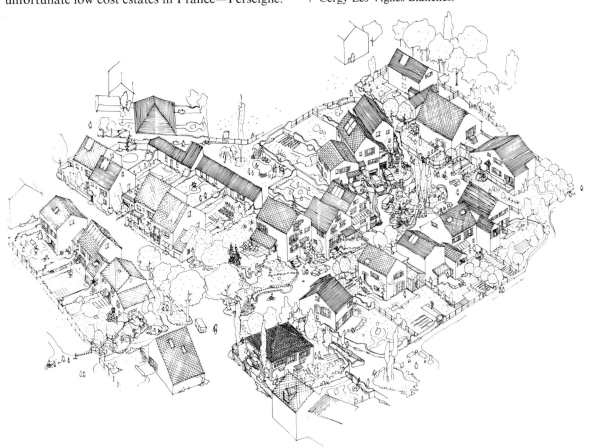

8 *Right:* The Factory town at Selestat, Alsace.

9 *Above:* Urban 'Rehabilitation' in Alençon.

persuading the people who put them forward that they were realistic, it was our function to translate them into programmes intelligible to architects and finally to ensure their realization.

Our first work on the scheme was to plan a college of secondary education for 600 pupils. If we had isolated it on a self-contained site, a confrontation would have occurred between a school area and a residential area. It was not enough that the college should share certain facilities with the community. More radically than this, we suggested breaking it up into several parts distributed around squares and streets to create a rhythmic sequence of small buildings linked by open spaces.

At the same time we worked on the flats. We were confident that if the tenants became owners in small cooperatives, all sorts of annexes, personal gardens and balconies would spring up. Small office complexes and craft workshops would appear, clustered round the buildings. Moreover, we felt that if we could break up rectilinear ways of feeling, introduce some new ideas, and fill in the gaps creatively, the whole appearance of the town would take on a new meaning.

The Housing Crisis in Western Europe: Britain – assessment and options

Walter Segal

In the last few years the number of annually completed dwellings and the rehabilitation of existing housing stock has steadily declined in Britain. It is likely to fall still further in years to come. At the same time the number of applicants on the housing lists of local authorities has dramatically increased. It would be even larger if many of those in need of a home were not deterred and plunged into apathy by the hopelessness of applying for one. Many of those that in the official view are 'adequately housed' wish to leave post-war dwellings in which the light fittings on the ceilings shake whenever there is a high wind.

The shortage of dwellings is accompanied by a disastrous and artificial shortage of land and as the ageing stock of existing housing, most of which of Victorian date, deteriorates rapidly as it nears the end of its natural life, the greater will be the legacy of slums which this century will bequeath to the next. Due to the inadequate rate of replacement of decaying buildings 'terminal maintenance' weighs heavily on shrunken resources.

These facts have emerged more clearly with every year in spite of dissimulation, concealment and official statistics. Hundreds of thousands of young people in their 20s and 30s without financial resources of their own face no better prospects than many years of waiting for housing vacancies. They are offered cold comfort by Government agencies: white papers, circulars and promises. The problem has reached proportions which are a scandal in a country of the Western World. To explain it, those in control make a practice of blaming the state of the economy. This homily has been trotted out time and again and it becomes less convincing the more it is quoted. The structural deficiencies of rigid and fossilized housing policies remain immune and enshrined in inflexible legislation. They are the sacred cows of administrations old in mind and body and increasingly unable to cope with the housing problems that confront them on all sides.

Inertia and mandarinism are the curses of British housing. None of the political parties possesses a housing programme that contains more than election promises. To put the needy into housing queues and keep them there for years is no better than to burden them with the 'ownership' of decaying dwellings and terminal maintenance while handing the job of providing new stock to the developer and speculative contractor.

In examining the post-war housing record of successive governments the methods of the old Duke of York come to mind. Thus to increase the supply of building materials for housing the brick yards were encouraged to stretch their output beyond capacity and a glut of poor quality bricks appeared on the market, cambered and wedge-shaped and often entirely unusable. At the same time other government agencies pursued dogmatically what they called 'industrialized building' and relied on imported assembly systems and the products of the cement industry. Methods of doubtful quality were imposed from above with, in many cases, disastrous consequences.

When such building methods gained preponderance in the housing of the 1950s and 1960s many brickyards were forced to close. Then, with the failure of 'industrialized building' the mandarins of central Government who had been blind to all warnings panicked, turned face and marched downhill just as they had done in the immediate post-war years when the short-lived 'prefabrication' euphoria came to a halt and when, now as then, firms engaged in system building shut-down. Traditional methods returned under a new name: 'rationalized traditional'. The right epithet was all-important but the new slogans produced little improvement of the housing shortage. By contrast the Victorians with a comparable labour force, with more flexible organization and better use of pre-made elements such as porches, bay windows, sills, copings and the like had achieved a phenomenal output of houses many of which, though visually detestable in our eyes, performed much better than our post-war housing is likely to do.

In the planning field Britain's post-war record was no better. Dogmatic and often contradictory directions were imposed by central Government and its higher civil servants whose background and thinking was rooted in ideologies no longer valid and who were entrusted with the exercise of powers that exceeded their talents and capacity for judgment. The catastrophic failure of 'comprehensive development' is a glaring example of this. It prevailed right into the 1970s and left a legacy either of sterile housing or later one of empty open spaces that were created by excessive demolition and condemned to lie fallow for years to come. Conflicting theories dominated the environmental patterns of housing of the post-war years. They were based on the powerful concepts that formed the tenets of a generation of politicians, legislators, administrators, planners, architects and other experts whose minds were formed and conditioned by the theorists of the 1920s and 1930s whose doctrines they tried to put into practice in the 1950s and 1960s. Many of them are still in key positions. Not too old to be disillusioned yet no longer able to apply the lessons of their failures, these men and women in senior and responsible positions constitute formidable obstacles to the introduction of housing policies that will be the needs of coming years. The thought patterns and images of the 1920s and 1930s were intoxicating. They brought hope, an infectious optimism and a boldness of scale that conjured up visions which cast their spell and later their blight over the entire field of environmental activity. It was a time of panaceas. Collectivist thinking was prevalent. It led to a preference for large structures and comprehensive agglomerations in which the individual became a cipher. The meandering slab block and the tower made their entry into housing. In Britain these were frequently used as density boosters to permit a limited provision of small houses and gardens, so much preferred by the nation to the new jungles that were rising everywhere. This was called 'mixed development' and an imbalance of housing conditions ensued in the new quarters when many families had to stay in cramped flats while others enjoyed the advantages of houses.

To humanize huge structures by architectural means is an unrewarding task. The loss of identity, the divorce from the ground and the collectivization of open space pose dilemmas that cannot be dis-guized by shape, texture, colour and proportion. A good view over landscaped spaces compensates only a few. The human animal does not appreciate being reduced to the scale of a termite.

Standards for design, construction and equipment of dwellings are nowadays more rigidly controlled than at any other time and while it is pretended that they operate with flexibility, they are in fact little more than straightjackets and utterly non-adaptable. Since 1918 when in the admirable Tudor Walters Report Raymond Unwin defined for the first time in the world standards to be achieved in state-subsidized housing and did so with wisdom and restraint, the quality of successive recommendations for housing has sadly declined till in the end it became drowned in the rigidly enforced trivia of present-day guide-lines. However priorities are subject to change. Targets that seemed desirable in the immediate post-war period have become questionable; targets that seem now essential are not covered by governmental standards.

Due to poor liaison between the many agencies in charge of different aspects of the housing programmes contradictions between aims and resources became more and more difficult to reconcile requiring constant adjustments. The inefficient manipulation of cost yardsticks developed into a major bottleneck and caused intolerable delays with hosts of officials holding up agreement on subsidies under central Government control. Thus state-aided housing projects may take more than a decade to complete.

The decline in building legislation brought with it the colossal amount of building failures that bedevil Britain's housing progress and that in the 1970s reached preposterous proportions. One of the reasons for this lies in the poor quality of legislators and their stunning lack of building experience usually obtained second hand relying on 'democratic' procedures of information gathering. If each of those responsible for framing building by-laws had personally designed, constructed, detailed and supervised the execution of at least 50 buildings together with satisfactory maintenance and final accounting and if, after ten years, could claim users' content, then, and only then, could a body of practical economical and easily administered building laws be put together. Where, however, quantity is the predominant element of concern in the devising of controls, the proliferation of poor-quality bureaucracy follows unavoidably. Nowhere is there more bureaucracy in government than in planning and building control and nowhere is there more inefficiency.

Two years and more can pass before a modest project can be started on site. It is the controllers' requirements and not those of the users that are paramount and buildings are designed in the first place to satisfy the demands of officials. In terms of human misery and in waste of resources such operational delays are unforgiveable and it is no wonder that the output of housing falls in Britain from year to year.

It would appear that a considerable amount of trivial legislation springs from the design urges of frustrated officials. Some of it may be due to import from abroad, from some of the over-governed countries of Northern Europe where the pace and the quality of life are totally different. Planning procedure on the other side is encumbered with complexities that are a deterrent to applicants and controlled by private interests that are present in decision-making. Voting on submissions is often vitiated by political allegiances and party lines encouraged by an excess of delegated power misused locally by parochial influence.

Taken in all a stage has been reached when the paralyzing effect of controls strangles all attempts to resolve the problems of the housing crisis. New thinking and a new policy are needed. A few facts may now be cited. The population of Britain is unlikely to grow to 70 million during the 1980s. Density studies made in recent years indicate that most housing targets can be met with two-storeyed houses. Cost comparisons have shown that for every two flats in large blocks, three or even four houses could have been built. While the average size of family has shrunk, the total number of families is increasing. Experience with living in flatted dwellings has confirmed in the average citizen's mind that houses are much to be preferred. Since the market values control the price of land and zoning legislation restricts the supply, building land has become more and more inaccessible for low-cost housing; and the unchecked escalation of prices continues. Local authorities have begun to sell council land at vast profits. Likewise there is a rise in the cost of building stimulated by the 'improved' standards devized by officials and imposed on users and industry from time to time as Government agencies think fit. As a result fewer and fewer people of limited means can afford to pay for 'amenities' that compel them to lower their standards of living in other spheres of their existence.

The answer to all these problems and impasses lies in the need for the public in this country to gain control of its controllers, to limit not only the scope of their activities but also their numbers and to bring order and efficiency into the jungle of housing that successive governments have allowed to develop. Public opinion must be informed and mobilized to put pressure on the Government. In this it will have the full support of the industry and professions; in a democratic country concerted action can produce changes. Hitherto the Government has reacted to all protests evasively and with futile promises or even lies, mainly because the public is not yet involved and its level of awareness of the state of condition that prevails in planning and housing is too low. However resistance is growing. There is unison of opinion among all those that had contact with the web of conspiracy that protects the existing control apparatus and its manipulators.

It is obvious that present housing policies will not achieve any effective reduction of the housing shortage for many years. That means that the intolerable housing queues will continue unless a new housing policy can be forced upon the Government.

The first priority of such a policy would be a complete overhaul of the subsidy structure which would enable local authorities to receive and to distribute and administer funds for new housing and the rehabilitation of old by themselves and with minimal interference from central Government. Such funds should be made available on a provisional basis and be accounted for after the completion of contracts. This would save the endless and protracted negotiations that in present usage precede agreements between central Government and local authorities and both delay operations and increase costs. Local authorities should have the option of using such funds for projects of their own or to make them available to groups and individuals intending to assist themselves: this would mean a return to practices operated in the not so remote past. Users would thereby regain protection for their plans and the advantages which local authorities can offer: among them the provision of building land of which nowadays they hold large stocks. Such land could be supplied on the basis of a valuation which would join the cost of houses to the costs of the land and thereby protect land values from the inflation that dominates the open land market. It appears that under the present circumstances this would be the only way in which building land could be made available to people of limited means and particularly to those that would undertake to build their own houses. For such users local authorities could further make available supplies of the necessary funds to purchase building materials and such transactions would be covered by leasehold agreements and mortgages. The required labour content would be provided by the applicants working either themselves or using sub-contractors. Local authorities would with the introduction of such measures into housing acquire a new role which could free them from many of the burdens they carry at present and which have their origin in the housing policies advocated and applied since the early years of the century chiefly by protagonists of the Liberal and, later on, the Labour Party. Instead of providers they would become, where practicable, enablers.

By permitting the population to take the building of their houses into their own hands as it was done in the past and is still practised in the USA and Scandinavia a much better use of national resources can be envisaged; in particular young people willing to work with their hands could acquire houses for which otherwise they could not hope to get a chance. A project on such lines is at present in operation in the London Borough of Lewisham and, if it succeeds, may provide an example which might be applied on a wider scale.

However not everyone will wish to build his own house and local authorities will have to continue to be responsible for housing the poor, a task which cannot and should not be left to the speculative contractor. Morover with traditional methods, people of little and no skills cannot be expected to build for themselves and where, in spite of all such handicaps and with the help of professionals such enterprises are undertaken, up to three years may be needed to reach completion of the works: a truly deterrent prospect. Therefore the employment of an appropriate technology for the construction of houses with semi-skilled or entirely unskilled labour is all important as is the need for rapid production for the stresses on family life caused by excessive building periods can be unbearable. Not in months but in weeks should the time for building such houses be counted.

Planning control of small house projects which will be the majority of the housing schemes of the near future and, one may hope, beyond must at long last be abandoned and be replaced by what may be called 'amenity control' which would cover practical matters such as access, parking, spacing of buildings in relation to sunlighting, daylighting and privacy, private and common open spaces and the like. At a time of such diversity in the visual appearance of buildings it is absurd to enforce conformity which merely degenerates into uniformity. With the acceptance of the principles of the gradual renewal of environment it is desirable to follow the practices of the past in which they were applied: each period putting its new buildings next to those of earlier times and without taking up design elements formerly in use. This is healthy practice, unaffected by lack of confidence or by the morbid desire to let the past control the present. It has protected the urban and semi-urban areas of bygone ages from becoming museums and it makes for the delight of so many English towns where the buildings of different periods stand cheek by jowl together and where the history of the towns can be read from the difference of their buildings. Whoever has walked along the rue de Rivoli, the most depressing street in all Paris, will understand what is meant by 'living diversity', small-scale planning, intimacy and other environmental values which are gradually being rediscovered. Therefore no more 'design guides', no more control of visual appearance by officials of limited visual education and sensitivity or by neighbours who wish to impose their own tastes or, as estate agents contend, to protect their 'investments' and whose ulterior motives bear no examination. If such forces had been able to cast their blight in the past, even St Paul's Cathedral would not have been built; for the City Fathers objected violently to the 'horrible modern architecture' of Sir Christopher Wren. Fortunately then, there was no such thing as the power of visual control in our meaning of the word. While old buildings must be conserved as long as this is reasonable and practicable, conservation and pastiche should not overgrow living design and in no way determine the visual appearance of the buildings and in particular the housing of our own time.

On a more serious level is the question of building control. This has gone completely awry with officials without building experience taking a hand at designing and constructing and where a continuous flow of legislation, not written to be understood, together with enshrined bad practices of the time of yore, will, if unchecked, eventually bring production in the field of housing to a standstill. At present it is merely putting years on completions and throws costs out of balance. There are very few officials in this country that possess a thorough-working knowledge of the vast number of trivial regulations that constitute this impossible body of legislation which, applied *in toto*, can strangle almost any building project. Fortunately, most building inspectors are not entirely aware of this.

What is most urgently needed is a ten-year moratorium to stop any further legislation. Necessary, too, as an immediate temporary measure, is the introduction of automatic relaxations to precede the revocations that will eventually have to be applied. Such relaxations will assist in bridging the gap between the present legislation and the practical instruments that will replace it. Unwinding the apparatus should defer redundancies. In both planning and building control new policies are bound to reduce the amount of required administration and to result in economies from which this country will draw considerable benefit. This will not only speed up production in housing by freeing it from its present straightjacket and by giving the public a proper share in the determination of targets but also help to reduce the endemic unemployment in the building industry which in part, at any rate, stems from the intolerable delays that were artificially created. While, however, such policies can be expected to ease the housing crisis, and this in itself has much merit, they cannot be regarded as a panacea. The structural problems of Britain which are embedded in a changed position in an uncertain world and in outworn institutions require adjustments that reach deeper than the housing crisis. Any easing of the burdens, however, contributes to a desirable aim: the rejuvenation of this country.

There is in Britain a wealth of talent and vital energy which if properly tapped can produce astonishing results from its people. The dormant spirit of innovation can be resuscitated and in a sphere like housing which can be made easily accessible to all people with the removal of the cobwebs of expert-mystique, pseudo-science and the blight of over-administration the present apathy can vanish and a new era of housing begin.

Models of Man in Casterbridge and Milton Keynes

Peter Stringer

Most of our everyday dealings and discourse depend on a common-sense psychology. We are all psychologists of a sort when we observe and predict people's behaviour and form our own ideas or theories of what makes people tick. These common-sense notions often involve unspoken assumptions about the nature of Man and of his place in society. We see man as active or passive; as rational or irrational; as governed by instinct and other innate characteristics or by patterns of response which he has learned; as an autonomous creature or one living in interdependence with others. There are numerous assumptions of this kind that can be detected beneath our words and actions.

In everyday life the assumptions may not be held consistently, nor be independent of one another. But in our professional lives they are more likely to be. The theories and methods which we adopt as architects, psychologists, and so on, are usually sufficiently formalized to ensure this. Taken together, a set of assumptions constitutes a 'model of Man'. What follows was assembled in order to sketch out three models of Man which may lead to quite different views of architecture for people.

The assumptions, and the model which they constitute, are important for a number of reasons. They are often implicit even in professional matters. They regulate the kind of architectural or psychological theories we might develop, and as a result determine our practical strategies for designing buildings or studying and developing people's behaviour and experience. Most importantly, they are normative. However, a model may be chosen from a number of alternatives, and there is often no reason for us to adopt a particular version.

In psychology, models of Man are increasingly discussed. There is a growing interest in the philosophical and 'meta-aspects' of the subject. A reaction against a dominant school (especially behaviourism) is accompanied by a search for strong arguments to justify the reaction. A discussion of models of Man may be used to provide the justification. The value-contingent nature of psychological 'facts', concepts and theories is slowly being appreciated. A classification of alternative models in psychology does not concern us here. Sometimes they are discussed in terms of arch-proponents, for example contrasting Freud, Skinner and Rogers; or in more general terms, psychoanalytic, behaviouristic, cognitive and humanist psychologies, perhaps. Here I have chosen to look at three models highlighted by the Swedish sociologist Joachim Israel, in his examination of the ideological functions of social sciences.[1] They usefully point up some of the significance of models of this kind. I shall call them 'organismic', 'role' and 'relational' models. Of course, these models are neither exclusive nor exhaustive in practice; nor are they as crude as they are depicted here.

The organismic model is characterized best (though not definitively) by behaviourism. The model treats man as a passive object; as determined by his basic biological nature; and as an individual rather than as a social being. There is a 'mechanical' flavour to the model. It deals with the present and future as essentially a replication of the past. Static conditions or equilibrium are assumed to be the appropriate mode. Ergonomic and anthropometric approaches to architecture are organismic, as are certain aspects of functionalism. Organismic architecture defines the built environment as a set of stimuli to guide and contain the human individual, without regard for his own powers or his relations with others.

Israel described the role model as follows: 'Man has certain positions within the social system and related to these positions are normative expectations concerning the individual's behaviour and concerning relevant attributes. Positions are independent of a specific occupant. The same is true of the expectations directed towards a position; they are defined as the role of the incumbent of a position.' In an extreme form of the role-model man is seen simply as executing learned and internalized roles. He is a passive recipient of the forces and influences of society. His definition is in social terms, without reference to his individuality or to his relations as a person with others. Architecture which is conceived in predominantly organizational, institutional or categorical terms adopts the role model. Thus, a hospital may be designed for doctors, administrators, nurses, orderlies, patients and visitors. Or a house for parents and children; housewife, brother and sister; middle-class trendy; or local authority tenant.

In the relational model, man is active and acting. He is both a subject and an object, influencing and being influenced by his social environment. He is seen not as a bundle of traits or other properties, but as his social relations. He is the sum of his social interactions. Throughout its constant interaction with others, the self is continuously changing. Interaction is fully reciprocal. Unlike the assumptions of the other two models, relational assumptions give priority neither to the individual nor to social processes. A relational architecture has a similar emphasis. The design goal is to produce built form which facilitates and encourages man's own attempts to relate to other individuals and to find his place in social and political institutions.

These three different views of man will be illustrated here in two ways. Later in the article I shall draw on some examples of contemporary architectural design. But before that I shall examine Thomas Hardy's development of plot in four chapters of his novel *The Mayor of Casterbridge*. My argument will not be without architectural reference points. In this novel Hardy was describing the market-town of Dorchester, in Dorset. Hardy, who was involved in architecture professionally, was as interested in built and urban form as in the country landscapes with which his work is associated.

Lucetta, with whom the Mayor Henchard has some years previously had a love affair, inherits a fortune and travels from Jersey to settle in Casterbridge. She hopes to resume her relationship with Henchard. In the event she marries Farfrae, the protégé and subsequently the business rival of the Mayor. Before that Farfrae had seemed likely to marry Henchard's step-daughter, Elizabeth Jane.

On her arrival Lucetta rents a mansion, High-Place Hall, in the centre of Casterbridge. This becomes the scene of some of the most important events in the changing relations between the principal characters:

'The house was entirely of stone, and formed an example of dignity without great size. It was not altogether aristocratic, still less consequential, yet the old-fashioned stranger instinctively said, 'Blood built it, and Wealth enjoys it'. . . . Yet . . . the house had been empty for a year or two, while before that interval its occupancy had been irregular. The reason for its unpopularity was soon made manifest. Some of its rooms overlooked the market place; and such a prospect from such a house was not considered desirable or seemly by its would-be occupiers.' (Chapter 21)

The prospect is used by Hardy as the *mise-en-scène* for the realization of Lucetta's attraction to Farfrae. Corresponding exactly to this development, progressive descriptions of the market-place illustrate views of people and places which move from the organismic to the role-based to the relational.

It is in Chapter 9 that the market place is first described:

'It was about ten o'clock, and market-day, when Elizabeth paced up the High Street. . . . The old-fashioned fronts of these houses, which had older than old-fashioned backs, rose sheer from the pavement, into which the bow-windows protruded like bastions, necessitating a pleasing *chassez-déchassez* movement to the time-pressed pedestrian at every few yards. He was bound also to evolve other Terpischorean figures in respect of door-steps, scrapers, cellar-hatches, church buttresses, and the overhanging angles of walls which, originally unobtrusive, had become bow-legged and knock-kneed.

In addition to these fixed obstacles which spoke so cheerfully of individual unrestraint as to boundaries, movables occupied the path and roadway to a perplexing extent. First the vans of the carriers in and out of Casterbridge, who hailed from Mellstock, Weatherbury, The Hintocks, Sherton-Abbas, Kingsbere, Overcombe and many other towns and villages round. Their owners were numerous enough to be regarded as a tribe. . . . Their vans had just arrived, and were drawn up on each side of the street in close file, so as to form at places a wall between the pavement and the roadway. Moreover, every shop pitched out half its contents upon trestles and boxes on the kerb, extending the display each week a little further and further into the roadway, despite the expostulations of the two feeble old constables, until there remained but a tortuous defile for carriages down the centre of the street, which afforded fine opportunities for skill with the reins.'

This description coincides with Elizabeth-Jane's first impression of the market-town as she goes to see Henchard for the first time. It is the scene as it would appear to a stranger. The account is much more of a detached, objective record than later descriptions of the market-place in the novel. People are presented primarily as organisms. There is no particular attention to their roles in society, other than to the fact that they are at market. There are no indications of their relations, in the sense intended here. In the immediately following paragraph, which could almost be read as an introduction to a present-day study of non-verbal communication, the market men are vividly described as isolated individuals signalling to one another across empty space. The social and relational context is as minimal as in a psychological experiment.

The physical setting in the passage quoted has a similar significance. Buildings and other objects are described as obstacles to free movement. Hardy is giving a highly literary account of circulation problems. But again the circulation has no particular social or relational significance. The problems are ones that a designer might approach with anthropometric or ergonomic information, which typically considers only organismic and highly predictable aspects of human behaviour.

This, then, is an illustration of what is termed in this essay as the 'organismic' model of Man.

In the next chapter, shortly after Lucetta has taken up residence in High-Place Hall, she is found waiting with Elizabeth-Jane for a call from Mr.

Henchard. She watches him move about in the busy market-place below:

'They sat in adjoining windows of the same room in Lucetta's great stone mansion, netting, and looking out upon the market, which formed an animated scene. . . . The farmers as a rule preferred the open *carrefour* for their transactions, despite its inconvenient jostlings and the danger from crossing vehicles, to the gloomy, sheltered market-room provided for them. Here they surged on this one day of the week, forming a little world of leggings, switches, and sample-bags. . . .

All over-clothes here were worn as if they were an inconvenience, a hampering necessity. Some men were well-dressed; but the majority were careless in that respect, appearing in suits which were historical records of their wearer's deeds, sun-scorchings, and daily struggles for many years past. Yet many carried ruffled cheque-books in their pockets which regulated at the bank hard by a balance of never less than four figures. In fact, what these gibbous, human shapes specially represented was ready money—money insistently ready—not ready next year like a nobleman's—often not merely ready at the bank like a professional man's, but ready in their large plump hands. It happened that today there rose in the midst of them all two or three tall apple-trees standing as if they grew on the spot; till it was perceived that they were held by men from the cider-districts who came here to sell them, bringing the clay of their county on their boots. . . .'

The scene becomes significant for Elizabeth-Jane when she catches sight of Farfrae behind one of the apple-trees. For Lucetta it is less charged. She is introduced to the roles, the occupations, of the people observed. At first she supposes that they are all farmers, but Elizabeth-Jane puts her right, and singles out a wine merchant, a horse dealer, a pig breeder and an auctioneer, as well as maltsters and millers. The greater part of this passage is concerned with observations that bear upon the social status of the market-goers. The built environment is referred to in social terms; 'mansion, open *carrefour* for their transactions', 'sheltered market room provided'. Clothes have always been indicators of social roles, and fashion has been interpreted by social scientists as primarily a device for communicating aspects of the wearer's position in society. The market-place is now 'a world of leggings, switches and sample-bags', with every man's story told by what he wears or carries. The man who sells cider-apples advertizes himself and his trade by appearing with his trees. Money, for some the entire key to the analysis of social roles, is also highlighted.

Two chapters further on Lucetta's interest has also turned to Farfrae: ... in addition to Lucetta's house being a home, that raking view of the market-place which it afforded had as much attraction for her as for Lucetta. The *carrefour* was like the regulation Open Place in spectacular dramas, where the incidents that occur always happen to bear on the lives of the adjoining residents. Farmers, merchants, dairymen, quacks, hawkers, appeared there from week to week, and disappeared as the afternoon wasted away. It was the mode of all orbits. From Saturday to Saturday was as from day to day with the two young women now. In an emotional sense they did not live at all during the intervals. Wherever they might go wandering on other days, on market-day they were sure to be at home. Both stole sly glances out of the window at Farfrae's shoulders and poll. His face they seldom saw, for either through shyness or not to disturb his mercantile mood, he avoided looking towards their quarters.

Thus things went on till a certain market-morning brought a new sensation.

Within four chapters of the novel, the significance of the market-place has moved from being simply a bustling, crowded setting for human figures seen from afar to being a place with deep, emotional resonance for the two women through whose eyes it has been presented. The mansion is now a home— the focus of threads of interpersonal relations rather than a sign of affluence and social position. The location of High-Place Hall, disagreeable to most

prospective tenants, is ideal for Lucetta and her companion. At the beginning of the passage just quoted Hardy is quite explicit about the part being played in his narrative by the house and by the market-place.

A new element appears when a new-fashioned agricultural implement, a horse-drill, is brought into the market-place. The world of work is one of the major components of a market-place, and indeed of *The Mayor of Casterbridge*. Now it is given its significance as the context for the relationship between Lucetta, Henchard and Farfrae. The two women leave the house to look at the instrument, and they listen to Henchard, who is in the crowd that the novelty has attracted, ridicule both the machine itself and Farfrae, who has recommended it. Henchard leaves and the women speak with Farfrae. The exchange concludes with a remark by Lucetta:

'Lucetta, discerning that he was much mixed that day, partly in his mercantile mood and partly in his romantic one, said gaily to him—"Well, don't forsake the machine for us", and went indoors with her companion.' (Chapter 25)

Until now Lucetta has observed the world of work from above, but here she actually comes down into it. However, she leaves when she finds Farfrae unable to disentangle his relationship with her from his business concerns.

The world of work also envelops the incident which had catalysed Lucetta and Farfrae's mutual attraction in the previous chapter. It perfectly illustrates my argument because it encapsulates in a developing sequence of events a transition from an organismic to a role to a relational view of people and their actions.

It is the day of the great Candlemas fair. Farfrae visits High-Place Hall to see Elizabeth-Jane. He finds only Lucetta, with whom he discusses her habit of looking at fairs and markets from her window:

'Do you look out often?', he asked.

'Yes—very often'.

'Do you look for anyone you know?'

Why should she have answered as she did?

'I look as at a picture merely. But', she went on, turning pleasantly to him, 'I may do so now—I may look for you. You are always there, are you not? Ah—I don't mean it seriously! But it is amusing to look for somebody one knows in a crowd, even if one does not want him. It takes off the terrible oppressiveness of being surrounded by a throng, and having no point of junction with it through a single individual'. (Chapter 24)

Lucetta herself is made to comment directly on the transition from the market place as a setting for undifferentiated human beings to its being a place with particular relational meaning. And in doing so she admits her interest in Farfrae, for the first time to his face. They talk briefly about their past histories. Then:

'The fair without the windows was now raging thick and loud. It was the chief hiring fair of the year. . . . Among the rest, at the corner of the pavement, stood an old shepherd, who attracted the eyes of Lucetta and Farfrae by his stillness. He was evidently a chastened man. . . . He had planted the stem of his crook in the gutter, and was resting upon the bow, which was polished to silver brightness by the long friction of his hands. . . . A little way off negotiations were proceeding which had reference to him. . . .'

The negotiations were between a farmer from a distant county and the old man's son. In these there was a difficulty. The farmer would not take the crust without the crumb of the bargain, in other words, the old man without the younger; and the son had a sweetheart on his present farm, who stood by, waiting the issue with pale lips.

'I'm sorry to leave ye, Nelly', said the young man with emotion.

'But, you see, I can't starve father, and he's out o'work at Lady-day. 'Tis only thirty-five mile'.

The girl's lips quivered. 'Thirty-five mile', she murmured.

'Ah! 'tis enough! I shall never see 'ee again!' . . . and she turned her face to Lucetta's wall to hide her weeping. . . .

Lucetta's eyes, full of tears, met Farfrae's. His, too, to her surprise, were moist at the scene.

The old shepherd is introduced against the background of the organismic throng. Initially he too is simply a figure, read through his posture, a human organism who supports himself on a stick which has been polished by his hand in use. But the stick is a crook—a sign of his occupation, just like the apple-trees of the cider farmers; and his role in society is at the heart of the negotiations which are going on. Finally, the relational or interpersonal aspect of these negotiations is produced. They mean a break-up for the young man either with his father or with his sweetheart. Thus, in no more than a page, people at the hiring fair are successively seen in the guises of all three models of Man.

It is the final, relational guise which appropriately gives rise to emotion and involvement on the part of Lucetta and Farfrae. The latter goes down to the group and manages their sorrowful situation by hiring the old man and the son himself. He returns to Lucetta in her house. But the world of work not only brings them together, it intervenes between them, for Farfrae is reminded of an appointment with a farmer and has to depart.

'What has happened to us is very curious.'

'Something to think over when we are alone, it's like to be?' . . .

'Well, whatever it has been, it is now over; and the market calls you to be gone.'

'Yes, yes. Market-business! I wish there were no business in the warrld.'

Throughout the episode and at its end the significance of the market as a place of business is clarified. As we have already seen, the theme of business takes on more and more importance as the novel progresses.

This analysis of a small part of Hardy's novel was intended to illustrate the different models of Man which were introduced at the beginning of the chapter. One cannot claim that Hardy was applying the models self-consciously, nor that he conceived the market-place in the three layers which have been uncovered. An account has been drawn, from a fictional, imaginative source, of how a place, buildings, urban forms *might* be seen to be defined, in varying ways, by human activities and purposes. This is many steps removed from actually designing built form with the models in mind. I will turn now to an analysis of two sets of real-world design intentions and then give an indication of people's responses to the resulting environment.

Two housing schemes at Milton Keynes—Netherfield (by Chris Cross and others) and Eaglestone (by Ralph Erskine)—have already been compared by Robert Maxwell, and their architects' approaches examined.[2] Although Maxwell's appraisal deals with architectural design and physical forms, some of his comments on the meanings of the two estates point in the direction of a 'models of Man' analysis. The estates are seen as 'intended to project an attitude towards life.'

In Netherfield 'the individual house shares, not in a community, but in a life-style'; the 'estate is not a model of a community, but of a class'. On the other hand, Eaglestone is community-orientated: Starting with the individual family we progress through the shared playgroup space, the garage court, the first school, the second school, and the community centre. The spatial structure models not the regularity of these steps as abstract concepts, but their fields of association as concrete precepts. If we can try to interpret the language of architecture, this architecture speaks of community, of social identity and cohesion, of the self-reliance and exclusivity of the tribe.

The contrast in Maxwell's reading of the architecture of the two estates is already apparent in the architects' statements of their attitudes and aims, which are reproduced on pp. 185–86. However, it

should be added here that these statements reveal something much more fundamental and less bland than 'attitudes and aims': they put forward the architects' basic assumptions, their model of Man and society. The Netherfield designers' espousal of a role model is taken almost to the point of alienation from Man's other aspects. Social meaning is delivered in the form of bureaucratized, large-scale development, embellished with an arcane eighteenth-century aesthetic. The brief is interpreted in terms of the bureaucratic infrastructure of Milton Keynes, and the master development plan is readily accepted after a brief struggle. As if in sympathy the scale of the scheme is allowed to engender its own bureaucracy within the office, conveying a specious appropriateness upon the highly regimented design solution. Several of the aesthetic principles stated are straightforwardly reactionary in tone. The emphasis on repetition and tradition is oriented towards residents who know what is expected of them and like to be reminded that the expectations are well-established and widely shared. The social order of Georgian and Victorian architecture is called up. We are reminded of a design aesthetic for patrons who could and would wait for the landscape to establish itself before passing judgement. Where the individual and his deeds are considered—as in reference to the car and to gardens—they are so privatized as to be more an instance of a contemporary life-style than of simple organismic requirements. A relational emphasis is equally suppressed in the dislike of confusion of the public and private.

Whereas the Netherfield architects appear to see community values as the domain of the planners, in Eaglestone they are of the essence of architecture. The key expression of Erskine's attitude is: 'the physical structure must give a sense of social community, and must identify both "place" and "community".' Instead of the repetitiveness of Netherfield, the stress is on homogeneous variety, endless and apparently haphazard permutations of standard building elements. Socially, too, the two schemes are poles apart. Netherfield assumes that social institutions will be taken care of by other

1a–b Netherfield, Milton Keynes. Architects Chris Cross and others. Photos B. Mikellides.

professions or accedes to the master plan's statement about them. Eaglestone constructs its own social structures as a complement to those already provided as part of the New Town's social policy. Here, architecture is treated as a way of designing places which will facilitate the integration of the individual into society. The physical environment is associated with social episodes which carry meaning for the individual and for society alike. Eaglestone exemplifies a relational model of Man and society.

It is not the purpose of this comparison to judge one estate as more successful than the other. Maxwell reported that there was general satisfaction with both estates. What is of interest is the extent to which the residents responded to or shared the architects' assumptions. In conditions of free and equal choice, would people decide to live on the estate which exemplifies their model of themselves? Unfortunately the question cannot readily be answered in Eaglestone and Netherfield. There are differing conditions of tenancy and ownership. However, an indication can be given, of how people viewed their own estate. From their descriptions, it is possible to infer the extent to which they are employing one or other model in their response to their neighbourhood.

Dan Bucsescu, an American architect who recently studied with me, collected a number of descriptions of the two estates.[3] His concern was with the concept of 'place' as a way of understanding people's cognitions, rather than with the models which are discussed here. However, one of his protocols will quite adequately serve the purpose of illustrating the models.

Residents were interviewed individually in their homes. They were asked to describe a familiar trip taken on foot from home to some activity site on the estate—usually a community facility. Each person marked his route on a transparent sheet laid over a coloured land-use plan of the estate. He was asked to reconstruct the trip in words, detailing all the events, people, places, landmarks and so on, which he could recall. The map served as a device to structure people's accounts and help them to recall the details of the trip. They were encouraged to give a description entirely in their own terms. Once they realized that there were no 'right' answers, and that no particular skills or standards of response were being looked for, they were able to give accounts of considerable colour and variety.

To some extent the architects' aims and attitudes are reflected in these narratives. Residents on Eaglestone tended to give richer and more detailed

2a–b Eaglestone, Marlborough street, Milton Keynes. Architect Ralph Erskine. Photos B. Mikellides.

explanations. Their descriptions of the physical environment were continually interwoven with comments on the social life of the community. The Netherfield accounts tended to lack this feature. But the significance of the Eaglestone account which is reproduced here (pages 185–86) lies in the resident's recourse to all three models of Man.

The annotations against the account should be taken as only one interpretation of what the woman is saying about what her neighbourhood means to her. Entirely different underlying models might be more appropriate as a framework for analysis. The models chosen probably have implications which are not pinpointed in the right-hand column. One may disagree sometimes with the model which has been diagnosed. Children's play, for example, which is such an important component of the woman's appreciation of her surroundings, can be taken variously as a simple organismic activity, as the role-appropriate behaviour of a particular social category, or as actions which help define a relation between the woman and her daughter or other children. In some cases it is highly debatable which interpretation should be used. Indeed, it would probably be more proper to admit that more than one model is implied in some of the remarks which are treated here as having a single significance.

In the context of a housing scheme by Ralph Erskine it is appropriate to introduce the issue of 'participation'. And participation in architecture as in any other sphere, brings to the fore stipulations about the nature of Man. It would be easy to assume that a participatory approach to architecture was fundamentally a 'relational' matter. But it need not be. Participation is a mode through which buildings can take shape; it can rest on any model of Man. Much will depend on the model adopted by each of the two parties involved, the architect and the client/user.

Let us assume that each has an 'organismic' view of Man. Both sides will take a rational and positivistic stance. The architect will look to the client as the source of valuable technical information about his requirements. This will be treated as value-free. It will often be cast in terms of 'needs', with biological connotations. The client's position in society and his relation to the architect or to others will not be seen as relevant to the problem at hand. The architect will ask the client to specify those parts of the problem and of potential solutions which he seems qualified as an individual to give advice on. The client's contribution could extend to suggesting a complete design—in theory there are no limits to it.

At the centre of this approach to architecture is the formation of a *product*, uniquely fit for its use. The architect is producer, the client is user. For the architect it is as much 'my' building as it is for the client. The crucial test for each is that the building works, like an efficient machine, without any further adaptive intervention or thought by themselves. The ultimate goal of this kind of architecture is the effective implementation and persistence of an optimal solution. Strict adherence to biological and individualistic principles seems to be the surest way to achieve it when dealing with so wilful and variable a creature as Man.

The recognition that the technical content of architecture is not value-free and that architect and client have a position in society can lead to a more socio-political approach. Participation is a matter then of enabling different groups to identify themselves and their interests. It is accepted that underlying their different roles will be values which the building in question should satisfy. The roles of different categories of people in society or in a social institution carry expectations to be fulfilled. The building should serve as a *vehicle* in which they can behave as is required of them. Both architect and client/user are role-bearers or 'actors', whose primary concern is with the efficient *performance* of their roles.

The role approach to Man looks as though it is consensual. Participation is treated as a way of fitting together the varying roles and requirements of different groups. Indeed, social guilt drives the architect to question and reshape his own professional role as well. But the approach is only possible if it ignores inherent conflicts between groups. Power has an important say in how the conflicts are managed. Allowing all interests to be represented, even if they were capable of being fully articulated, would nearly always defeat the architect's end. In this particular guise, participation has very strong political undertones. The principal benefit to the architect of role-model participation is his integration into social and political institutions.

The focus of a relational approach to participation, on the other hand, is a moral one. Both parties acknowledge that the other is an active agent, not passively subject to the dictates of biology or society. They find a part of their identity as persons in their relation to one another, in the context of the business of designing a building. This model is followed when it is accepted that the primary purpose of the building is not to produce an anthropometric or institutional fit to certain activities, but to act as a catalyst for development of the *being-in-relation* of people who use the building.

An important question in these varying perspectives on models of Man is the extent to which a dogmatic adherence to a simple model is adopted. The social sciences have certainly tended to argue for the exclusive validity of one model or another. The Milton Keynes architects similarly chose to base their aims and attitudes on a single principle, even though they would never wish to deny that they were designing a residential estate for human organisms with characteristic behaviours, powers and needs. Only in *The Mayor of Casterbridge* and in the account of the Eaglestone resident is there an integrated awareness of more than one aspect of Man's nature and his relationship to society. This observation is not intended as evidence of a fundamental difference between the professional and non-professional viewpoints. What is interesting is the varying importance attached to each model by different people at different times. The architect, and other professionals, must decide whether they wish to match the viewpoint of the people for whom they are designing, to extend, or even to contradict it. Each path is equally feasible, though the consequences will be very different.

Notes to the text

[1] 'Stipulations and construction in the social sciences' in J. Israel and H. Tajfel (ed.), *The Context of Social Psychology* (Academic Press, London, 1972).

[2] 'Two housing schemes at Milton Keynes', *The Architects' Journal*, 10 December 1975, pp. 1247–60.

[3] Dan Bucsescu, 'Concept of "Place"—a tool for investigating environmental cognitions', unpublished M.Sc. dissertation, University of Surrey, 1977.

Architects' statement on Netherfield

The attitudes and aims of the team which designed Netherfield have been expressed as follows:

Although certain city ground rules had already been established when we began work (the interval of access from the grid roads with the 100 m *cordon sanitaire*, the catchment placing of key social buildings, a pedestrian underpass system, and so on), our initial studies involved the investigation of ideas to achieve spatial continuity in spite of the grid system, but this proved an immutable barrier. On closer examination the housing densities were less relaxed than implied by the master plan and, rather than inventing new forms for an imaginary suburbia, the sources that came to mind were more familiar. Also implicit in a scheme of this size was the problem of developing an organization in which a number of different people at the design stage, and later, could contribute at different scales. The need for this kind of comprehensible idea underlies the apparent rationalism of the layout.

The following summarize some of our preoccupations:

* Pattern of streets: the inevitability of the car in the house or on the plot as a solution to housing layout, as opposed to the Radburn principle [of separating pedestrians from vehicles] with its semi-exclusivity and confusion of the public and private domains.
* Terrace housing: conventional house plan with as many variants as possible—fronts and backs; one formal side addressing public space; the Regent's Park analogy; one side open with possibilities for future extensions; a private garden having a sense of being connected to other open spaces.
* Landscape: the large scale interplay between informal landscape (existing hedges and trees reinforced by new planting) and the harder geometry of buildings—English landscape tradition. This is further established by the constant roofline, the interplay of which, with the undulating ground plans, begins to offer variety in sections (1–4 storeys) and plan types (there are 17 variants).
* Repetition: to make the most of the formal collective qualities of social repetition. The straight line of the terrace accentuating the low curves of the natural topography; the sum of the parts etc. as in the 18th to 19th century street architecture or as in Oud's little houses at Kiefhook in Rotterdam.

We believe it would be premature to evaluate Netherfield fully before the landscape had established itself and the evolutionary process had played its part.

Architect's statement on Eaglestone

The architect of Eaglestone gave the following account of his attitudes and aims:

Contact with a group larger than a family from early childhood is vital. 'Isolated' families are all too common and can help to create the social problems, fear and aggression found in many townships. 'Social' people, living in groups from early years, help form a coherent society where each age group has its place—combating old age and loneliness with its consequential need for social rehabilitation.

More than half those living in a district—small children, housewives, the elderly and infirm, invalids and sick—are there all day. Schools, shops, community centres, open spaces and, above all, places of work, should all be incorporated into a housing district. Lack of work places leads to suburban character—to incomplete communities in housing estates. A living area must be a complete and vital organism capable of change and growth. In Eaglestone, as in earlier schemes, an attempt has been made to integrate dwell/work/shop/play/relax environments.

The physical structure must give a sense of social community and must identify both 'place' and 'community'. In Eaglestone the main and the temporary centre (which may become permanent) as well as the housing groups are planned around major open spaces on the hill and in the valley. Groups are subdivided into recognizable 'gossip groups' (30–50 dwellings) around pedestrian streets and squares, car courts with arrival bays, community rooms and play places.

Work places, schools, play spaces and front door contact create activity along main pedestrian streams—strong social lines with urban qualities. These are offset by quiet semi-private interiors within groups of houses. Individual privacy in the gardens and the houses is protected as far as possible.

Statement by Eaglestone resident*
Well, if I was making my most usual trip through the estate, I would be travelling from my house, down to the Market Hill area, probably to go to the old Community

---

*Shortened version of a longer statement.

185

House for one of the activities involving the children. So my daughter would invariably be with me. So I would be travelling very slowly. And spend a lot of time on that trip talking to people that I meet just because I travel so slowly. I know a lot of people around.

Role—environment perceived predominantly through social category.

I come out of the house almost always through the front door and cut across the Ferndale play area. That usually means at least a ten-minute stop, partly so I can look up the children I know there, and partly because my daughter likes to play on the swings and seesaw. From the Ferndale play area there is a fairly straight downhill path all the way through the estate down to Market Hill. There are two other play areas on the right-hand side of that path. My daughter doesn't play there very often. But usually when on our way to Market Hill, we are continually brought into the things the children who live in the surrounding houses and are out, are doing.

Relational—the trip through the estate is seen in terms of meeting people.

Organismic—environment defined simply in terms of movement patterns.

Relational—both *vis-à-vis* own daughter and other children. (Daughter's use of play area is defined organismically.)

In front of my house I turn left. . . . To get to the Ferndale playground I usually come on this side of the houses. I could go around this way, but this way takes me close to the garages and I do not want to encourage my daughter to go in that direction. And that is actually not the most direct route to the swings.

Organismic—route followed from A to B.

Relational—to daughter.

Relational—to other children.

Lots of children use this play area. It's the biggest on the estate. So we spend a lot of time here. If you look at it, you'll see it's a bit derelict just now. Because of the drought and children running all over the grass, it got pretty bald. They also dug a few holes in it for playing marbles. The trees are also in very poor shape. But in spite of all this it's a kind of lively area. I like the way the houses look onto the central space. It's a sort of safe feeling. I mean, I let her go out there on her own. It's nice for me to feel like I can give her more freedom than one would usually a two-year old in any other environment. Firstly, the area is well-protected from traffic. And there's also a lovely circle of supervising adults peeking out the windows at regular intervals. If there was an accident there would be somebody on the spot very quickly. But that huge area of bald grass does look somewhat desolate. I think it should either be grassed for people to sit and enjoy the grass with a small protective fence around it; or they should say, 'Alright, it's a playground', and put tarmac down.

Organismic

Relational

Organismic—apart from physical features the description is primarily of activities.

Organismic and relational.

Role—the supervising adults.

Organismic—again an activity-focused description.

Also in the area there's the 'dial-a-bus' 'phone. And then we come down across this corner where the main path down to the Market Hill area begins. It is at this point that the private housing begins. I am very much aware of this. For one, because the houses up here which are for rent are surrounded mostly by brick walls, while the houses for sale have wooden fences. It makes quite a stark transition. I actually prefer the brick walls. I like them because they provide shelter against the wind. I think a brick wall is a real asset, especially with children— there are a lot of games you can play against a brick wall which you could not do with a slatted wooden fence. You can't play cricket against it, for example. . . .

Role—conditions of tenure.

Organismic—shelter.

Organismic and role—use of wall for games, and expectation that children will use it for play.

The Biosphere and Man: some reflections on technology and tact

Gösta Ehrensvärd

On the expansive tendencies of Man

During the last ten thousand years the vast system of plants and animals in interaction—in a word the *biosphere*—has become infected by an organism with an extraordinary rate of growth and expansion of the areas of its habitats. Infection is, I think, the right biological term for the process, whereby a new mutation of an organism, after a long stable phase of life in symbiosis with its biological environment, suddenly develops explosive tendencies for independent growth at the expense of its surrounding eco-systems.

If we—metaphorically speaking—regard the whole biosphere as a gigantic host-organism, the recent growth of Man and the logarithmic expansion of his habitations is reminiscent in a way of the sudden appearance of malignant metastases in a human body with a certain risk that one or several vital cell-systems and organs will be invaded by alien cell-communities of cancerogenous organization and metabolism. If not checked in time the situation might accelerate and the prognosis for the host organism would be doubtful, to say the least.

We may begin our analysis of Man's plight and our exposition of how that might be reflected before long in the built environment by looking back to his circumstances 200 years ago. At that time solar energy was the sole energy source for his support, with regard to both food and power for his various activities. The forests provided a seemingly inexhaustible supply of fuel and as their resources were tapped the land that was left behind was agriculturalized to raise plants for capture of more solar energy, now in the form of varieties of cereals with the prospect of annual harvests. We could add, as auxiliary methods of solar energy capture, the use of water-wheels and windmills. Also, of course, we must remember the utilization of winds driving sailing vessels at sea.

These energy sources, together with the variations on the theme of agriculture, were quite sufficient to cater for around 1,000 million individuals. In spite of considerable adverse infiltration into the biosphere as the forests were cut back, its capacity to provide $5 \cdot 10^{12}$ kilowatt-hours per year of captured solar energy for human use enabled at least 1,000 millions to live and continue their expansion into the virgin realms of nature in search of more fertile soil, more valuable materials. Over the next 200 years, however, the picture changes dramatically.

It is a common fallacy to regard the start of the Industrial Revolution of the 1800s as a result of Man's discovery of the potentialities of fossil fuel as an energy source for the newly invented power-machines. As a matter of fact, coal as energy source did not overtake firewood, either in the industries or in communication systems, until the late 1850s. The growing demand for firewood for engines (stationary and mobile), for sleepers for expanding railways, pit-props for newly opened mines and charcoal for the iron industry, results during the nineteenth century in marked destruction of virgin forests on a grand scale. When coal finally took over as the prime driving force for industry in general, later to be superseded by oil and gas, the erosion of forests within easy reach of human settlements was a sad, incontrovertible fact. Subsequent events, for example the advent of super-highways making their scarring inroads into the biosphere, have not contributed to the remedy of the situation. The forests recede, the acreage of agriculture expands, the urban areas spread—all owing to the fact that Man, having found vast deposits of fossil fuel (stored solar energy!), is happily exploiting this bank-account of easily utilizable energy, and is displaying his expansive tendencies in full force. The total energy budget of 1980 works out as follows: $100 \cdot 10^{12}$ kilowatt-hours per year per 4,100 million persons. This includes by now $15 \cdot 10^{12}$ kilowatt-hours per year of utilized solar energy as the result of effective utilization of water power and improved agricultural techniques. The rest, around $85 \cdot 10^{12}$ kilowatt-hours per year, is based on fossil fuel and, to a minor extent, on nuclear power.

To sum up: Man has during the last 200 years succeeded in tripling his energy output from the biosphere, yet the population expansion is at least fourfold. This statement gives ample food for some thoughts about the future.

It is an unpleasant fact that the population might rise up to around 6,000 million persons around A.D. 2000 and that the definite and documented decline in fossil fuel and fissionable material will have a grave impact on the world's economy by A.D. 2050. Modern technology must therefore activate every means of solar energy capture, in all regions of the globe. (Obviously I am again thinking here of all facets of solar energy capture for the future, not only the biological systems, but also *all* manifestation of solar power on our planet, including water power, wind and wave power and direct radiation capture via photocells and mirror systems.) We now begin to see the necessity of a *friendly* confrontation between the biosphere and Man; between the solar energy-capturing eco-systems and technology in general. The days of conquest are definitely over for Man in the biosphere. The question is no longer how we might *utilize* the biosphere, but rather how we are going to *live with* the biosphere.

A vision of the future integration of human settlements within the biosphere
Let us assume, and accept as a harsh fact, that we are living in a future when accessory energy sources, such as fossil fuel and even material for generation of nuclear energy, are extinct or at any rate very scarce. Our energy resources are mainly based on intelligent utilization of solar energy in different manifestations. Water power has slowly become supplemented by wind and wave power, generating electricity to extensive power-grids. Careful forestry technology is by now the source of combustible material and timber products of all types. Agriculture at an advanced technological level provides our daily bread, and food products in general—nothing new on this frontier, although a hybrid between agriculture and forestry, the cultivation of rapidly growing trees on marginal lands, harvested in cycles of 3–5 years, could perhaps be described as new. The harvested material is directly used in energy 'power-stations': that is, through combustion or pyrolysis it is chemically transformed into liquid fuel and/or electricity.

That is all we can expect from the technological

utilization of solar energy on a large scale. So-called 'direct capture' of solar radiation via photocells and synchronous mirror systems directed towards 'solar towers' in certain regions is a method that gives only a minor input of electricity. Those of us who in a bygone age, around 1980, keenly argued for solar energy as a panacea for the energy crisis can now see what has happened to their innocent dreams. The world I am trying to depict here in realistic terms is a world where Homo Sapiens *has been forced* to live on solar energy as the sole energy source. The energy output is at the most 40 % of the global energy consumption in 1980—just sufficient to support 2,000–3,000 million human beings, at a reasonable standard of living, round the globe. (The question, 'What became of the rest of the population around year 2000?', can be asked in passing.)

Man, in our imagined period of the future, must make the best of a situation in which three facts cry out to be heeded:

1 That the strictest economy with regard to sources of energy and material is a must;
2 That the organization of human life and human settlements has to be accomplished along biological guidelines;
3 That the integration of Homo Sapiens into the biological system of the biosphere as a whole has to be achieved with great tact.

Now we may proceed to some guidelines as to how these desiderata may be answered. Since we are familiar with advanced ideas about biological organization of cells, cell systems and organs, and about biological communication between organs and the organism, we are aware that the guidelines for human settlements have to start with communication systems.

Long distance transport and communications joining 'productive regions' (areas of mining, forestry, agriculture) with 'towns' have to be strategically planned to utilize a minimum of available electricity. In other words, we must envisage a few well-kept *electrified* long-distance railway systems to take the main load of the transport of material (and to a lesser extent persons) between production and consumer centres. The days of the fuel-consuming super-highways, with their innumerable vehicles driven by liquid fuel, are definitely over. In some cases new railways (electrified) will be built on the foundations of deserted roads or highways. In this way we may utilize intelligently the solar energy we harvest as electricity generated by water power. (As an extension of this philosophy, it would not be technologically impossible to construct an electricity-powered system for heavy barge-traffic upstream along trafficable waterways. This is just a suggestion.)

When we come to intercontinental exchange of material, and to some extent of persons, perhaps it would be desirable to bring about a renaissance of sailing ships in modern and probably computerized versions. Wind-power as a valuable manifestation of solar energy could here make a practical come-back. Experiments are already under way in the construction of sailing ships of more than 20,000 t.d.w. with a minimum of crew and computerized setting of sails. A small amount of liquid fuel would be used as an accessory energy source.

In our vision of the future, long-distance air traffic is a rarity. This is because the use of liquid fuel is heavily controlled for what we might term 'middle-distance communication'. Under this heading we place all traffic in the distance-range of 50–100 kilometres. Such distances are too small for electrified branch-lines from the main arteries of the railways and waterways, and too great for man-powered vehicles, for instance bicycles. However, middle-distance traffic lanes are essential for local transport between town centres and networks of small communities spread along the main arteries. As I see it (and take my view for what it is worth), the middle-distance traffic networks will become *the main consumers of the liquid fuel* derived from organic material farmed chiefly in forests. The fuel will be a sort of 'gasoline'—probably based on methanol—and will be used to power small cars and trucks. These vehicles will be absolutely necessary for small-scale contacts between the large population centres and the diffusely distributed rural

areas. The car is here to stay—yet for middle-distance purposes only. And in limited numbers.

The 'towns' of the future (in our present sense of organized settlements for a concentrate of human individuals) are limited to local areas of around 300 square kilometres, giving a radial distance from the periphery to centre of 10 kilometres. If this were the case, traffic and transportation of minor loads could mostly be carried out by bicycles, tricycles and modern modifications of the ancient rickshaws. This means that urban traffic would utilize to a great extent what is nowadays an almost forgotten power-source: the energy of the human body (50–100 watts/person). The requirement of energy conservation implies that the population of every 'town' has to be limited to 100–300 thousand persons.

Concentric 'growth' is achieved around towns, if possible: that is to say, belts of active agriculture, forestry and mining industries. Harbour towns obviously occupy a semi-circle around the water front. This is obviously a schematic outline. The main theme is that energy expenditure within the transport and communication sector is kept at a minimum. Here is another suggestion for what it may be worth: in order to spare valuable productive areas let two or three *high buildings* occupy the centre of each town, housing administration, offices, and at ground level, warehouses, maybe supermarkets—in short housing for trade and administration. Around these 'cones', possibly reaching up to the 50–100 metres level, would be the low family-homes, preferably one house per family, with garden plots of considerable variety. Biologically speaking, variety is a must, for it is a *stimulus*, conducive to the senses to be active under all conditions.

Turning to the daily occupation of the inhabitants of the towns, many of them will carry out their work in the various types of production belts around the settlements. Here, efficiency is improved by utilizing modern electrical trains of the London Underground type, maybe interspersed with old-fashioned trams in the communication network in order to achieve swift contact with expanding rural areas, forest regions and possibly industrial sites.

I should emphasize here that I am not speaking as an architect well-versed in town planning: my views are those of a technologist with a biochemical background. My vision of the future, in its details, is very much my own.

I should now like to make a few comments about housing. It think it is time to emphasize that Man as a zoological specimen has a considerable variability with regard to likes and dislikes in his living habits, and there are considerable variations in traditional rules for eating, feeding, neighbourliness and social behaviour in general. Building for people should therefore automatically have its more human counterpart: building for human individuals. Of course, I know full well how much economics comes into this. Even in the energy-rich 1970s, incongruent and incompatible bunches of individuals are placed in housing projects whose structures and facilities are products of the holy principle of standardization, with the excuse of economic necessity. In the future time we are discussing, the economic argument for still more standardization will gain further ground, since the energy budget will hold less than half of the present funds for energy expenditure and around half of materials available. Yet still I protest against the holy dogma of standardizing human habitats. The social principle that everyone should have everything that everyone else has, is based on the sociopolitical argument that everyone is intrinsically alike. Wrong! We as human beings are definitely *unequal*.

Even under a strict austerity plan for a society, in towns or in the regions outside, there will exist *some* amenities for equal share among the inhabitants. I am thinking of electric power, telecommunications, water supply, drainage facilities, etc. This should not, however, imply that every person in the community or region has to utilize all these commodities to the same extent. Some people with unusual energy and inventiveness may transgress the limits set for individual use of social amenities for comfort. Let them have their way. Others like to exercise a usually forgotten social right: to *abstain* from this or that. They do not want to keep up with the Joneses and are willing to share their surplus of small extras. Let them have their way too; in the long run the budget for the society in question evens out to a healthy mean between the citizens of higher economic status and those with a self-imposed low social standard.

This is good democracy, where sharing without envy is the main theme. This brings a variety of lifestyles—and thus flexible architecture for *different* people could very well become a reality, even in times of economic hardship. Expanded in an intelligent way, this programme of providing for society, as far as lifestyles go, is no more expensive than programmes of standardized living and standardized housing.

If 'standardization' raises its head again in the far future, therefore let us express respect for the *unequality* of individuals, by providing every townhouse with a sufficient lot of various facilities to be utilized variously to greater or lesser extent: an open fireplace, yet a chance to benefit from central heating; input contacts for electric light, telephone, radio, TV, running water; and various facilities for disposal of human debris and every kind of rubbish. As a most important item, every individual house should by law have a well-stocked storage unit as a buffer system in case something 'goes wrong' in the energy system serving a large region; this should contain reserve fuel, food and transportation means. The times are hard and may be harder, and every individual from the status-rich to the status-poor must be prepared for some catastrophe. This spirit of *preparedness* permeating towns and rural communites in the far future may well compensate for some sacrifices in general comfort. It is, however, everybody's individual right to choose between the two concepts of comfort and security. This choice will be an acute reality for architects at work some hundred years from the time of writing. The given factors will be these: a global energy harvest of a mere $40 \cdot 10^{12}$ kilowatt-hours per year—or 40% of the 1980 consumption; one third of now available structural metals; and some thousand millions of persons with individual profiles craving food, housing and respect for their individuality.

Appendix on Human Needs

Byron Mikellides

Man is a social animal. We associate, interact, belong; we join, influence, dominate, control, like, love people. Do we have a 'herd instinct' which draws us together? Are there psychic dynamic forces which pull us, or gradually acquired drives we develop for survival purposes? Are we to talk of a few basic general drives which energize our behaviour, or a vast number of motivating influences directed towards the satisfaction of our goals?

These are some of the questions to which psychology and evolutionary biology have failed to provide clear answers. Whether the human needs which express these drives are basically physiological, or basically psychological, or a fairly even mixture of the two, remains obscure. The extent to which such needs can be explained simply in terms of territory alone is also far from settled.

F. F. Darling in an article 'Social Behaviour and Survival' (1952), suggested that the provision of territory satisfies not only our physiological needs but mainly our psychological ones. In this 'castle and border' interpretation of territory the nest site provides for *security* (as opposed to anxiety) and at the border, the periphery, for *stimulation* (as opposed to boredom). R. Ardrey in his book *The Territorial Imperative* (1967) added a third need, that of *identity* (the need of the animal to defeat anonymity and to differentiate itself from all others of its species). Ardrey further suggests that these three needs motivate behaviour of all higher animals including Man, and that there is a definite hierarchy amongst them: identity is the most powerful, followed by stimulation, then security, which could be sacrificed if need be for the sake of the other two. Psychologists who consider needs in terms of social behaviour, such as W. C. Schutz, propose three basic interpersonal needs that the developing child gradually acquires: *inclusion* (synonymous to interaction), *control* (dominance) and *affection* (love).

But if we are to trace the various attempts to explore human needs, we need to turn back to the work of Sigmund Freud who conceived Man as a dynamic system of energies—the *id*, the *ego* and the *superego*, all three dynamically interacting to produce an individual's behaviour. The id is the original system and the source of all psychic energy (*libido*) out of which the other two evolved. This energy takes the form of unconscious instincts that drive the organism. The ego is the system which deals with the realities of the external world at the conscious level; it is the system of cognitive processes—perceiving, thinking, deciding. The superego is the system of restraining and inhibitory forces acting on our id impulses, such as sex. It expresses the values, rules and morals that society

and parental control provide; it becomes our 'conscience'. When the id, the ego and the superego are in conflict they lead to arousal and anxiety, which are dealt with through characteristic 'defence mechanisms'. (See how our couple dealt with the situation in the 'wall game', p. 22.)

By stressing these biological rather than social determinants of personality, Freud stimulated interest in others either to build upon his own theory or to develop alternative theories in an attempt to demolish psychoanalysis. A. Adler, a student of Freud, stressed the social rather than the biological determinants of personality by arguing that the main source of Man's motivation is his *striving for superiority* and that all other motives are expressions of this aim: Man's goal is to perfect himself, to compensate for his deficiencies and inferiorities. Similarly, D. McClelland postulates as our main driving-force the *need for achievement*: we behave in a way which shows effort to accomplish something, to do our best, to excel over others. Postulating one or two instincts or needs as basic motivational forces (e.g. Freud's libido or Adler's 'striving for superiority') is an approach that is in direct contrast with the identification of multi-motivational influences by other psychologists such as H. Murray, G. Allport and A. Maslow. Murray's tentative list of psychological needs or motivational energies published in 1928 gives an idea of their rich variety, though we should remember that the relative strength of each need *as well as their organization* varies from person to person.

G. Allport develops this richness and multiplicity even further, and argues that these forces are limitless in number and variety. To account for their diversity he proposes the concept of *functional autonomy*, which maintains that activities serving an original motive may later become *motivating in their own right*.

Kurt Goldstein (1947), followed by A. Maslow, adopted as Man's main driving-force the idea of *self-actualization* developed earlier by Carl Jung—the drive to make actual what is potential in the self, i.e. towards maximum realization of one's potentialities. Maslow believes that there is a 'natural unfolding' of our needs in a gradual and progressive fashion from the 'lower needs' to the 'higher needs'. The individual follows this development as he matures, ideally arriving at self-actualization. There are basically five levels in a hierarchical order:

1 Physiological needs: hunger, thirst.
2 Safety needs: security, order; freedom from pain, discomfort and threat.
3 Belongingness and love needs: love, sex, affection, friendship, identification.
4 Esteem needs: fame, prestige, recognition, success (self-esteem and respect of others).
5 Need of self-actualization: Man's desire for self-fulfilment; 'to become everything that one is capable of becoming'.

To these five needs Maslow adds the desire to know and understand and the aesthetic need as an afterthought. Once a person is freed from the domination of the lower needs he is in a position to allow his rich potentialities to flourish — he is free to come 'self-actualized.'

Finally, Michael Argyle (1967, 1978), a social psychologist from Oxford, takes an intermediate position and offers a provisional list of seven motivational sources of interpersonal behaviour in terms of the goals that are sought in each case. The origins of these drives are to be found both in childhood experience and in innate tendencies. Argyle considers his list, given below, as 'moderately well established':

1 Non-social drives which can produce social interaction: e.g. biological drives such as the need for food may lead to various kinds of interaction.
2 Dependency: submissive relations towards others who provide help, guidance, protection.
3 Affiliation: this refers to friendship, physical contact, and is related to extroversion.
4 Dominance: need for power, status, recognition.
5 Sex: biological purpose of reproduction; pleasurable end in itself.
6 Aggression: to harm other people physically or verbally.
7 Self-esteem and ego-identity: the need for self-evaluation and approval by others.

The Danish psychologist Ingrid Gehl in her book *Bo-Miljo* (*Living Environments*) isolated three different types of needs which she considered should be satisfied in living environments:

1 Physiological needs: of sleep, rest, food, drink, hygiene, sex, light, air, sun.
2 Safety needs: of general house safety, safety precautions. Avoidance of pollution, noise and accidents, and traffic safety.
3 Psychological needs: of contact, privacy, experience (involving all our senses), activity, play, structuring (to be capable of orientation, to be able to place objects in one's surroundings in relation to oneself), identification (to identify oneself with something in one's environment, to project oneself into it) and aesthetics (to receive stimuli which are considered beautiful).

In order to bring these psychological needs into sharper focus in relation to our living environments, Gehl divided the environment into four components: dimension, arrangement, location, and sensory stimuli. She then proceeded to show how each psychological need is related to each of these components. For example, with regard to the need for 'contact', the *dimensions* of the environment (height, width, length) influence the possibilities for contact. Smaller spaces or shorter distances make it easier for people to meet and talk. Secondly, the *arrangement* of the environment (that is, the objects in it such as benches, trees, play facilities) may facilitate the satisfaction of contact needs if carefully considered. Thirdly, the *location* of the environment may facilitate passive contacts leading to friendships as a result of using common pathways or through the orientation of kitchens with regard to semi-private spaces. Fourthly, *sensory stimuli* from the environment can be used to create contact, as for instance through the sounds of footsteps, voices, music, textured surfaces, colour, etc.

Finally Gehl considers these psychological needs in relation to different age groups. Very young children up to six years of age have predictable needs, and require both contact with their own families and with other children; they need varied experiences in the physical and social environment and activity involving sensory and motor functions. Old people's needs on the other hand, are less predictable, and highly variable. Some old people are active and mobile, others very dependent. But the need for experience and activity is very important with the aged, many of whom spent a great proportion of their time in their own neighbourhood. The environment should allow them to meet young children and relatives.

On the understanding that such approaches do not claim to have developed an adequate theory about the complex nature of personality, lists of psychological needs such as Ingrid Gehl's are helpful as simple practical guides for checking and identifying needs within the context of a defined problem. Further research on the relative strength of such needs between cultures could provide us with useful information leading to greater understanding about the nature of human needs and the ways in which the environment can facilitate their expression.